Teacher Education around the World

Changing policies and practices

Edited by Linda Darling-Hammond and Ann Lieberman

Routledge
Taylor & Francis Group

LONDON AND NEW YORK

First published 2012
by Routledge
2 Park Square, Milton Park, Abingdon, Oxon OX14 4RN

Simultaneously published in the USA and Canada
by Routledge
711 Third Avenue, New York, NY 10017

Routledge is an imprint of the Taylor & Francis Group, an informa business

British Library Cataloguing in Publication Data
A catalogue record for this book is available
from the British Library

Library of Congress Cataloging in Publication Data
Darling-Hammond, Linda, 1951–
   Teacher education around the world: changing policies and
   practices/Linda Darling-Hammond and Ann Lieberman.
      p. cm.—(Teacher quality and school development)
   1. Teachers—Training of—Cross-cultural studies.   2. Education
   and state—Cross-cultural studies.   3. Educational change—Cross-
   cultural studies.   I. Lieberman, Ann. II. Title.
   LB1707.D37 2011
   370.71'1–dc23   2011039873

ISBN: 978-0-415-57700-7 (hbk)
ISBN: 978-0-415-57701-4 (pbk)
ISBN: 978-0-203-81755-1 (ebk)

Typeset in Galliard
by RefineCatch Limited, Bungay, Suffolk

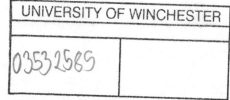

MIX
Paper from
responsible sources
FSC
www.fsc.org   FSC® C004839

Printed and bound in Great Britain by
TJ International Ltd, Padstow, Cornwall

Teacher Education around the World

Teachers ar
does it take

Around t
schools to n
in Finland le
teacher educ
of European
quality teach
are doing the

The leadir
and practices
dealing with
countries tha
Kong, Canad
practices that

- emphasi:
- focus or
  professic
- curriculu

In addition
shape the prep
  Teacher Ed
countries, wha
particulars of t
tries, documer
and sustaining
essential for all

Linda Darli
Stanford Univ

Ann Lieberm
and Senior Scl

THE UNIVERSITY OF
WINCHESTER

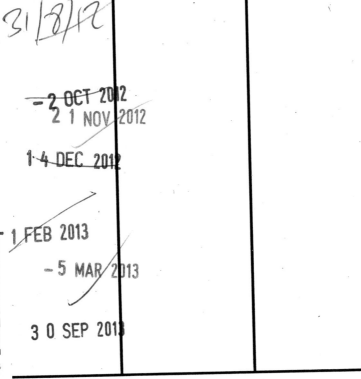

Teacher quality and school development series
Series Editors: Christopher Day and Ann Lieberman

Contents

List of illustrations

Figures

Tables

Contributors

Linda Darling-Hammond is the Charles E. Ducommun Professor of Education at Stanford University, CA, where she launched the Stanford Center for Opportunity Policy in Education and the School Redesign Network, and served as faculty sponsor for the Stanford Teacher Education Program. She is a former President of the American Educational Research Association and a member of the National Academy of Education. In 2008–2009, she headed President Barack Obama's education policy transition team. Her research, teaching, and policy work focus on issues of school reform, teacher quality, and educational equity. Among Darling-Hammond's more than 300 publications are *The Flat World and Education: How America's Commitment to Equity Will Determine Our Future* (Teachers College Press, 2010); *Powerful Teacher Education: Lessons from Exemplary Programs* (Jossey-Bass, 2006). Among recent recognitions, she is recipient of the 2011 Brock International Prize in Education and the 2009 McGraw-Hill Prize for Innovation in Education.

Janet Draper has been Professor of Education Studies at Hong Kong Baptist University since 2007, following a long career in teacher education in Scotland at Moray House Institute of Education, then at the University of Edinburgh, and later at the University of Exeter in England. Her research interests are teacher development and teachers' work, careers and professionalization, including the induction of staff at all career stages, school leadership, and the work–life balance. She has been a member of the Council of the General Teaching Council for England since 2005.

A. Lin Goodwin is Professor of Education and Vice Dean at Teachers College, Columbia University, New York. Her research and writing focus on the connections between teachers' identities and their development; between multicultural understandings and curriculum enactments; and on the particular issues facing Asian American teachers and students in U.S. schools. She has published widely in key education journals and is the editor of several books. Recent articles include: "Curriculum as colonizer: (Asian) American education in the current U.S. context" (*Teachers College Record*), and "Globalization and the preparation of quality teachers: Rethinking knowledge domains for teaching" (*Teacher Education*). She has served as a consultant to a wide variety of organizations on issues of teacher education, diversity, and assessment. She has been privileged to collaborate with educators in the Middle East, Europe, and Asia to bring about school, teaching, and curriculum reform.

Karen Hammerness is an Associate Professor and the Director of Program Research in Bard College's Master of Arts in Teaching Program, New York, USA. Her research focuses on the design and pedagogy of teacher education as well as on the role of vision for teachers and teacher education programs. She is the author of *Seeing Through Teacher's Eyes: Professional Ideals and Classroom Practices* (Teachers College Press, 2006).

Ben Levin is a Professor and Canada Research Chair in Education Leadership and Policy at the Ontario Institute for Studies in Education, University of Toronto. His career consists of half as an academic and half as a senior civil servant. He served as Deputy Minister (chief civil servant) for Education for the Province of Ontario from 2004 to 2007 and again in 2008–2009, and from 1999 through 2002 played a similar role for the province of Manitoba. As an academic, he has published six books, most recently, *How to Change 5000 Schools* (with Avis Glaze and Ruth Mattingly) and *Breaking Barriers to Equity*, and has written more than 200 other articles on education, conducted many research studies, and has lectured and consulted on education issues around the world. His current interests are large-scale change, poverty and inequity, and finding better ways to connect research to policy and practice in education.

Ann Lieberman is an Emerita Professor from Teachers College, Columbia University, USA. She was a Senior Scholar at the Carnegie Foundation for the Advancement of Teaching for the past ten years and is now a Senior Scholar at Stanford University. She is widely known for her work in the areas of teacher leadership, networks and school–university partnerships and the problems and prospects of educational change. Her recent books include: *Teacher Leadership* and *Teachers in Professional Communities* (with Lynne Miller) and *How Teachers Become Leaders* (with Linda Friedrich). She is a past president of AERA. Her unique contribution has been that she has been able to go between schools and universities—embracing the dualities that plague our field—between theory and practice as well as the lack of connection between research policy and practice. She has fashioned a way to be both scholar and activist, practitioner and theoretician.

John MacBeath is Professor Emeritus at Cambridge University where he has held the Chair of Educational Leadership since 2000. Prior to that, he was a Director of the Quality in Education Centre at the University of Strathclyde in Glasgow. From 1997 to 2001, he was a member of the Blair Government's Task Force on Standards. Other consultancies include OECD, UNESCO and

ILO (the International Labour Organization), the Bertelsmann Foundation and the European Commission on school self-evaluation. He has been working as a researcher and a consultant to the Education Bureau in Hong Kong since 1997. He is Past President of the International Congress on School Effectiveness and Improvement, and Director of Leadership for Learning. He was awarded the OBE for his services to education in 1997 and an honorary doctorate from the University of Edinburgh in 2009.

Diane Mayer is Head of the School of Education at Deakin University in Australia. Her current research and scholarship focus on the policy and practice of teachers' work and teacher education, examining issues associated with the professionalism of teaching and what that means for the policy and practice of teacher education within the context of economic and cultural globalization. She is co-editor of the journals *Teaching Education* and the *Asia Pacific Journal of Teacher Education*, and has worked extensively with the profession of statutory bodies in Australia and the USA.

Nicole Merino serves as the Director of Performance Assessment in California Teachers at the Stanford Center for Assessment, Learning and Equity (SCALE)—a center that supports innovation in performance assessment for teachers and students. She also works on the development and implementation of the Teacher Performance Assessment Consortium, and is a lecturer in the Stanford Teacher Education Program. She received her PhD at the University of California, Santa Barbara. Her specializations include teacher assessment and child development, with a research interest in social cognition in early childhood. She has served as the local PACT coordinator and teaching associate in the Teacher Education Program at the University of California Santa Barbara.

Ray Pecheone is founder and Executive Director of the Stanford Center for Assessment, Learning and Equity (SCALE), a new center focusing on the development of performance assessments for teachers and administrators and the development of a performance-based system for student assessment to support the next generation of formative and summative assessments at the district, state and federal level. He has held a variety of roles in the Connecticut State Department of Education, including Bureau Chief for Curriculum, Research, Testing and Assessment, Co-director of the first Assessment Development Lab for the National Board for Professional Teaching Standards (NBTS), and lead consultant to the Chief State Schools Officers (CSSO). He is currently leading a national assessment for pre-service teaching which includes 22 states and 85 universities as well as directing a large-scale student assessment research project in New York City that is designed to prepare all students for college and career success.

Pasi Sahlberg is Director General of CIMO (Centre for International Mobility and Cooperation) in Helsinki, Finland. He has global experience in educational reforms, training teachers, coaching schools and advising policy-makers. He has worked as a teacher, teacher educator, policy advisor and director in Finland and for the World Bank in Washington, DC, and the European Commission in Turin, Italy, as an education specialist. His fields of interest include educational change, school improvement, cooperative learning and international education policy. His recent book is entitled *Finnish Lessons: What Can the World Learn about Educational Change in Finland?* He sits on the Board of Directors of ASCD and IASCE. He has a PhD from the University of Jyväskylä and is an Adjunct Professor at the Universities of Helsinki and Oulu.

Marco Snoek is Professor in the School of Education at the University of Applied Sciences Hogeschool van Amsterdam, the Netherlands. His research focuses on the professional quality and professional development of teachers in the context of school innovation. He has published articles on teacher education policies, in both the Dutch and European context. Marco is a member of the boards of the Dutch Association for Teacher Educators (VELON). As a representative of the Dutch Government, he is a member of the European Commission's Thematic Working Group on the Professional Development of Teachers.

Jan van Tartwijk is Professor of Education in the Faculty of Social and Behavioral Sciences at Utrecht University, the Netherlands. Before coming to Utrecht, he worked in the teacher education department of Leiden University Graduate School of Teaching. At Leiden, he taught classes in classroom management and was involved in the management of the teacher education program. His research focuses on teacher–student communication and classroom management, but he is also involved in research on educational topics, including coaching and assessment in teacher and medical education, and the development of teacher knowledge over the course of a teaching career.

Preface

This book is an attempt to show what a variety of countries around the world are doing in pre-service and in-service education as they introduce and implement programs that deal with *teacher quality, new ways of thinking about learning, professional development, and 21st-Century skills and abilities.* We have both found that the idea of teacher quality is part of the education discussion in countries all over the world, but their definitions, policies, and practices differ, depending on the country. Part of what we learn is the way different cultures see education in general, and teacher quality in particular. History, size, culture, teacher preparation, policies in teacher education, and the changing nature of assessment are only some of the issues that are raised in the chapters in this volume.

Our idea was to try to get inside these different countries and see how policies are formed and how innovative practices are supported and what we could learn by this examination. In a few countries there is almost a seamless connection between policy and practice and an insistence that teachers be well educated with a master's degree in order to teach (Finland, Singapore), while, in other places, people can teach with a minimum of preparation, yet with a new set of expectations for what education should be in the 21st Century (Australia, the USA, Hong Kong). In some places new slogans represent a new way of thinking about schooling (Hong Kong, Singapore), while in other places new ways of implementing new programs are changing the very relationship between policy and practice (Canada, the UK).

Continuous learning for teachers is also handled variously, as in some countries teachers have been given more of a voice in how professional development is organized and implemented (Canada). For some countries, there is a national dialogue on preparing, inducting, supporting and assessing beginning teachers (Australia). In each case, the countries represent varied approaches to teacher quality, different definitions and different programs of teacher preparation and professional development, and raise various ways of handling the process of change.

It is our aim to show this array of countries and how they deal with the quest for teacher quality, to learn from the various descriptions of their contexts, cultures, and commitments in teacher education, and to synthesize the themes that cut across these countries, noting their similarities and differences as a way to educate us all.

We have shared the responsibilities for producing this book in true collaborative fashion.

Chapter 1

The most wanted

Teachers and teacher education in Finland

Pasi Sahlberg

Introduction

Finland is regarded as one of the world's most literate societies. As a nation of modest people, Finland never actually intended to be the best in the world. Finns like to compete, but *collaboration* is a more typical characteristic of this nation. In the early 1990s when Finnish education internationally was nothing but average, the Finnish Minister of Education visited her colleague in Sweden to hear, among other things, that by the end of that decade Swedish education system would be the best in the world. The Finnish Minister replied that the Finns' goal is much more modest than that. "For us", she said, "it's enough to be ahead of Sweden." And that, indeed, is what happened. This episode is an example of close sibling relationships and coexistence between Finland and Sweden. In fact, collaboration is more common than competition, also, between these neighboring Nordic nations.

High levels of participation and completion of education at all ages, equitable access to publicly financed education and high student achievement in recent international assessment studies indicate Finland's sound overall educational performance. All these accomplishments have been established in a relatively short time and at modest expense. As a consequence, policy-makers and researchers are pouring into the nation to study this "Finnish miracle." How did a country with an undistinguished education system in the 1980s surge to the head of the global class within just few decades?

Many factors have contributed to Finland's current educational fame, of course, such as unified nine-year compulsory schooling that ensures equal educational opportunities for all in good schools with modern learning-focused curricula that successfully address students with varying needs, and local autonomy and responsibility for both delivery of educational services to citizens and also continuous development of schools. But research and experience both suggest one factor that trumps all others: *excellent teachers*.

This chapter examines the crucial role that teachers play in Finland and describes how teacher education is making major contributions to the transformation of Finland's educational system into a global point of interest and object of study in this decade. Before describing the current structures and policies of

Finnish teacher education, however, it is useful to review some historic and cultural aspects of teaching and teachers in Finland.

The traditions of teaching

Education has always been an integral part of Finnish culture and society. While access to basic education became a legal obligation and right for all as far back as 1922, Finns have understood that without becoming literate and possessing broad general knowledge, it would be difficult to fulfill one's aspirations in life. Before formal public schooling, since the 17th Century, cultivating public literacy was the responsibility of priests and other religious brethren in Finland. Catechist schools offered religious-oriented initial literacy education in Sunday schools and itinerant schools in villages and in remote parts of Finland. By tradition, the ability to read and write was required for legal marriage by the church for both women and men. This is beautifully described by Aleksis Kivi in the first Finnish novel, *Seven Brothers*, published in 1870 (Kivi, 2005). Becoming literate, therefore, marked one's entry into adulthood, with all its duties and rights. Teachers gradually too assumed these responsibilities as the public school system began expanding in Finland in the early 20th Century. Primarily due to their inherited high social standing, teachers enjoyed great respect and also trust in Finland. Indeed, Finns continue to regard teaching as a noble, prestigious profession—akin to physicians, lawyers, or economists and driven mainly by moral purpose, rather than by material interests or rewards.

Teachers are the main reason why Finland now leads the international community in literacy, as well as in science and mathematics achievement. Of course, many other factors have contributed to Finnish high educational performance, as well.

Until the 1960s, the level of educational attainment in Finland remained rather low. For example, in 1952, as Finland hosted the Summer Olympics and Armi Kuusela was crowned as Miss Universe, 9 out of 10 adult Finns had only completed seven to nine years of basic education — a university degree was regarded as an exceptional attainment at that time in Finland (Sahlberg, 2007). In other words, the educational level of the nation was comparable to that of Malaysia or Peru, and lagged behind its Scandinavian neighbors, Denmark, Norway and Sweden. In the 1960s, elementary school teachers were still educated in two- or three-year teacher-preparation seminars, not by academic institutions, but rather by units that offered shorter practical training in teaching. One graduate of a teacher-preparation seminar in the 1950s is Martti Ahtisaari, formerly a primary school teacher in Oulu, then President of Finland, and now a Nobel Peace Prize laureate. Today, when celebrating its educational achievements, Finland publicly recognizes the value of its teachers and implicitly trusts their professional insights and judgments regarding schools. To put it quite plainly, without excellent teachers and a modern teacher education system, Finland's current international success would have been impossible.

Those educational accomplishments seem all the more remarkable given that Finnish children do not start primary school until the age of 7. The educational system in Finland today consists of an optional pre-school year at the age of 6, followed by nine-years of *basic school* (*peruskoulu*), compulsory for all. In principle, basic school consists of six years of primary school and three years of lower secondary school (junior high school). This is followed by voluntary three-year upper secondary education that has two main optional streams: general (*lukio*) and vocational school (*ammattikoulu*). Both streams lead to higher education, either in a university or polytechnic. Content experts and subject-focused teachers provide instruction in the upper grades of basic school as well as at general and vocational upper-secondary levels.

Enrollment and completion rates in Finland are, by international comparisons, very high. According to data from Statistics Finland (2009), nearly 98% of the six-year-old cohort attend pre-school classes, 99% complete compulsory basic education (mostly without repeating grades or delays), and 95% of basic school graduates immediately continue their studies in the upper secondary school of their choice. Drop-outs from general and vocational upper secondary school (high school) have become rare, declining from high figures in the 1980s. Intensive student counseling and personalized study programs help Finland attain an average 95% graduation rate compared to 82% in the OECD countries on average (OECD, 2011; Välijärvi & Sahlberg, 2008). The challenge in Finland is to make more young people complete their upper secondary studies on time. There is a considerable gap between intended graduation time and actual graduation time particularly in vocational schools.

All Finnish education is publicly financed, including higher education. About 2% of all expenditures in Finnish educational institutions are paid for by private resources (OECD, 2008). This is significantly less than comparable averages in industrialized OECD countries (14%) or in the European Union (10%). Local authorities and municipalities assume primary responsibility for providing public education. Local tax revenues, on average, finance 58% of all pre-tertiary education, with the national budget financing the rest. In short, Finland's education administration is decentralized.

The Finnish education system has many differences compared to public education in the United States or the United Kingdom. The Finnish system lacks rigorous school inspection, does not employ external standardized student testing to inform the public about school performance, and has adopted equality of educational opportunities as the main driver in its education policies. A National Matriculation Examination at the end of upper secondary education is the only external high-stakes instrument used in Finnish schools. Teacher education is fully congruent with these characteristics of educational policy in Finland.

Finland defines five categories of teachers:

1 *Kindergarten teachers* work in kindergarten classrooms and are also licensed to teach pre-school classes.
2 *Primary school teachers* teach in grades 1 to 6 of unified nine-year basic schools. They normally are assigned to one grade and teach several subjects.

3   *Subject teachers* teach specific subjects in the upper grades of basic school (typically grades 7 to 9) and in general upper secondary school, including also vocational schools. Subject teachers may be specialized to teach one to three subjects, e.g. mathematics, physics, and chemistry.
4   *Special education teachers* work with individuals and groups of students with special needs in primary schools and upper grades of basic schools.
5   *Vocational education teachers* teach in upper secondary vocational schools. They must possess at least three years of work experience in their own teaching field before they are admitted to a vocational teacher preparation program.

In addition to these five teacher categories, there are also teachers in adult-education institutions where similar pedagogical knowledge and skills are required. There are approximately 5700 new openings in all teacher education programs in Finland each academic year. This article focuses on the education of primary and subject teachers, who constitute about two-thirds of all teacher-education students in Finland.

Dreaming of teaching and teachers

Teaching as a profession is closely tied to Finnish national culture. Indeed, one aim of formal schooling is to transfer the cultural heritage, values, and aspirations from one generation to another. Teachers are, therefore, essential players in nation-building. Throughout the centuries, Finland has struggled for its national identity, mother tongue, and its own values: first, during four centuries under the Kingdom of Sweden, then for more than a century under the Russian Empire and its five czars, and then for yet another century as a newly independent nation positioned between its former patrons and powers of globalization. There is no doubt that this history has left a deep mark on Finns and the desire for personal development through education, reading, and self-improvement. It has become part of the cultural DNA in Finland.

It is no wonder, then, that teachers and teaching are highly regarded in Finland. The Finnish media regularly report results of opinion polls that document favorite professions among general upper-secondary school graduates. Surprisingly, among young Finns, *teaching* is consistently rated as the most admired profession, leading the ratings of medical doctors, architects, and lawyers (*Helsingin Sanomat*, 2004). Teaching is congruent with core social values of Finns: social justice, caring for others, and happiness. Teaching is also regarded as an independent profession that enjoys public respect and praise. It is a particularly popular career for young women—more than 80% of those accepted for study in primary teacher education programs are talented women.

Indeed, teachers are admired individuals in Finnish society. In a national survey, about 1300 adult Finns (ages 15–74) were asked if their spouse's (or partner's) profession had influenced their decision to commit to a relationship with them (*Helsingin Sanomat*, 2008). Interviewees were asked to select five professions from a list of thirty that would be preferred for a selected partner or spouse. The findings were rather surprising. Finnish males viewed a teacher as the most desired spouse, rated just ahead of a nurse, medical doctor, and architect. Women, in turn, admire only a medical doctor and a veterinarian ahead of a teacher as a profession for their ideal husband. In the entire sample, 35% rated a teacher as among the top five preferred professions for their ideal spouse. Apparently, only medical doctors are more sought after in Finnish mating markets than are teachers. This clearly documents both the high professional and social status teachers reached in Finland—in and out of schools.

Only Finland's best and brightest are able to fulfill those professional dreams, however. Every Spring, thousands of Finnish general upper secondary school graduates submit applications to Departments of Teacher Education in eight Finnish universities, including many of the most talented, creative, and motivated youngsters. Thus, becoming a primary school teacher in Finland is highly competitive. It is normally insufficient to complete general upper secondary school successfully and pass a rigorous Matriculation Examination, an external upper secondary school graduation examination. Successful candidates must also possess the highest scores, positive personalities, and excellent interpersonal skills. Annually only about one of every ten of such students will be accepted to prepare to become a teacher in Finnish primary schools. The annual total of applicants in all five categories of teacher education programs is about 20,000.

The selection of primary school teacher education candidates consists of two phases: first, all candidates take a national entrance exam that is based on selected articles on various aspects of teaching and education. Then, based on their Matriculation Examinations scores, Upper Secondary School Diploma issued by the school, and relevant out-of-school merits the top candidates are selected to the second phase. These applicants are invited to an interview in which their understanding of educational issues and their personality are examined by the university faculty. Candidates are asked, among other things, to explain why they have decided to become teachers.

As these two selection phases suggest, access to Finnish teacher education is highly selective and only the most capable candidates are admitted. Normally, at least some prior experience in teaching or working with children is required. The Departments of Teacher Education in Finnish universities accept just over 700 new primary school teacher education students annually. Figure 1.1 summarizes the trend in total annual applicants since 2001, disaggregated by gender. Two phenomena are apparent (also reported in Kumpulainen, 2008). The Finnish teaching profession in primary schools is becoming increasingly attractive except for a slight decline in the middle of this decade. Then, the proportion of male primary school teachers remains relatively small. Although the total students who do not complete their primary school teacher Master's degree program is small, a relatively larger number of male students appear elsewhere—not as primary school teachers.

Until the mid-1970s, primary school teachers were taught in teacher colleges. Lower and upper secondary school subject teachers studied in specific subject-focused

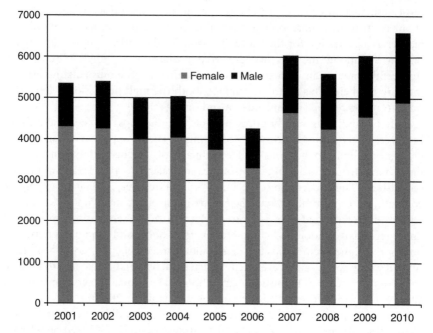

Figure 1.1 Total annual applicants to Finnish primary school teacher education programs, 2001–2010.

Source: Sahlberg (2011).

departments of Finnish universities. By the end of the 1970s, all teacher education programs had become part of academic higher education and, therefore, take place in universities. Simultaneously, scientific content and educational research advances began to enrich the teacher education curricula. Teacher education is now *research-based*, meaning that it must be supported by scientific knowledge and be focused on thinking processes and cognitive skills employed in conducting research (Jakku-Sihvonen & Niemi, 2006). A particular principle of research-based teacher education in Finland is systemic integration of scientific educational knowledge, didactics (or pedagogical content knowledge), and practice in a manner that enables teachers to enhance their pedagogical thinking, evidence-based decision-making, and engagement in the scientific community of educators. Consequently, the basic requirement today for permanent employment as a teacher in all Finnish basic and upper secondary schools is possession of a Master's degree, as shown in Table 1.1. This is described in more detail in the following sections.

Salaries are not the main reason young people become teachers in Finland. Teachers earn very close to the national average salary level; on average, typically equivalent to what mid-career middle-school teachers earn annually in OECD

Table 1.1 Required teacher qualifications by type of school in Finland

Type of school	Pupils' ages	Grades	Required teacher qualifications
Kindergarten	0–6		Kindergarten teacher (BA)
Pre-school	6		Kindergarten teacher (BA) Primary school teacher (MA)
Basic school	7–16	1–9	Basic school teacher (MA)
Primary school	7–12	1–6	Primary school teacher (MA)
Lower secondary school	13–15	7–9	Subject teacher (MA)
General upper secondary	16–18	10–12*	Subject teacher (MA)
Vocational upper secondary		10–12	Vocational teacher (BA) Subject teacher (MA)
University	19–		Higher academic degree (MA/PhD)
Polytechnic			Higher education degree (MA/PhD)

Note: * General upper secondary school is based on a non-graded structure, enabling students to complete studies independent of the pacing of traditional grades or classes.

nations—about US$44,000, just above the OECD average (OECD, 2011). More important incentives than financial reward are factors such as high social prestige, professional autonomy in schools, and the ethos of teaching as a service to society and the public good. Thus, young Finns perceive teaching as a career on a par with other professions where people work independently and rely on scientific knowledge and skills that they acquired in university studies. That is one reason why teaching in schools has remained autonomous in terms of teachers' professional judgment regarding curriculum, student assessment, professional development, and reporting progress of one's work.

Educating teachers for a knowledge-based work

International indices suggest that Finland is one of the most advanced knowledge societies (Sahlberg, 2011). Well-educated Finns are a cornerstone of knowledge, research, and innovation. Education policies since the 1960s have emphasized knowledge and skills as conditions for success in Finland (Aho *et al.*, 2006). Schools have played an important role in transforming Finland from a traditional industrial-agrarian nation into a modern innovation-based knowledge economy. This would not have been possible without considerable improvement in how Finnish teachers are prepared.

Teacher education is an important and recognized part of higher education in Finland. In many other nations the situation is different: teacher preparation is frequently viewed as a semi-professional education arranged outside of academic universities. In the Finnish Acts on Teacher Education in 1978–1979, the minimum requirement for permanent employment as a teacher became a Master's

degree that includes an approved Master's thesis with similar scientific requirements as in any other academic field. This legislative policy was the impetus to
transfer all teacher education programs from colleges to Finnish universities. The
seeds were sown for believing that the profession of teacher is based on scholarly
research. An important side-effect of this transition was the unification of the
Finnish teaching cadre, which had been divided in the Basic School Reform of
1972. Since the beginning of 1980, all teachers have earned Master's degrees and
they are all members of the same teacher union.

All teachers today, as holders of Master's degrees, are automatically qualified
for post-graduate studies. The major subject in the primary school teacher-education program is *education*. In subject-focused teacher education programs,
students concentrate on a particular subject, e.g. mathematics or foreign
languages. Subject-focused teacher candidates also study didactics, consisting of
pedagogical content knowledge in their own subject specialty. There are no other
ways to gain a teacher's diploma in Finland; the university degree constitutes a
license to teach. Successful completion of a Master's degree in teaching today
takes, according to the Ministry of Education (2007), on average, from five to
seven and a half years.

Finnish teacher education focuses on the balanced development of the prospective teacher's personal and professional competences. Particular attention is
devoted to building pedagogical thinking skills, enabling teachers to manage
instructional processes in accordance with contemporary educational knowledge
and practice (Niemi, 2002; Westbury *et al.*, 2005). In primary teacher education,
this is led by the study of education as a main subject, composed of three major
thematic areas: (1) the theory of education; (2) pedagogical content knowledge;
and (3) subject didactics and practice. Research-based teacher education programs
culminate in a required Master's thesis. Prospective primary school teachers
normally complete their theses in the field of education. Subject-focused
prospective teachers, in turn, select a topic within their major subject. The level
of scholarly expectations for teacher education is similar across all teacher-
preparation programs, from elementary to upper secondary school.

Teacher education in Finland is aligned to the framework of the European
Higher Education Area (Jakku-Sihvonen & Niemi, 2006; Pechar, 2007; Zgaga,
2007) that is being developed under the ongoing Bologna Process. Currently,
Finnish universities offer a two-tier degree program. First, an obligatory three-year
Bachelor's degree program qualifies students for graduate studies, followed by a
two-year Master's degree program. These two degrees are offered in multi-disciplinary programs consisting of studies in at least two subjects. Studies are quantified
in terms of credit units within the European Credit Transfer and Accumulation
System (ECTS) in 46 European nations. ECTS, which will become a guiding
policy for the European Higher Education Area, is a student-centered system based
on student workload required to achieve the objectives of a program. The objectives are normally specified in terms of learning outcomes and competences to be
acquired. ECTS is based on the assumption that 60 credits represent the workload

of a full-time student over one academic year. The student workload for a full-time study program in Europe equals, in most cases, about 1,500–1,800 hours annually. Therefore, one ECTS credit represents about 25–30 working hours. Teacher education requirements are 180 ECTS credits for a Bachelor's degree (which does not meet qualifications for a Teaching Diploma or enable permanent employment as a teacher), followed by 120 ECTS credits for a Master's degree.

A broad-based teacher education curriculum ensures that newly prepared Finnish teachers possess well-balanced knowledge and skills in both theory and practice. It also implies that prospective teachers develop deep professional insight into education from several perspectives, including educational psychology and sociology, curriculum theory, assessment, special needs education, and didactics (or pedagogical content knowledge) in selected subject areas. To illustrate what teachers study during their preparation program, Table 1.2 summarizes primary school teacher education topics with required credit units, as offered by the Department of Teacher Education, University of Jyväskylä (Sahlberg, 2011). All eight Finnish universities have their own nationally coordinated teacher education strategies and curricula, ensuring coherence, but encouraging local initiative to make best use of each university's resources and nearby opportunities.

As a general rule, primary school teacher education preparing teachers for the lower grades (typically, grades 1–6 of basic schools) includes 60 ECTS credits of pedagogical studies and at least 60 additional ECTS credits for other courses in educational sciences. An integral part of these additional educational studies is a Master's thesis requiring independent research, participation in research seminars, and presentation of the final educational study. The common credit assigned to this research work within all universities is 40 ECTS credits.

The revised teacher education curriculum in Finland requires primary school teacher candidates to complete a major in educational sciences and earn 60 ECTS credits in minor studies in subjects included in the National Framework

Table 1.2 Primary teacher education Master's degree program at the University of Jyväskylä in 2009

Curriculum component	ECTS credit
Basic Studies in Education*	25
Language and Communication Studies	25
Intermediate Studies in Education*	35
Multidisciplinary School Subject Studies	60
Minor Subject Studies	60
Advanced Studies in Education**	80
Elective Studies	15
TOTAL ECTS CREDITS	300

Notes:
* Includes 12 ECTS credits from teaching practice.
** Includes 16 ECTS credits from teaching practice.

Curriculum for Basic Schools, which is regularly updated by the National Board of Education and the Ministry of Education.

It is worth noting that most Finnish students in primary teacher education programs enter their studies with solid knowledge and skills in a range of subjects studied in upper secondary school. In Finland, unlike in the United States or the United Kingdom, students are obliged to successfully accomplish a curriculum that includes seventeen required subjects—among them physics, chemistry, philosophy, music, and at least two foreign languages. Normally, students accepted in primary school teacher education programs have earned higher than average marks in these subjects. For example, in the University of Helsinki, more than 10% of students select mathematics as their minor subject, which provides them a license also to teach mathematics as subject teachers in grades 7–9 (Lavonen *et al.*, 2007). It is easy to see that primary school teachers in Finland, in general, possess a strong mastery of subjects that they teach due to their broad-based upper secondary school curriculum and primary teacher education program that builds on that solid base.

Subject teacher education follows the same principles as primary school teacher education, but is arranged differently. There are two main pathways to become a subject teacher. Most students first complete a Master's degree in their academic programs with one major subject, e.g. Finnish language, and one or two minor subjects, e.g. literature and drama. Students then apply to the Department of Teacher Education for their subject teacher education program. Pedagogical studies, where the main focus is on subject-oriented teaching strategies, is equivalent to 60 ECTS credits and requires one academic year. The other pathway to become a subject teacher is to apply directly to teacher education when students apply to pursue a major subject in their academic program. Normally, after the second year of subject studies, students start their pedagogical studies in their university's Faculty of Education. The curriculum for this second pathway is identical to the first route, only scheduled differently within the Bachelor's and Master's tracks, typically over four academic terms as illustrated by the program at the University of Helsinki (Table 1.3).

Prospective subject teachers decide to major in fields that they will be teaching, for example, mathematics or music. For this major subject, advanced studies involving 90 ECTS credits are normally required. In addition, 60 ECTS credits are required in a second school subject. Generally, the Department of Teacher Education organizes courses in pedagogical studies in collaboration with subject-matter programs offered by university subject departments that also are responsible for teacher education of their own students (Lavonen *et al.*, 2007). Exceptions include teacher education, as some specific subjects included in the National Framework Curriculum for the Comprehensive, such as textile work and crafts, special education, student counseling, and music are also organized by the Departments of Education. Teacher education for music, arts, and physical education usually takes place in separate departments or institutes in the university. It is worth noting that academic subject faculties—not the Department of

Table 1.3 Structure of the pedagogical component of the subject teacher education program at the University of Helsinki in 2011

Bachelor's level (25 ECTS credits)	Master's level (35 credits)
First Term (18 credits) • Developmental psychology and learning (4) • Special education (4) • Introduction to subject didactics (10)	Third Term (17 credits) • Social, historical and philosophical foundations of education (5) • Evaluation and development of teaching (7) • Advanced teaching practice in Teacher Training School or Field School (5)
Second Term (7 credits) • Basic teaching practice in Teacher Training School (7) As part of Master's program: • Research methodology (6)	Fourth Term (12 credits) • Research seminar (Teacher as a researcher) (4) • Final teaching practice in Teacher Training School or Field School (8)

Teacher Education—that have an important role in teacher education in Finland issue Master's degrees for subject teachers.

Instruction in Finnish teacher education departments is arranged to support pedagogical principles that newly prepared teachers are expected to implement in their own classrooms. Although each university teacher has full pedagogical autonomy, every Department of Teacher Education in Finland has a detailed and often binding strategy for improving the quality of their teacher-education programs. Subject-focused pedagogy and its research in, for example, science education within Finnish universities are well advanced by international standards (Kim, Lavonen, & Ogawa, 2009). Moreover, cooperative learning, problem-based learning, reflective practice, and computer-supported education are implemented today—at least to some extent—in all Finnish universities. A Finnish higher education evaluation system that rewards effective, innovative university teaching practice has served as an important driver of these positive developments.

Research-based teacher education means that integration of educational theories, research methodologies and practice all have an important place in Finnish teacher-education programs. Teacher education curricula are designed so that they constitute a systematic continuum from the foundations of educational thinking to educational research methodologies and then on to more advanced fields of educational sciences. Each student thereby builds an understanding of the systemic, interdisciplinary nature of educational practice. Finnish students also learn the skills of how to design, conduct, and present original research on practical or theoretical aspects of education. An important element of Finnish research-based teacher education is practical training in schools, a key component of the curriculum, as documented in Tables 1.2 and 1.3.

There are, in principle, two kinds of practicum experiences within teacher education programs in Finland. A minor part of clinical training occurs in seminars and small-group classes in the Department of Teacher Education (part of the Faculty of Education), where students practice basic teaching skills with their peers. Major teaching practice experiences occur mostly in special Teacher Training Schools governed by universities, which have curricula and practices similar to conventional public schools. Students use a network of selected Field Schools for practice teaching. In primary school teacher education, students devote approximately 15% of their intended study time (for example, in the University of Jyväskylä, 40 ECTS credits) to practice teaching in schools. In subject teacher education, the proportion of teaching practice in schools represents about one-third of the curriculum.

The Finnish teacher-education curriculum, as summarized in Tables 1.2 and 1.3, is designed to integrate teaching practice in theoretical and methodological studies systematically. Teaching practice is normally divided into three phases over the five-year program: *basic practice, advanced practice*, and *final practice*. During each phase, students observe lessons by experienced teachers, conduct practice teaching observed by supervisory teachers, and deliver independent lessons to different pupil groups that are evaluated by supervising teachers and Department of Teacher Education professors and lecturers. Evaluations of Finnish teacher education repeatedly identify the systematic nature of teacher education curricula as a key strength and a characteristic that distinguishes Finnish teacher education from that of many other nations (Darling-Hammond, 2006; Jussila & Saari, 2000; Saari & Frimodig, 2009).

The Finnish teacher education program is a spiral sequence of theoretical knowledge, practical training and research-oriented enquiry of teaching. Teacher-education responsibilities are integrated within the activities of academic university units. For example, at the University of Oulu, three academic units shown in Figure 1.2, namely Science, Humanities, and Education, deliver teacher education courses for their students. They include staff (normally lecturers and professors)

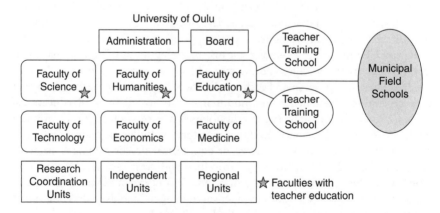

Figure 1.2 Structure of the University of Oulu and the organization of teacher education in 2011.

specialized in subject-oriented teaching methodologies. Their curricula are also coordinated with the Department of Teacher education, which has responsibility for the overall delivery of teacher education.

Although Teacher Training Schools constitute the main portion of the network within which Finnish students complete their practice teaching, some normal public schools (called Municipal Field Schools) also serve the same purpose, as illustrated in Figure 1.2. One-third of all teaching practice at the University of Oulu occurs in Municipal Field Schools (MFS). Teacher Training Schools where practice teaching occurs have higher professional staff requirements; supervising teachers must prove their competency to work with student teachers. Teacher Training Schools (but not MFSs) are also expected to pursue research and development roles in teacher education in collaboration with the university's Department of Teacher Education, or sometimes also with the academic units' teacher education staff. For example, in the University of Oulu, Faculty of Science and Faculty of Humanities assume teacher-education roles and support appropriate staff. All Teacher Training Schools can, therefore, introduce sample lessons and alternative curricular designs to student teachers. These schools also have teachers who are well prepared in supervision, teacher professional development, and assessment strategies. There are no specific qualifications to become such a teacher—it is each individual's responsibility to build the needed knowledge and skills required for employment in a Teacher Training School.

Teachers' work and professional development

Since teaching is a much sought-after profession in Finland, most new graduates from Finnish Departments of Teacher Education and subject-focused programs seek immediate school employment. During their studies, students already have built an impression of what school life from a teacher's perspective may be like. However, graduates do not necessarily acquire the experience of participating in a community of educators, taking full responsibility for a classroom of students, or interacting with parents. All these considerations are part of the curriculum, but many licensed graduates discover that there is a gap between lecture-hall idealism and school reality.

Induction of new teachers into their first full-time teaching assignment is relatively less developed in Finland, although research and development work is rather active (Jokinen & Välijärvi, 2006; OECD, 2005). It is up to each school and municipality governing these schools to address their new teachers' induction into their teaching responsibilities. Thus, practices regarding Finnish teacher induction are, admittedly, diverse. Some schools, as part of their mission, have adopted advanced procedures and support systems for new staff, whereas other schools merely bid new teachers welcome and show them to their classrooms. In some schools, induction is a well-defined responsibility of school principals or deputy principals, while in other Finnish schools, induction responsibilities may be assigned to some experienced classroom teachers. Teacher induction is admittedly an area that requires further development in Finland, as recent European recommendations have correctly pointed out (European Commission, 2004).

Finnish teacher education programs have been praised for their systematic academic structure and high overall quality by several international reviews and evaluations (Jussila & Saari, 2000). However, in Finland, it is widely recognized that professional development and in-service programs for teachers are not aligned with initial teacher education and often lack focus on essential areas of teaching and school development. Perhaps the main criticism deals with weak coordination between initial university teacher education and ongoing professional development programs in schools. Municipalities, as the overseers of primary, lower and upper secondary schools, are responsible for providing teachers opportunities for professional development or in-service training, based on their needs. In practice, there is an allocation of three mandatory days for professional development that must be provided by the municipalities. Today, however, it is up to individual teachers or school principals to decide how much beyond those three days and what type of professional development are needed and whether such interventions can be funded.

In Finland, there is significant disparity between municipalities' and schools' relative ability to finance professional development for their teachers. The main reason for this situation is how Finnish education is financed. The central government has only limited influence on budgetary decisions by municipalities or schools. Therefore, some schools receive significantly more allocations for professional development and school improvement than others, where, particularly during times of economic downturn, professional development budgets are often the first to vanish.

Governance of Finnish education is not consistent throughout the nation. Some schools experience relatively higher autonomy over their operations and budgeting; others do not. Therefore, teacher professional development takes many forms in Finland. Ideally, the school is the prime decision-maker regarding how professional development should be arranged and provided. Schools may also be motivated to lower their operating expenses, such as for textbooks, heating and maintenance, and, rather, to divert those funds to teacher development priorities. On the other hand, some Finnish municipalities still organize in-service programs uniformly for all teachers and allow little latitude for individual schools to decide what would be more beneficial to them. According to a large national survey conducted by the University of Jyväskylä in 2007, on average, teachers devoted about seven working days annually to professional development; approximately half was taken from teachers' personal time (Piesanen, Kiviniemi & Valkonen, 2007).

Finnish teachers are paid on the basis of total instructional time. Their annual duties also include three days focused on planning and professional development. According to a Finnish national survey, approximately two-thirds of primary and secondary school teachers in 2007 participated in professional development (Kumpulainen, 2008). This suggests that from a total Finnish teacher population of 65,000, more than 20,000 failed to participate in any professional development during that year. Participation in professional development, according to a recent report by the Ministry of Education (2009), is decreasing. The government, therefore, is considering ways to strengthen the legal grounds for teacher professional development by requiring that all teachers must have access to adequate professional in-service support, funded by municipalities.

The Finnish State Budget annually allocates some US$30 million to professional development of teachers and school principals through various forms of pre-tertiary education. The main purpose of this allocation is to ensure equal access to further training, particularly for teachers working in more disadvantaged schools. This professional development support is contracted out to service providers on a competitive basis. The government initially determines the focus of the training, based on current national educational development needs. The Finnish Ministry of Education (2009), in collaboration with municipalities, plans to double public funding for teacher professional development by 2016.

Finnish teachers who possess Master's degrees have rightful access to postgraduate studies to supplement their normal professional development opportunities. Primary school teachers can easily begin their doctoral studies in education; their doctoral dissertation will focus on a selected topic in education. Many primary school teachers take advantage of this opportunity, often while they simultaneously teach in schools. Post-graduate studies in education for subject teachers require more work. For doctoral studies in education, students must complete advanced studies in the educational sciences. The main subject must be changed from the student's initial academic concentration, e.g., chemistry, into education, so that students become qualified to complete their doctoral dissertation in education.

Time for collective responsibility

Teaching is commonly viewed in Finland as a demanding profession requiring high academic qualification even for teachers of very young students. Since teacher education became part of academic university studies in the 1970s, Finnish teachers' identity and sense of belonging to highly regarded professionals have gradually increased. During the course of Finland's education reforms, as reported by Aho and colleagues (2006), teachers have demanded more autonomy and responsibility for curriculum and student assessment. The professional context of teaching in Finland differs significantly from that in other countries regarding how teachers experience their work. The professionally respectful environment that teachers experience in Finland is an important factor not only for teacher education policies but also in explaining why so many young Finns regard teaching as their most admired future career.

Curriculum planning is the responsibility of schools and municipalities. Most Finnish schools today have their own curriculum that has been coordinated with and approved by their local education authorities. This correctly implies that teachers and school principals have key roles in curriculum design. The National Framework Curriculum for Basic School and respective documents for upper secondary education provide guidance and necessary regulatory aspects that each school must keep in mind in its curriculum development activities. However, there are no strict national standards or descriptions of learning outcomes that schools must include in their own curriculum, as is true in the United States, for example. That is why curriculum practices vary from school to school; curricula designed by schools are very diverse. The teachers' key role in curriculum planning clearly requires teacher education to instill in all teachers well-developed knowledge and skills related to curriculum issues. Moreover, it has shifted the focus of teacher professional development from fragmented in-service training toward more systemic school improvement that provides a better ethical and theoretical basis for teaching.

Another important teacher responsibility is student assessment. As mentioned earlier, Finnish schools do not employ standardized assessments to determine their progress or success. There are three primary reasons for this: (1) education policy in Finland gives high priority to individualized education and creativity as an important component of school operations. Therefore, students' progress in school is primarily judged against their respective characteristics and abilities, rather than by using statistical indicators; (2) education developers insist that curriculum, teaching and learning are priority components in education that should drive teachers' thinking and school practice, rather than assessment and testing, as is the case in some other education systems. Student assessment in Finnish schools is embedded in teaching and learning processes and is thereby used to improve both teachers' and students' work in school; and (3) determining Finnish students' academic performance is regarded as the responsibility of the school, not of external assessments or assessors. Most Finnish schools acknowledge some shortcomings, such as comparability or consistency, when teachers do all student assessments and grading. At the same time, there is wide acknowledgment in Finland that problems often associated with external standardized testing can be even more troublesome. These problems include a narrowing curriculum, teaching for tests, and unhealthy competition among schools and teachers. Classroom assessment and school-based evaluation are therefore important and valued components of the teacher education curriculum and professional development in Finland.

The only "standardized" assessment of student learning is the national Matriculation Examination established in 1852 (Sahlberg, 2011). It takes place at the close of upper secondary education and serves as a general requirement to academic higher education. It assesses students' knowledge, skills, and competences through essay-type exams in various subjects and is fully financed by students and administrated by an external examination board. It has, many Finnish education specialists argue (Häivälä, 2009), a discernible effect on curriculum and teaching in general upper secondary school; its influence also reaches the closing years of lower secondary school.

Although Finnish teachers' work consists primarily of classroom teaching, many of their duties are outside of class. Formally, teachers' working time in

Finland consists of classroom teaching, preparation (in the case of lab-based subjects such as biology), and two hours weekly collaboratively planning school work with colleagues. Unlike in many other nations, Finnish teachers do not need to be present at school if they do not have classes or if the school principal has not requested them to perform some other duties. From an international perspective, Finnish teachers devote less time to teaching than teachers in many other nations do. For example, a typical middle-school teacher in Finland teaches, on average, about 600 hours annually, corresponding to four 45-minute lessons daily. In most other OECD countries, by contrast, a teacher at the same level spends up to 1000 hours teaching, which means longer periods of time daily in the classroom. Figure 1.3 compares average net teaching time in Finland, the United States, and the OECD countries, according to the OECD statistics (OECD, 2011).

This, however, does *not* imply that teachers in Finland work less than comparable teachers do elsewhere. An important—and still voluntary—part of Finnish teachers' work is devoted to school improvement and work with the community. It is worth remembering that Finnish schools are responsible for the design and continuous development of their curriculum. Unlike in many other nations, Finnish teachers serve as the main assessors of students' school achievement. Indeed, Finland does not employ test-based accountability to monitor and control its schools. Instead, students receive their grades from teachers whose duties include designing and conducting appropriate assessments to document student progress. Finnish teachers have accepted curriculum development, experimentation with teaching methods, and student feedback strategies as important aspects of their work outside of classrooms. In fact, many schools are close to emulating what have been called *professional learning communities* among teachers and school administrators.

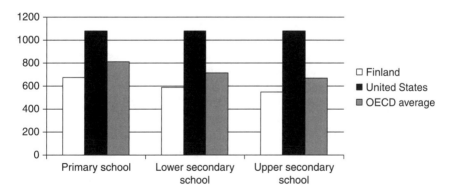

Figure 1.3 Average net teaching hours per school year in Finland, the United States, and in OECD nations.

Source: OECD (2011).

The future of teacher education in Finland

What, in summary, are the relative strengths of teacher education in Finland, based on international perspectives? First, though the Bologna Process directs overall European higher education structures and policies, it does not stipulate how signatory nations should design curricula or arrange their teacher education. There is, and will continue to be, significant differences in national teacher education policies and practices among European education systems. Within this mosaic of European teacher education systems, Finland has these three peculiarities.

First, since it allocated primary school teacher education to the universities and upgraded the teacher diploma to a required Master's degree, Finland has been able to attract some of the most able and talented youth to become teachers. As described earlier, there is a strong cultural influence in the career planning of young Finns, but that alone does not explain this sustained popularity of teaching careers in Finland. Two other factors may be identified. On one hand, the required Master's degree in educational sciences provides a competitive professional foundation not only to become employed as a teacher in primary school, but also in many other careers, including education administration and the private sector. All graduating teachers are automatically eligible to enroll in postgraduate studies, still tuition-free in Finland. On the other hand, many young Finns select teaching as their primary career because work in Finnish schools is perceived as an autonomous, independent, highly regarded profession comparable to working as a medical doctor, lawyer, or architect, for example. Increased external control over teachers' work in schools through test-based accountability or centrally mandated regulation would likely deflect more bright young people into other professional careers where they have freedom to make use of their own creativity and initiative.

Second, there is an extraordinary close connection between the teacher education departments and the subject faculties in Finland. Subject teacher education is organized in a collaborative and coordinated manner that guarantees both solid mastery of subjects to be taught and state-of-the-art didactic competences for all graduates. Faculties in the universities perceive teacher education as an important part of their function and university lectures and some of the professors have specialized in a pedagogic study of their own disciplines. Faculties of education and various subjects in the university are also positively interdependent: they can achieve sustainable success only when both of them do their best.

Third, teacher education in Finland is also recognized because of its systematic and research-based structure. All graduating teachers, by definition of their degree, have completed a research-based Master's thesis that has equally as tight academic requirements as any other field of study in Finnish universities at that level. Research orientation to teacher education prepares teachers, at all levels, to work in complex and changing social and educational environments. Research-based academic training has also enabled implementation of more radical national education policies. For example, enhanced professional competences have led to increased trust in teachers and schools regarding curriculum planning, assessment and reporting of student performance and school improvement. Finland has successfully integrated into its teacher education programs research, knowledge of content and didactics, and practice.

Indeed, research carries a twofold significance for teacher education. Research findings establish a professional basis for teachers to teach and work effectively in a complex knowledge society. Teacher education—in any society—has the potential to progress as a field of science only through and from robust contemporary scientific activity. *Professionalism* as the main descriptor of teaching requires that teachers can access and follow ongoing development of their own craft and that they can freely implement new knowledge within their own professional work. Thus, further development of Finnish teacher education must necessarily be built upon high-quality international research and development.

Current research in and on Finnish teacher education is not well enough focused and coordinated to respond adequately to that call (Jakku-Sihvonen & Niemi, 2006; Ministry of Education, 2007). Most doctoral dissertations focused on teacher education are sourced by individual teachers or by activities of the Departments of Teacher Education, not from externally funded research projects that is the common practice in medicine or economics, for example. Research grant proposals that focus on teaching or teacher education seldom successfully compete against research proposals that address health, technology, or the environment. Furthermore, in Finnish universities, professors in the Faculties of Education devote much more time to supervising students' theses and dissertation work than do professors in other academic units. Table 1.4 shows that Faculty of Education professors' average workload is double that of their colleagues in other academic units, as far as the total Master's theses supervised are concerned.

Continuous national and international reviews suggest that although teacher education in Finland stands as a good example in the international context,

Table 1.4 Master's degrees vs. professors in various academic fields in Finland in 2006

Faculty	Total no. of professors	Master's degrees	PhD degrees	Degrees per professor	Master's degrees per professor
Social Sciences	248	1 784	107	7.63	7.19
Education	130	1 630	77	13.13	12.54
Political Sciences	205	1 261	95	6.61	6.15
Natural Sciences	352	1 496	308	5.13	4.25
Medical Sciences	260	415	228	2.47	1.60

Source: Adapted from Ministry of Education (2007).

several aspects of Finland's program could be improved. Finnish authorities are particularly concerned about the fact that many students enroll in teacher education too long after graduating from upper secondary schools. This is due to intense competition at entry that often requires that an applicant has to have at least some experience of school practice. It is also argued that Finnish students spend too long at their studies and are therefore much older than their peers elsewhere when they finally enter the labor market. The main model for further improving teacher education in Finland today are European policies that are not binding directives, but rather recommendations on building more coherent teacher education as part of the European Higher Education Area. The main policy issues to be addressed regarding Finnish teacher education, according to the Ministry of Education (2007), include:

1   *Responding to the changing society.* Declining age cohorts and many teachers who are retiring create a complex challenge for preparing needed new teachers by 2020. At the same time, Finnish schools must accommodate a growing number of immigrant and special needs students. Teacher education should be based on a thorough needs analysis to prepare educators for their work in a changing social and cultural world. Weakening social networks in Finland are also increasing the upbringing and caring aspects of teachers' work. As a result, many teachers feel overloaded by these new responsibilities and some suffer from burn-out. Even more than previously, initial and in-service teacher education must address the social and psychological issues in teachers' work.

2   *Systematic professional development for all teachers.* Teacher education in Finnish universities and ongoing teacher professional development should constitute a better continuum. Induction should be available to all teachers and included as part of lifelong professional development. The responsibility of Finnish municipalities in providing professional development opportunities should be strengthened by requiring that each teacher can have access to relevant professional development.

3   *Teacher education strategy for each university.* Each university offering teacher education programs should have an up-to-date, comprehensive teacher education strategy. These plans should stipulate, for example, the program's aims, functions and quantitative targets, describe needed coordination among the university's various units, outline operational principles of practice teaching in Teacher Training Schools, and ensure mobility for teachers and students among other institutions. These strategies should also strongly focus on enhancing the university's role in providing in-service training and professional development for teachers.

4   *Strengthen research on teacher education.* Teacher education is part of academic higher education and the responsibility of the entire university. Research on teacher education should be strengthened through a better, more highly coordinated national research program; that may mean

concentrating teacher education in a smaller number of departments, improving leadership, as well as teacher education research and expanding multi-disciplinary graduate and post-doctoral programs. Research on teacher education should become more competitive in seeking and receiving financing for research projects.

Finnish teacher education's greatest potential lies in the hundreds of talented and motivated young people who, year after year, seek enrollment in teacher education programs. This is a crucial factor for the continued and future success of teacher education in Finland. Young Finns gravitate toward teaching because they consider it an independent, respected, and rewarding profession where they will have the freedom to fulfill their aspirations. But general upper secondary school graduates also weigh the quality of teacher education programs when making decisions about their future career. It is therefore paramount that Finnish teacher education continues to develop to ensure that, in the future, it remains an attractive and competitive option for highly able young people.

No single feature can explain good educational performance in Finland, but, rather, a network of inter-related factors. Excellent teachers, as most analysts argue, play an important part in current educational excellence. Teachers' professional status in Finnish society is a cultural phenomenon, but how teachers are prepared to teach in classrooms and work collaboratively in professional communities is attributable to systematically planned and implemented academic teacher education. For other nations, imitating the Finnish curriculum system or organizational aspects of schools may not be a wise strategy. However, a positive lesson that the Finns themselves have learned by raising the level of teacher education to be on a par with other academic pursuits is certainly something that merits closer examination. A critical condition for attracting the most able young people year after year to teacher education, however, is that a teacher's work should become an independent and respectful profession rather than merely a technical implementation of externally mandated standards, mindless tests, and administrative burdens.

Chapter 2

Quality teachers, Singapore style

A. Lin Goodwin

We the teachers of Singapore pledge that:

We will be true to our mission to bring out the best in our pupils.

- *We are committed to our pupils' holistic development and regard them as unique individuals with different learning needs and styles.*
- *We will provide our pupils with opportunities to discover new interests, cultivate their special talents and inspire them to realise their potential.*

We will be exemplary in our discharge of our duties and responsibilities.

- *We will demonstrate moral courage and integrity, take pride in our work and uphold the professionalism of our teaching fraternity.*
- *We will be purposeful in what we do and our passion to care for our pupils and educate them will be the source of our motivation.*

We will guide our pupils to be good and useful citizens of Singapore.

- *We will guide our pupils to become resilient, responsible and resolute citizens who love Singapore, our home.*
- *We will journey with our pupils and guide them to become confident, thinking and innovative individuals who are committed to serve, improve and defend our country, Singapore.*

We will continue to learn and pass on the love of learning to our pupils.

- *We are committed to our professional growth, and possess the open-mindedness and drive for continuous learning.*
- *We believe that true learning is a joyful experience which we will share with fellow teachers and our pupils.*

We will win the trust, support and co-operation of parents and community so as to enable us to achieve our mission.

- *We will involve parents and the community in providing rich learning experiences for our pupils.*
- *We will forge and sustain effective and meaningful relationships with parents and the community to help our pupils discover and develop their talents.*

The Teachers' Pledge, Ministry of Education, Singapore
http://www3.moe.edu.sg/purposeofteaching/teacherPledge.html

So where in the world is Singapore? (And why should we care?)

It was not so long ago that I would confront the first question when I mentioned that I was going to visit my mum in Singapore. I was just as likely to have a colleague or some acquaintance from "the West" tell me to have a nice trip to China or Hong Kong prior to my departure. It is still not outside the realm of possibility for "Occidentals" to perceive Singapore as embedded in the "universal oriental" (Goodwin, Genishi, Asher, & Woo, 1997) and to identify it as a part of China, or some other Asian country in "the Far East." However, in our newly globalized world, things have changed, especially in terms of how we know and what we know of "the Other."

What we in the U.S. now may know more keenly is that Singaporean students have consistently outperformed their counterparts on international assessments (Luke *et al.*, 2005; Ministry of Education (MOE), December 2008; National Center for Education Statistics, n.d.). According to TIMSS (Trends in International Mathematics and Science Study) data, not only do they outperform their peers in scores of countries around the world, including the U.S., they consistently perform at or near the top. For example, in 2007 and 2003, fourth graders in Singapore were second and first respectively on the mathematics assessments, and achieved first place in science in both years (National Center for Education Statistics, n.d.). Partly as a consequence of the high performance of its students in these international comparisons, Singapore today enjoys much wider international recognition. President Obama's inclusion of Singapore in his recent visit to Asia is an indicator of the country's rising status as a global player. The consistently strong performance of its pupils, coupled with its high level of purchasing power parities (PPP)—ranked seventh just behind the U.S., according to an international comparison report of the World Bank (2008)— and its leap, literally, into the 21st Century in a single generation, has changed the question from "Where is Singapore?" to "How can we be more like Singapore?" Moreover, in an increasingly shrinking world context where countries are able to easily look across at international neighbors and measure themselves against common yard-sticks, we are all in a better position than ever to share knowledge and learn from one another.

As all nations strive towards excellence at all levels, be it economic, social, political, cultural, or, of course, educational, teacher quality has become a contemporary global concern (Buchberger, Campos, Kallos, & Stephenson, 2000; International Alliance of Leading Education Institutes, 2008; International Reading Association, 2008). While there is little argument about the need for quality teachers and the key role they play in the socialization of citizens and the conveyance of national priorities, there remains little consensus on what constitutes "excellence" or quality and how quality teachers might best be attained (Akiba, LeTendre, & Scribner, 2007). The stellar performance of Singaporean students appears to have captured the international imagination and naturally leads to the question of quality teachers, especially given mounting evidence that teacher quality is the key to student performance and achieving positive student outcomes. Certainly in the U.S., the issue of teacher quality is currently one of the most pressing concerns expressed by policy-makers, the media, the public at large, and by educators themselves, and has been a central focus of current Secretary of Education Arne Duncan (October 22, 2009). In the national educational discourse, there are a multitude of opinions about how teacher quality should be defined, and these opinions are not only varied but often contradictory (e.g., Darling-Hammond, 2001 vs. Walsh, 2001). We are immersed in debates regarding what teachers should know and should be able to do, the qualities and preparation teachers should have, where teacher preparation should take place (if at all), and what this preparation should include—or exclude (Cochran-Smith & Zeichner, 2005; Darling-Hammond & Bransford, 2005; Darling-Hammond & Youngs, 2002; Goodwin & Oyler, 2008).

This chapter takes a look at the question of teacher preparation of quality and for quality through a case study of teacher education in Singapore, with a focus on the past decade or so. The story relies on data from multiple sources including a wide range of documents: program handbooks and course of study outlines; scholarly articles and book chapters; reports; PowerPoint presentations. It also relies on observations conducted in Singapore, and conversations with or inter-views of teacher education faculty and university administrators, principals and teachers, and MOE personnel. Finally, it draws upon data from relevant internet sites. The chapter begins with an examination of the Singapore context framing teacher preparation. It then moves to a focus on recruitment, teacher prepara-tion, and professional development, paying attention to key structures, programs, and procedures. It ends with a broader look across the data to surface some possible intangibles that seem to support quality teachers Singapore style.

The Singaporean context for education and teacher preparation

Singapore is a very small South-East Asian country, a 710+ square kilometer island (Statistics Singapore, September 28, 2009) bookended by the southern tip of the Malayan peninsula 50 kilometers to the north and the nearest Indonesian island about 20 kilometers to the south. It is home to a multi-racial, multi-ethnic and multi-religious population of just under 5 million (Singapore Department of Statistics, 2009), the majority of whom are "Chinese (77%), Malay (14%) and Indian (8%)," most of whom speak at least two of the four official languages: Malay, Tamil, Chinese (Mandarin) and English. According to 2008 MOE data (September, 2009a), just over half a million children attend 356 primary and secondary schools, and are taught by about 28,000 teachers. The majority of teachers are female (73%), as are the majority of principals and vice-principals (64%). Literacy rates surpass 96% (Statistics Singapore, September 28, 2009) and "there are opportunities for every child in Singapore to undergo at least ten years of general education" (MOE, September, 2009a, p. v).

The physical landscape of Singapore is decidedly vertical, densely packed with hundreds of commercial skyscrapers and housing development blocks (government housing) where the majority of Singaporeans live, etched with an intricate network of roads and highways supporting a well-developed and efficient public transportation system—both above ground and below. As a modern, technologically advanced city-state, it displays many of the characteristics and trappings of urbanicity—throngs of people, an over-abundance of vehicles, hyper-commercialism, limited space, and a great diversity in terms of people, languages, cultures, food, traditions, and ways of life. Uncharacteristic of many urban centers, Singapore is also a clean, manicured garden city, well-organized and planned, efficient, and with low levels of crime and poverty. Much of the population is middle class and enjoys high standards of living including excellent health facilities and services, well-equipped and safe schools, smooth running government, public housing that is ever more sophisticated and amenity-rich, and myriad opportunities and options for professional, intellectual, and personal advancement.

Visitors to Singapore today would be hard-pressed to believe that in just about 50 years, Singapore has progressed from being a "struggling post-colonial society plagued with problems of survival," to a "vibrant . . . economy with a competitive edge in the world market" (Yip, Eng, & Yap, 1997, p. 4), often touted as an example for other nations, both "developed" and "developing."[1] As a witness to this transformation, I am hard-pressed at times to believe it myself, especially when I compare the physical, educational, economic, and social landscape of the Singapore of my childhood, and the landscape of the country where my parents still reside. "Simply, as a small economy with little primary industry and natural resources, [Singapore] has defined its future as an information/service/digital economy driven by educational investment and development" (Luke *et al.*, 2005,

p. 8). From the time I was in primary school through pre-university,[2] a period that paralleled the critical early years of Singapore's independence, the constant refrain was—and remains—that her people are Singapore's "most precious resource" and that "through education every individual can realise his [*sic*] full potential, use his talents and abilities to benefit his community and nation, and lead a full and satisfying life" (MOE, June 29, 2007; also Goh & Gopinathan, 2008; Gopinathan, 2007; Luke *et al.*, 2005; Yip, Eng, & Yap, 1997). Consequently, Singapore "has skillfully used education policy to both transform society and in that process to make education a valued social institution" (Gopinathan, 2007, p. 68), thereby cementing a national belief in education as the "prime engine of economy, nation and identity" (Luke *et al.*, 2005, p. 8).

While education has remained a perennial bedrock value in Singapore, the focus of educational initiatives and reform has shifted according to national imperatives and goals. Thus, the emphasis after independence from Malaysia in 1965 was "survival-driven education" (Goh & Gopinathan, 2008), aimed at achieving "universal primary education . . . and mass recruitment of teachers . . . to staff the rising number of schools" (Goh & Lee, 2008, p. 97). Teacher quality was much less a concern than recruiting sufficient numbers of teachers. The years from 1978 to 1997 saw a shift to "an efficiency-driven education," in response to Singapore's need to compete for multinational dollars and "produce skilled workers for the economy in the most efficient way" (Tan, 2005, p. 2). Quantity— enough schools with enough teachers—was now inadequate; attention was now on raising quality—upgrading schools, streaming (i.e., tracking) students according to their identified talents, designing curricula geared to students' skill levels and perceived capacities, expanding tertiary education. "Reducing educa- tional wastage" meant "teachers and children alike were mechanically fed by a bureaucratically designated and rigid curriculum" (Goh & Lee, 2008, p. 25).

All this changed in 1997 when Prime Minister (PM) Goh Chok Tong[3] announced *Thinking Schools, Learning Nation (TSLN)*, a new national vision for developing "the creative thinking skills and learning skills required for the . . . intensely global future" and making "learning a national culture" (June 2, 1997). This ushered in the current focus on "ability-driven education [which] aims to identify and develop the talents and abilities of every child to the maximum" (Tan, 2005, p. 5). Definitions of teaching and learning became more inclusive, expansive and flexible in order to embrace: diverse ways of knowing and thinking; multiple pathways and options for learning; and innovative pedagogies and technologies (Hogan & Gopinathan, 2008; Luke *et al.*, 2005; MOE, December 2008). Added PM Goh Chok Tong in his speech:

> [*Thinking Schools, Learning Nation*] will redefine the role of teachers . . . Every school must be a model learning organisation. Teachers and principals will constantly look out for new ideas and practices, and continuously refresh their own knowledge. Teaching will itself be a learning profession, like any other knowledge-based profession of the future.

Thus, educational reforms sparked by *TSLN* fueled significant changes in the recruitment, preparation, compensation, status, and professional development of teachers, changes that have had an indelible impact on teacher quality and the teaching profession in Singapore.

Teacher preparation in Singapore

Teacher recruitment

[Q:] Although teachers are in great demand, why are so many people unsuccessful in gaining admission to NIE [National Institute of Education]?

[A:] Each year, MOE receives many teaching applications. All applicants must first and foremost meet our minimum selection criteria. Our selection criteria have to be stringent. They are assessed based on the totality of their academic and non-academic achievement. Their applications are considered in competition with others.

(MOE, 2009b)

One of the reasons why there are many more individuals seeking to enter teaching than there are successful applicants is that "in 1996, the Singapore government implemented wide-sweeping changes in the salaries and promotion aspects in the education service" (Goh & Lee, 2008, p. 100). Salaries for new teachers rose steeply and are now commensurate with salaries for new graduates entering other fields that require equivalent preparation and study, such as engineering, law and business. In addition, all student teachers are appointed as MOE employees— General Education Officers—from the moment they are accepted into teacher preparation, and receive: a full salary for up to two years according to MOE pay scales and criteria; benefits (such as retirement,[4] health care); an annual bonus (given to all Singapore employees in accordance with Singapore's economic health); plus they are eligible for other bonuses tied to performance or other relevant work experiences. All student teachers' tuition fees are fully covered by MOE plus they are provided funds to purchase materials such as books and laptop computers. In return for the support they receive during their preparation, successful graduates are required to complete a bond of service for 3–5 years (the years of service required depends on the length of program completed). Student teachers who drop out or fail to complete the program for other than extraordinary reasons (e.g., serious health issues) must repay the government for compensation and tuition costs on a pro-rata basis.

However, salaries are not the only reason why "there are more applicants than vacancies" and "teaching is competitive."[5] Teaching receives a great deal of publicity and "personal interest shown by the Prime Minister" (Yip, Eng, & Yap, 1997, p. 4). The MOE uses a variety of media to advertise and recruit, has a "road show about teaching as a career," and hosts recruitment events at "nice hotels with tea." Teachers and teaching are consistently included in speeches made by government officials, ministers, and the Prime Minister, where their contributions and importance to nation-building are heralded (see http://www. moe.gov.sg/ for archives of speeches). The guarantee of employment is obviously a strong recruitment draw. The MOE not only organizes all recruitment efforts, but recruits according to vacancies in schools and in response to shortage areas. Thus successful applicants are not only salaried during their preparation, but are assured of employment upon program completion. At the same time, schools are assured of new teachers who are well prepared and have been specifically selected to meet their needs. Still, this does not mean that quality or preparation are sacrificed in order to fill shortages; schools and the MOE are prepared to "stay with a gap for a while"—a current example is the need for geography teachers—rather than fill shortages with less than qualified teachers. It is not surprising then that prospective teachers who enter the MOE website related to teaching careers first face the question "Are you the right one?" because "not everyone can be a teacher" (2009b). Similarly, the NIE website reminds applicants in several different places that "because of the large number of candidates seeking admission, we regret that no telephone or personal enquiries will be entertained" (NIE Foundations Programmes).

The selection process is stringent and begins with criteria—academic performance, educational background—for application to the various programs and pathways available for teaching different grade levels or subjects (described more fully later in the chapter). Prospective teachers who meet these criteria submit an online application which is processed by MOE. Applicants "found suitable" are interviewed by a panel which includes principals and faculty from the National Institute of Education (NIE). States the MOE 2009 website:

> The interview panel will assess your communication skills, interest in teaching, goals and aspirations, and your willingness to learn. More importantly, you must have the passion to teach and the belief that you can make a difference.

In addition, applicants who do not possess "basic proficiency in EL (English language) required for entering teaching"—with minimum pass scores at the "A" or "O" levels—or are applying to teach special subjects such as art, music, physical education or home economics, or a Mother Tongue Language (Chinese, Malay or Tamil) are required to pass an entrance proficiency (language) test or a drawing test, music audition, or physical proficiency test. While applications are accepted year round, there are two NIE intakes a year, "a major one in July for all programmes," and "a second intake in January only for the Postgraduate Diploma in Education" (Secondary) program. Consequently, applicants selected for teacher preparation before the start of the NIE term are posted to schools as contract teachers (full-time but temporary) during the interim with the help and guidance of "senior teachers in the respective schools." According to MOE

(2009b), this enables new recruits to "discover whether teaching is suitable for you . . . [and] in turn will help you to appreciate the NIE course better."

Teacher preparation pathways and requirements

Without exception, all student teachers are required to complete a university-based program offered by NIE. Established in 1991, NIE is one of the schools housed within Nanyang Technological University (NTU), one of Singapore's four universities, and the sole teacher preparation institution in Singapore. Annual intake of initial teacher certification (ITC) students has been fairly consistent since 1998 at about 2000 candidates (Goh & Lee, 2008). However, the 2009 cohort was increased to about 3000[6] in response to MOE's goal to reduce primary class sizes in Singapore from 40 to 30 students.

There are several Initial Teacher Preparation (ITP) program pathways offered by NIE for aspiring teachers, according to their educational background, prior academic performance, and career goal in terms of grade level (i.e., primary or secondary) or subject specialty. Table 2.1 presents the various options in brief, and indicates eligibility, pre-selection criteria, length of program, and teaching levels (distilled from NIE Foundation Programmes). What Table 2.1 reveals is that NIE offers "multiple pathways catering to student teachers with diverse educational backgrounds" (NIE Foundation Programmes). Candidates enter teacher preparation possessing different levels of academic and or technical prep-aration from the more basic to the more advanced (A-Levels or high school diploma; polytechnic diploma; Bachelor's or university degree). However, all are held to rigorous and specific admission standards, and are informed clearly that meeting minimal requirements does not guarantee admission.

The curriculum

It would be impossible, given the space limitations of a single chapter, to lay out in detail the curriculum for each of the ITP pathways along with their numerous specialization choices and options, available at NIE to student teachers. This section will therefore focus on: (1) the overall philosophy that underlies teacher preparation in Singapore; (2) the main curricular components common to all programs or pathways; and (3) the student teaching experience in general. The Diploma in Education is being phased out, so this pathway is not included in the discussion.

Underlying philosophy

The current framework for ITP—the VSK Model—is graphically represented by a central pillar of values (V) encircled by skills (S) and knowledge (K); skills and knowledge interact but are always anchored to and informed by values (see Figure 2.1, p. 32).

Table 2.1 Initial Teacher Preparation (ITP) programs offered by NIE

Program	Minimum eligibility criteria	Pre-selection criteria[1]	Program length	Grade level teaching
PGDE—Postgraduate Diploma in Education "to prepare university graduates to become teachers"	Bachelor's degree	Pass on Pre-Selection Test (subject) or Entrance Proficiency Test (language) as applicable; Proficiency tests/auditions for PE, Art, Music; GCE 'O'-Level passes in English, Mathematics and any Science (primary teaching)	One academic year (max. two academic years), 33–44 Academic Units (AUs); PGDE in PE is two academic years (max. three academic years), 67 AUs	Primary Secondary Junior College
BA/BSc in Education—" to integrate the best of an academic degree with a good foundation in the field of education"	A-Levels or polytechnic graduates (equivalent of high school diploma)	Minimum grades[2] in: 4 A-Level subjects + at least 5 O-Level subjects including English as a first language + mother tongue at the A- or O-Levels; passing grades in mathematics at either the A or O levels; other minimum grades in subjects according to reading subject selected (reading a subject = subject major)	Four academic years (max. seven & minimum 3.5 academic years), 122–131 AUs	Primary Secondary
BEd (part-time) "specially designed for non-graduate primary school teachers"	NIE Diploma, Certificate of Education, or NIE Advanced Diploma	Good A-Level or Polytechnic qualifications; letter of recommendation from principal	Four academic years (max. six & minimum 3.5 academic years), 138 AUs	Primary

Diploma in Education— "the first qualifications towards a meaningful teaching career"	A-Levels or Polytechnic graduates (equivalent of HS diploma) Note: Special Training Program in Mother Tongue Languages (Malay, Tamil, Chinese) offered to O-Level holders	Minimum grades in 4 A-Level subjects (one or more sittings of exams); passing grades in at least five O-Level subjects including English as a first language. In addition, according to specialization, passing grades in O-Level mathematics; minimum A- or O-Level grades in Chinese, Malay or Tamil; minimum grade and passing audition for music; minimum A- or O-Level grades and interview for art. Entrance Proficiency Tests as applicable.	Two academic years	General Track: Primary; Specialization Track: Primary and Secondary Mother Tongue Languages, PE; Lower Secondary: Art, Music, Home Economics

Notes:

[1] Candidates for ITP programs are typically drawn from the top-third of graduates.

[2] It is important to highlight that "minimum" grades should not be interpreted as minimal grades. The term is simply used as a way to inform readers that applicants need to have achieved subject grades of a particular level in order to be eligible for consideration, not just at the "A" level, but oftentimes at the "O" level as well.

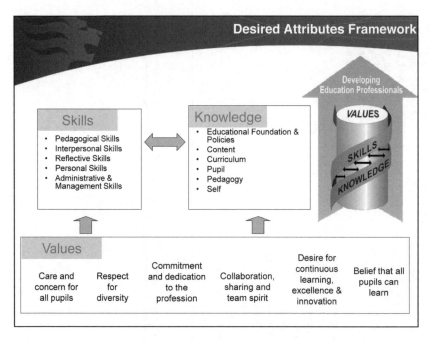

Figure 2.1 VSK framework for initial teacher preparation at NIE

So, for instance, Knowledge of "self" or of "pupils" is supported and enacted by "interpersonal" or "reflective" skills, and grounded by the fundamental values of "care and concern for all pupils" or "respect for diversity." The VSK model traces its genesis to *Teach Less, Learn More (TLLM)*, a call in 2004 by current PM Lee Hsien Loong for "transforming learning" in ways that

> would mean less dependence on rote learning, repetitive tests and a "one-size fits all" type of instruction, and more on experiential discovery, engaged learning, differentiated teaching, the learning of life-long skills and the building of character through innovative and effective teaching approaches and strategies.
>
> (Singapore Education Milestones, 2004–2005)

As one of several conceptual frameworks that have grown out of *Thinking Schools, Learning Nation* and have helped to carry this vision forward, *TLLM* initiated the 2005 re-design of ITP programs, resulting in the VSK (Values, Skills, Knowledge) model with an explicit emphasis on "Innovation, Independent Learning, Critical Thinking, Commitment and Service." The VSK model should resonate with U.S. audiences since the notion of knowledge, skills and dispositions is integral to U.S. standards for teacher preparation going back to the development of INTASC

(Interstate New Teacher Assessment Consortium) standards for new teachers in 1987. In keeping with "evidence-based curricula informed by research," teacher preparation curricula at NIE benefit from extensive reviews of international literature and research, as well as close examination of the histories and practices of peers in the global community. Thus, for example, the ground-breaking work of Lee Shulman (1986) on pedagogical content knowledge appears as a key component of the theoretical foundation for ITP programs. Indeed, NIE study teams regularly visit fellow educators and institutions around the world to conduct observations and keep pace with educational innovations, engage in mutual learning and sharing, and participate in cross-national/transcultural dialogues on common issues and concerns. The learning stance that NIE adopts is not simply outwardly focused, but is simultaneously locally grounded in research—large-scale and not, quantitative and qualitative—"to develop new and innovative ways of teaching and learning . . . aimed at enhancing practice in Singapore schools" (NIE Office of Education Research). Thus, teacher preparation at NIE is informed "glocally,"[7] that is both globally and locally.

ITP programs: common elements

Currently, there are two main preparation pathways into the classroom—the postgraduate pathway or PGDE, and the degree pathway or BA/BSc/BEd Other than the BEd which "is a degree programme for non-graduate primary teachers," all the other pathways prepare both primary and secondary teachers. Although the Diploma in Education is still in place, "there is an intention to close down the Dip Ed permanently by 2012 (last intake) except for certain specialisations in languages, art and music. This is in line with the Ministry's move to recruit a graduate teaching workforce." Students in ITP programs typically complete their programs on a full-time basis, with the exception of the Bachelor of Education that affords part-time study.[8] Still, BEd students are required to complete one semester of residency on the NIE campus and are permitted leave from their regular teaching positions to do so. All NIE student teachers are strongly encouraged to complete their programs in the time allotted, but are permitted to extend their program for one to three academic years, depending on the program. Students must maintain good academic standing in their program which means achieving a cumulative grade point average (CGPA) of 2.0 or C. It is important to note here that there is little grade inflation, and a C grade is not only acceptable but challenging to earn. Students who do not maintain a CGPA of 2.0 are put on academic warning after one semester and academic probation after two. If this continues for a third semester, students are terminated from the program.

Courses are counted in Academic Units (AUs) with one AU translating into an hour per week of lecture or tutorial plus three hours of laboratory or fieldwork. Most courses are offered for two or three AUs. Each program consists of core courses which are compulsory and prescribed electives "that form a certain field of specialisation in a particular subject. They add to the depth and/or breadth of knowledge and skills to be acquired by student teachers" (NIE Foundation Programmes). Student teaching or "teaching practice" is also required of every trainee and carries 10–12 AUs. While students may "read the subject/courses of their own choice, the final choice of subjects/courses sometimes has to be determined by the Dean" or program heads according to space and availability (NIE Foundation Programmes). Programs use "various modes of assessment [which] include tests/practical tests, essay assignments, project work, progress ratings and examinations" (NIE Foundation Programmes). Finally, all student teachers are expected "to participate actively in talks, seminars, workshops and other activities organised for them . . . activities [which] form an integral part of the programme" (NIE Foundation Programmes).

ITP programs, regardless of pathway, all include common curricular components: Education Studies, Academic Studies or Subject Knowledge, Curriculum Studies, and Practicum. Language Enhancement and Academic Discourse Skills (LEADS) are also compulsory for all student teachers. Table 2.2 describes in brief each of these components, summarized from program handbooks (NIE Foundation Programmes).

All courses are offered on campus at NIE, with the exception of teaching practice, by NIE "academic staff" who occupy a variety of "academic tracks" including "the Professorial Track, Lecture Track, Visiting Staff and Part time Professorial Fellows [and] MOE Seconded Staff." Faculty on the professorial track have their doctorates and experience the same breakdown of responsibilities as professors in the U.S., namely research/scholarship, teaching, and service. Lecturers need not have doctorates, "although progression in the career ladder on the teaching track to principal lecturership requires a doctorate." Visiting staff and professorial fellows typically hail from other countries and may or may not hold doctoral degrees. Finally, MOE seconded staff include teachers, principals or education officers from MOE who are assigned for service at NIE for a defined amount of time, usually one or two years. Some of these could include educators with doctoral degrees.

The core curriculum, as outlined in Table 2.2, consists of *Education Studies* courses designed to provide students with foundational "concepts and principles . . . necessary for effective teaching and reflective practice." In four courses, students learn about human development and learning theory, teaching diverse learners and creating positive learning environments, and the use of ICT (Information and Communication Technologies) in terms of instruction and pedagogy, skills and tools, and cyber well-being as an example of the *TLLM* focus on educating the whole child of and for the 21st Century. Students also take a social contexts course to learn about the education system in Singapore—policies, history, major reforms, socio-political concerns/impacts, teachers' possible roles within education.

All student teachers "will specialise in the methodology for teaching at either the primary school level, secondary school level or junior college level" (NIE Foundation Programmes) in at least one subject. Table 2.2 indicates the number

Table 2.2 Brief descriptions of common curricular components for all ITP programs

Curricular component	Brief description	Special considerations
Education Studies	"key concepts and principles of education that are necessary for effective teaching and reflective practice in schools"	Four core courses required of all students: Ed Psych 1 and 2, Social Context of Teaching & Learning, ICT for Meaningful Learning
Academic Studies	Defined as/by under-graduate major/degree	PE secondary teachers are required to engage in additional (specific) academic study. BEd students take Subject Knowledge instead of Academic Studies
Curriculum Studies	"designed to give student teachers the pedagogical skills in teaching specific subjects in Singapore schools"	Aligned with teaching subject(s) and dependent on subjects studied at university # of teaching subjects required: 3—BA/BSc primary 3–2—PGDE primary 2—PGDE or BA/BSc secondary 1–2—PGDE junior college
Practicum	"develop planning and delivery skills, followed by classroom management and evaluation skills . . . opportunities to explore other aspects of a teacher's life besides classroom teaching"	Mentoring by cooperating teachers, NIE faculty, part-time faculty (retired teachers and principals)
LEADS (Language Enhancement and Academic Discourse Skills)	"oral and writing skills necessary for effective communication as teachers in the classroom and in their professional interaction with colleagues, parents and the general public"	Additionally, MOE requires "a series of three English Language Content Enhancement courses" for PGDE Primary, or PGDE Secondary—English language"
GESL (Group Endeavors in Service Learning)	"compulsory project work . . . Student teachers in an assigned group are to collaboratively complete a project in a community service within the programme of study"	Not required of BEd students

of teaching subjects different programs require that student teachers select for *Curriculum Studies*. It is important to note that the teaching subjects PGDE students choose for Curriculum Studies must correspond to the academic subjects they read in university. Thus, while *Academic Studies* are not an explicit or separate component of the PGDE program because students enter NIE already holding a degree in an academic content area, Academic Studies are still an implicit aspect of the PGDE program and have an impact on students' Curriculum Studies selections. The situation is slightly different for BA/BSc students who, over their four-year programs, are engaged explicitly in Academic Studies alongside Curriculum Studies. However, like PGDE students, students in the degree pathways also engage in Curriculum Studies that align with their Academic Studies. Students in the BA primary track must choose one Arts subject (e.g., geography, art, Chinese language) as their first academic subject, just as BSc primary education students must select one Science subject (e.g., biology, mathematics). Similarly, BA students preparing to teach at the secondary level "must read an arts subject as Academic Subject 1 but can choose an Arts or Science subject as Academic Subject 2" (NIE Foundations Programmes); it follows then that BSc secondary students are required to read in the sciences for their first subject. Every program includes a course in communication skills (LEADS) that includes topics such as "vocal health care and quality . . . pronunciation . . . purpose, audience and context when communicating . . . making oral and written presentations in a variety of school contexts" (NIE Foundation Programmes). Finally, all student teachers, with the exception of BEd students, are required to work collaboratively with peers to complete the Group Endeavors in Service Learning (GELS) Project, which demands 20 hours of direct service in the community, including project design, planning and presentation.

Teaching practicum

As stated earlier, a teaching practicum is required of all student teachers and typically occurs during the second semester of the program (in the case of PGDE programs) or the second semester of each year (in the case of BA/BSc programs). The purpose of the practicum is:

> [To] provide student teachers with the opportunity to develop teaching competencies in a variety of instructional contexts and at different levels, under the guidance and supervision of cooperating teachers and university lecturers . . . develop planning and delivery skills, followed by classroom management and evaluation skills . . . [and] explore other aspects of a teacher's life besides classroom teaching.
>
> (NIE Foundation Programmes)

PGDE students complete one 10-week Teaching Practice placement during their year-long program. Placements are assigned by MOE because "it is better for [students] to be placed in schools that will have vacancies to absorb them immediately when they complete the programme." BA/BSc students are placed by the NIE Practicum Office because "they have more than one practicum spread across the number of years of the programme" and so there is less urgency to place them in schools that have vacancies until later in their programs. Cooperating teachers (CTs) are selected by the schools since "they know best which teachers have sufficient experience to serve that role." However the practicum office does suggest to schools "that the CTs should be teaching the same subject area as the student teacher and have at least 2–3 years of teaching experience." Each school designates the vice principal or senior department head as the School Coordinating Mentor who is the main liaison between NIE—specifically the NIE Supervision Coordinator—and the school, and between and among CTs and student teachers. The SCM also oversees and supports the work of student teachers and CTs, helps to facilitate observations, and plays a key role in student evaluations.

The Teaching Practice experience affords PGDE students "10 weeks of independent teaching" in two different grade levels, either upper and lower primary, or upper and lower secondary, and in two or three subjects. BA/BSc students have a similar experience during their final 10-week teaching practice, although primary track students teach three subjects and secondary students teach two. However, for degree students, the 10-week practicum represents the culminating field experience for their program; each student also completes three prior practicum experiences, beginning in the initial year of their program. In year one, BA/BSc students complete a two-week "school experience," a non-credit but required placement that introduces them to a primary and then a secondary school context. In the second year, students complete a "Teaching Assistantship, five weeks of observation and reflection at two different grade levels, either primary or secondary." Year three brings Teaching Practice I for "5 weeks of guided teaching" before "Teaching Practice II" in the final and fourth year.

Student teachers typically spend the first week of Teaching Practice/Teaching Practice II observing before beginning the "teaching of lessons for the remaining weeks"—20–24 lessons for students preparing to teach in the primary grades, and 16–20 lessons for secondary level students (NIE Practicum/FAQs). All students are observed by NIE Supervision Coordinators who "make at least 2 lesson observations per student teacher under their charge," plus NIE recommends that CTs conduct "a total of 8 (formal observations) for all the CS (Curriculum Study) subjects, spread over *10 weeks* of the TPII (Teaching Practice II) period" (NIE Practicum Office). Student teachers are assessed using the *Assessment of Performance in Teaching*, a rubric consisting of five performance criteria—"Lesson preparation, Lesson delivery and management, Classroom management, Feedback and evaluation, Professional qualities" along four standards of performance—distinction, credit, pass, fail. Assessors are reminded that each performance criterion "comprises some aspects of the VSK framework around which the Desired Outcomes of Initial Teacher Preparation were drawn up" and that the "indicators are meant as guidelines for assessors of student teachers' attitudes, skills and knowledge" (NIE Practicum/SCMs).

Student teaching evaluations occur at a final meeting chaired by the principal that brings together the SCM and the NIE supervisor "to discuss all cases." The grade assigned relies on summative reports written by CTs (and discussed with student teachers) and by NIE supervisors, as well as comments from principals and the SCM. The final grade must represent a consensus between NIE and the school. In addition, "Moderation is *compulsory* for DISTINCTION and FAIL cases" (NIE Practicum/SCMs), thus underscoring that the level of performance expected of students is "credit" or "pass." Students who experience difficulties during their student teaching are discussed and are "provided support." Discussions typically involve the principal and the SCM, and are moderated by the NIE supervisor. Those who fail student teaching can retake the practicum and make a second (and final) attempt to meet standards; however, their salary is suspended for the second student teaching period.

Professional development for Singapore teachers

Induction and mentoring for new teachers

Each year, new teachers are inducted into the profession, beginning with an investiture ceremony which is attended by the Minister of Education and is reported in the public media. They each recite "the Teachers' Pledge," (see above) voicing aloud their commitments and responsibilities as teachers. They enter schools which typically have a "structured induction programme" in place typically involving "4 core inservice courses that new teachers have to attend within their first 2 years of service (classroom management, basic counselling, working with parents, reflective practice)." Additionally, new teachers are "assigned a buddy, mentor and supervisor—the buddy is a peer teaching the same subject, the mentor is an experienced teacher also teaching similar subjects ... The supervisor is usually the HOD (Head of Department)." Schools also organize Staff Welfare Committees that offer support regarding "recreational activities." The principal, senior teacher, and department heads further provide a variety of orientations and supports.

The MOE also provides a wide variety of supports through the *Teachers Network* (MOE Teachers Network) to help new (and continuing) teachers manage the many stressors of teaching. One example is the "Teacher Renewal Journey." Over the course of four full and four half-days spread out over a year, the experience affords teachers the space and time "to engage in deep reflection ... as they seek deeper meaning behind teaching as a profession." The *Individual Consultation and Advisory Resource for Teachers (iCARE)* provides "information, advice or support" that is "directly available ... easily available ... care and support for work-related and personal issues." New teachers can talk to peer teachers or use on-line resources to help them with issues such as "starting on the job," "staying emotionally healthy," and "classroom know-how." Other MOE resources include *From us to you—Café OYEA* where "brewmasters" offer all manner of support such as inspirational stories or quotes from other teachers or students, teaching "tips" that mix the practical with the conceptual (such as a current discussion about reflection), downloadable resources, and so on, or *Edumall2.0*, an internet platform where teachers and students can "access . . . education digital content and interact with one another."

Professional development for all teachers

Beyond the "hand holding during the first year or so" that "helps to prevent the early exit of freshly trained teachers" there is "a comprehensive framework to provide different pathways for teachers to upgrade themselves" (Goh & Lee, 2008, pp. 102, 105). The professional development (PD) of teachers is an essential aspect of the national agenda, as evidenced by the government's "move towards an all graduate recruitment by 2015" and the goal for "30 percent of the teaching force [to] have Master's degree qualifications by 2020." These goals apparently spurred the development of the BEd to provide a mechanism for nongraduate teachers currently in the workforce, to upgrade and earn their Bachelor's degree while acquiring additional professional knowledge and skills, and the phasing out of Diploma of Education programs for "O" level holders. All teachers are also entitled to 100 hours of paid PD annually that is considered "office time" and therefore can happen during school hours with resources provided for "relief teachers." To meet the PD needs of Singapore's 28,000 teachers, NIE developed the Professional Development Continuum Model in 2004 which provides a menu of PD options, including advanced degree study (Master's and doctoral), professional development courses, and advanced diplomas.

The concept of a career ladder has been quite well developed in Singapore, offering teachers different routes for advancement and leadership. MOE developed *Edu-Pac* (Education Service Professional Development and Career Plan) "for teachers to develop their potential to the fullest" (MOE, 2009b). Teachers can select from among three possibilities:

> the Teaching Track allows you to advance to a new pinnacle level of Master Teacher. The Leadership Track gives you the opportunity to take on leadership positions in schools and the Ministry's headquarters. If you are inclined towards more specialised areas where deep knowledge and skills are essential for breaking new ground in educational developments, the Senior Specialist Track is available for you.

The Ministry also provides funding for scholarship and study leaves—both locally and abroad, facilitating teachers' movement along selected career ladders and learning along multiple dimensions. For instance, a teacher could take a study leave to attend university in another country, or could take a study leave to intern at a local gallery to learn more about art in communities. In turn, NIE designs and offers the in-service courses and the degree programs needed to help teachers take advantage of these MOE options. Just as with initial teacher preparation, NIE and MOE work together synergistically to meet teachers' educational and professional needs, to support teachers' advancement, and to respond to national imperatives and goals. Thus, NIE offers degree and diploma programs for school leaders, senior teachers and content specialists, as well as a plethora of ad hoc courses that support MOE initiatives. The MOE has also made it easier for teachers to be temporarily posted to NIE as teaching faculty for up to four years (previously, "secondment" was only available to schools or the Ministry), thus opening yet another PD route for teachers to learn and grow, and creating yet another mechanism for NIE and schools to be mutually informing and collaborative. Finally, through the Teachers Network, MOE offers numerous conferences and workshops, as well as grants for which teachers and schools can apply. Given all the support available to new and continuing teachers, it comes as no surprise that the annual teacher attrition rate is very low.

Lessons to ponder: what supports quality teacher preparation in Singapore?

This case study can only provide a very general overview of teacher preparation in Singapore because the teacher preparation enterprise is extremely vast, deep and complex. There is so much more that could be described and discussed, and yet cannot be in the space of a single chapter. Yet, this overall look at teacher preparation in Singapore has allowed some key lessons or factors to emerge, understandings about preparing teachers of quality that could inform the structure and content of teacher preparation elsewhere in the world. These take-away practices or strategies fall roughly into three categories: (1) teacher preparation curricula; (2) teacher identity and development; and (3) cross-institutional collaboration and communication.

First, in terms of teacher preparation curricula, what seems to stand out are:

- *The deliberate alignment of content knowledge (Academic Subjects) with pedagogical knowledge (Curriculum Studies):* ITP students engage in extensive study of their teaching subjects along with extensive study of *the teaching of* their teaching subjects.
- *The immersion of ITP students in both "professional" and "general" study from the start through the completion of their programs.* Academic Subjects and Curriculum Studies courses are not just aligned, they are taken concurrently and are mutually informing.
- *The range and depth of courses that teach content and/or integrate content and pedagogy.* Each content area offers 23–25 choices (example, 25 courses in geography, or courses such as "Economic Botany" or "Teacher Talk"),

affording students the (required) opportunities for rich and deep study in their teaching subject and of teaching.

- *The availability of multiple pathways into teaching without any apparent compromise of quality or requirements:* ITP programs enable students to enter teaching at different points in their academic journey, and to choose many different specializations. However, each student, no matter the pathway or specialty, is held to the same standards and must meet the same requirements.
- *Careful attention to the unique kinds of preparation teachers at different levels may need beyond the shared and compulsory curricular components:* For instance, teachers preparing to teach in the lower primary are required to take two courses specifically designed to develop their understanding of integrated curriculum for young children.
- *A curriculum that is ordered and sequenced with prescribed choices as well as required courses:* This ensures that ITP students are continuously building upon previous learning.

Second, teacher identity and development are deliberately nurtured through:

- *National attention to nurturance and celebration of teaching, teachers and education:* Through the media, generous resource allocation, public ceremonies, national competitions and scholarship programs, traditions and rituals such as the teachers' investiture ceremony, use of the internet to highlight teachers' work, accomplishments, stories, etc. A current example is the *Teachers' Vision Statement:* Singapore Teachers—Lead. Care. Inspire. For the Future of Our Nation Passes through Our Hands. "Written by teachers for teachers through an envisioning exercise in which schools islandwide participated" (MOE Teachers Network), the statement represents the culmination of hundreds of school-zone and school building level conversations facilitated by the MOE and involving 28,000 teachers. Launched by Ms. Ho Peng, Director General of Education at the 2009 annual "Teachers' Mass Lecture" (Peng, August 2009), her speech celebrated the "teaching fraternity" and "community of practitioners," but also deliberately underscored "emerging teacher leadership" and "Singapore teachers as beginning to chart the future of our profession." To support teacher leadership, Director General Ho has called for a "Teacher Development Centre to be set up, as a home to all Singaporean teachers."
- *Deliberate and concrete support for new teachers:* Mentoring, in-service courses, and a buddy system that acknowledge that all new teachers, no matter how well prepared, need induction and on-the-job support.
- *A well-defined career path that provides leadership opportunities for teachers within the classroom as well as outside the classroom.*
- *Generous financial assistance to teachers during preparation as well as for further professional development:* This ensures that teachers can focus on

growing and learning because they have fewer financial worries, plus they are allowed time to engage in PD.

Finally, in terms of cross-institutional communication and collaboration:

- *NIE, MOE and the schools are all engaged as partners* in the preparation of teachers, plus all three institutions are deliberately engaged in enacting a national vision of education, students and teachers for the 21st Century.
- *There are concrete structures in place that are designed to support exchange, shared decision-making and responsibility:* For example, the insistence on school–university consensus on student teaching grades, or the opportunities for teachers to serve at NIE (and for faculty to serve in schools through a "school attachment" opportunity).
- *Careful attention to and descriptions of every programmatic detail accompanied by extensive informational resources and materials, all designed to keep everyone on the same page, aligned in terms of definitions and tasks:* Even as a relative outsider, I was able to gain a clear understanding of different requirements, roles, visions, etc. simply by reviewing all the handbooks, PowerPoints, videos, materials, etc. in print and on-line.

Conclusion

A look at the history of educational change in Singapore reveals multiple cycles of reform and numerous campaigns, beginning in the post-colonial era of the 1950s and continuing through to today. This history highlights the importance of education to Singapore, and how much energy, people hours and resources have been devoted to creating an excellent infrastructure and developing a literate and forward-moving population. It is also a history that says education is not only a serious concern in Singapore, but education is always evolving and changing, fueled deliberately by a vision of nationhood and global membership, the citizens needed to enact this vision, and the teachers Singapore requires to develop her people, these citizens. Thus, as of this writing, teacher preparation is in the process of undergoing another metamorphosis, changes that bear brief mention but must wait for another chapter for a more complete exploration and discussion. On December 1, 2009, NIE made public the report *A Teacher Education Model for the 21st Century* (*TE21*) that describes, "NIE's enhanced and updated teacher education model," and "puts forward six broad recommendations" including the "V3SK Model [that] focuses on three value paradigms: Learner-Centred, Teacher Identity and Service to the Profession and Community . . . at the centre of teachers' work" (NIE, 2009, pp. 11, 23). The report is "the culmination of a review initiative which began in November 2008," involved many NIE "academic staff, as well as education officers from the schools [and] considered local and international educational trends, policies and research data." *TE21* marks a new era of teacher preparation at NIE and in Singapore and undoubtedly will sharpen, improve, extend, and enrich the impressive work Singaporean educators have accomplished in their definition of and deliberately rapid progress towards quality and qualified teachers.

Acknowledgments

I am very grateful to the many Singaporean colleagues who were so generous with their help and were so willing to speak with me about teacher preparation in Singapore. I am especially grateful to NIE colleagues Associate Dean Low Ee Ling and Academic Head of Curriculum, Teaching and Learning, Christine Lee for their helpful review of this chapter.

Chapter 3

Teacher preparation in the Netherlands

Shared visions and common features

Karen Hammerness, Jan van Tartwijk and Marco Snoek

Introduction

The Netherlands provides a particularly interesting context for examining teacher preparation for several key reasons. First, students in the Netherlands perform quite well academically in comparison to their peers in Europe and in the United States. Second, the Netherlands faces a series of challenges shared by other countries, in particular, regarding teacher quality and recruitment. Finally, teacher preparation in the Netherlands is somewhat unique, in that the faculty at some of the best-known and most highly regarded universities share a common vision for—and approach to—teacher preparation. While the Netherlands is a small country (employing roughly 135,000 primary teachers, and 75,000 secondary teachers in 2006) taken together, these features suggest the importance of better understanding the nature of Dutch teacher preparation. In order to set the stage for this case, we first provide an overview of the educational context.

The educational context

The Dutch educational system

Primary schools provide primary education for children aged 4–12 in the Dutch educational system. Although education is compulsory at the age of 5, 98% of children start at age 4 (Snoek & Wielenga, 2003). The first two years are more "play oriented" and the more systematic schooling in reading, writing and mathematics begins at age 6. At the end of primary education, students take a final exam, such as the CITO test, which is necessary for acceptance into a school for secondary education.

The education system at the secondary level splits into three different streams—the VMBO, the HAVO and the VWO—which vary in degree of academic difficulty level and length but are all required to address some of the same topics included in "basic" secondary education for approximately three years. VMBO is a four-year secondary education program that prepares students for secondary vocational education. VMBO graduates can also continue their secondary education in the second last year of the HAVO. The HAVO is a five-year secondary education program that prepares students for higher professional education. HAVO graduates can also go onto the second last year of VWO, a six-year program, which prepares students for university education. One important feature of primary and secondary schooling is that for nearly 100 years, public and private schools have been funded equally by the government and all are free to pupils. Indeed, there are more private schools than public schools— Roman Catholic and Protestant schools represent about two-thirds of all primary schools (30% each, respectively), but there also are some Islamic, Jewish and Hindu schools, as well as schools guided by a particular philosophy, such as Steiner schools. One-third of the primary schools are "public" schools, implying that they are the responsibility of the city council. At the secondary level, private schools represent almost half of all schools (Ministry of Education, Culture and Science, 2008, p. 22). At the same time, the degree to which many of these private schools draw upon religious values or beliefs varies considerably from minimal to strong—and while some private schools may have a strong identity and curriculum based on a particular religion, this is not the case for all. The quality of the education of all primary and secondary schools, both public and private, is monitored by the Inspectorate of Education.

The Netherlands compared with other countries

While there are concerns in the Netherlands about a recent decline in students' scores on international tests, the scores in the Netherlands remain high in comparison to many other countries. Dutch students score well above the international average in tests of reading, particularly at the primary level (Mullis *et al.*, 2007; OECD, 2007, 2010; PISA, 2006). In the 2009 PISA report the Netherlands ranked second in Europe and tenth worldwide (OECD, 2010). In mathematics, Dutch students outrank many countries on the TIMSS tests, and older students achieve some of the highest test scores on the PISA, only outranked by Finland in Europe (Mullis *et al.*, 2007; OECD, 2010). Interestingly, a recent study conducted by UNICEF found that children in the Netherlands ranked the highest on all measures of well-being which they assessed, leading some newspapers to proclaim the fact that Dutch children are the happiest in the world (UNICEF, 2007; Zeller, 2007; Comiteau, 2007). Finally, the level of education of Dutch people has been rising; the percentage of young people leaving school without qualifications at the secondary level dropped from 16% in 2000 to 12% in 2007, which is well below the European average (Centraal Bureau voor de Statistiek, 2009).

Educational reforms

In the past two decades, the Netherlands has witnessed three major reforms aimed at secondary education that have had a major impact on how the public and politicians perceive and experience education and educational reform in the country.[1] The first of these reforms, in 1993, introduced standardized goals and tests for all 14 subjects—the "basisvorming" (basic curriculum) that had to be covered in the first three years of all secondary education. The overall goal of this reform was to improve the general quality of education, but its aim also was to pay more attention to the development of skills in the curriculum, and on postponing the choice of study and profession to 15 years (from 12).

The second reform, in 1998/99, involved the introduction of the "tweede fase" (second phase), a reform of the curriculum in the last two years of HAVO and the last three years of VWO, with the aim of better preparing students for higher education. This reform consisted of two innovations. The first was the introduction of four "profiles," clusters of subjects, that students can choose to study in these last years of HAVO and VWO. Four profiles were developed: culture and society, economics and society, science and technology, and science and health. Depending upon the profile students chose, subjects would then be tailored to their interests and ambitions. The second innovation was the intro-duction of the "studiehuis" (study house). This innovation implied a shift towards *active and self-regulative learning* (Simons, 2000) which would prepare students better for higher education and the labor market. Underlying this reform were theoretical notions derived from constructivism, which were called *new learning* (Simons, van der Linden, & Duffy, 2000). This new learning implied a shift in the classroom towards independent inquiry and away from factual learning. For the teacher, it meant a shift in role from being the source of knowledge to being a supervisor, coach, and facilitator.

The third reform, in 1999–2002, involved the reorganization of the lower levels of secondary education, suggesting the combination of junior general secondary education (MAVO) with lower vocational education in one stream (VMBO) with the aim of creating more pathways for students in these schools.

Despite the good intentions of these reforms, the implementation was problematic. Teachers felt that these reforms had been imposed on them and that their professional opinion had not been considered. The basisvorming (basic curriculum) in particular met much resistance and ultimately was abolished in 2006. When it was proposed, many teachers were positive about the study house, but in practice it turned out to be difficult to implement (cf. van Veen, Sleegers, & van de Ven, 2005). As a consequence, the reforms became the subject of a heated debate in the Netherlands (NRC, 2006, 2007). Politicians called for a parliamentary committee that was charged with investigating the implementation and results of the reforms and with formulating guidelines for future educational policies (Commissie Parlementair Onderzoek Onderwijsvernieuwing, 2008). Based on the literature, their own research, and hearings, this committee concluded that while there had been considerable political support for the innovations, support among teachers, parents, and students was lacking or that the implementation of the reforms had been too much top-down, and that, as a consequence, many teachers felt that the innovations had been forced upon them.[2] The parliamentary committee recommended that these kinds of reforms should never be implemented again without support from the field.

Challenges

While these debates about the reforms continue both in the public arena and in the field of education (Simons, 2006; van der Werf, 2006), the Dutch government has identified teacher shortages, with the related and equally pressing issues of controlling teacher quality and retention, as an additional challenge facing the educational system (Commissie Leraren, 2007; Meesters, 2003; see also Ministry of Education, Culture and Science, 2008). The Commissie Leerkracht (Commission on Teaching) noted that by 2014 about 75% of the present teachers in secondary education will have left the profession because of retirement and attrition. As a consequence, serious teacher shortages are predicted because the influx of new teachers in the profession cannot replace this substantial attrition. Complicating this situation is the growing diversity of the population—approximately 20% of the population were ethnic minorities as of 2007 (Central Bureau for Statistics, 2011)—and the struggle to provide a good education to ethnic minorities, a challenge the Netherlands shares with other European countries. A recent report found that the dropout rate of non-Western ethnic minorities was twice as high as that of native Dutch students (Ministry of Education, Culture and Science, 2008). However, while these concerns have been identified at a policy level, these issues have had little direct influence upon teacher education in the country thus far.[3]

Finally, while Dutch students have been doing quite well in international tests comparatively, the public is becoming concerned about their international rankings and performance (Ministry of Education, Culture and Science, 2008). Over the past decade, the country's relative position in a number of international rankings has been declining. These issues have led to considerable discussion and concern in the country about how to improve Dutch children's performance. Very often, the concern focuses on the competence and the quality of teachers. For instance, a recent study investigated the results of using "traditional" methods of teaching mathematics compared with methods relying on solving authentic problems (KNAW, 2009) upon children's mathematical proficiency. The researcher concluded that the children's lower mathematical proficiency was not related to differences in the quality of the teaching methods, but rather to the teachers' insufficient calculating skills. Studies such as these have fueled debates and questions about the characteristics and abilities of teachers. The quality of teachers—as is the case in a number of countries around the world—is becoming an important policy issue seen as intimately related to educational improvement. And, in turn, for teacher education, the quality of its graduates is increasingly on the country's political agenda.

Teaching in the Netherlands

Some policy efforts to develop the profession

Although historically, teachers in the Netherlands have been highly regarded in the country, similar to other well-respected professions, the profession seems to have been decreasing in status over the past decade. Recent reports suggest that teachers themselves do not believe themselves to be as highly appreciated or valued, although they attach much value to the work they do. Public perception of teachers also appears to be falling—more than half of the public appear to be concerned about the quality of teachers. Reports suggest that the percentage of public respondents who thought highly of teachers fell from 68% in 2006 to 55% in 2007. At the same time, parents report confidence in their children's own schooling, scoring their own schools quite highly, leading the Ministry to report that "The impressions of the general public do not chime with the actual situation experienced by parents." Furthermore, data examined by the Ministry reveals that fewer young people are applying to teacher preparation programs (Ministry of Education, Science and Culture, 2008).

Thus, as is the case in many countries, the Netherlands Ministry of Education, Science and Culture has been increasingly concerned about attracting qualified, well-prepared individuals into the profession. As a consequence, a series of committees has been set up and measures have been taken which focus upon the development of teaching as a profession. As early as 1993, when concerns about the decreasing status of teaching and the teacher shortages were just coming to the fore, the government established the Committee on the Future of Teaching. This committee recommended a move from perceiving teaching as an isolated activity and that rather, teachers should have opportunities to cooperate, learn from each other, and become members of schools that serve as learning organizations (Maandag et al., 2007; Verloop and Wubbels, 2000). The committee also suggested the introduction of *career lines*, related to teacher salaries, so that a career path would be more visible for teachers. Finally, the committee also developed a series of recommendations that would better prepare teachers for their challenging work in schools and for this demanding role. In light of research that suggests that new teachers often struggle with reality shock when they first enter teaching, which may ultimately lead to attrition (e.g. Veenman, 1984; Britzman, 1986), the committee also called for teacher preparation programs to offer more intensive, practice-based experiences in schools prior to full-time teaching (Commissie Toekomst Leraarschap, 1993; Vermeulen & Koopman, 2000).[4] In particular, the proposal to introduce more practice-based experiences in teacher preparation programs was in line with reforms that teacher education programs were already carrying out, and has been adopted by teacher educators in the Netherlands. Indeed, the concern with mitigating new teachers' *practice shock* through increasing opportunities to learn in practice, has become the focus of substantial efforts by a teacher educators in the Netherlands (Korthagen & Kessels, 1999; Korthagen *et al.*, 2001; Stokking *et al.*, 2003; see also Brouwer & Korthagen, 2005; Koetsier & Wubbels, 1995; Veenman, 1984).

A second, more recent attempt to professionalize teaching has involved the articulation of competencies that all Dutch teachers are expected to meet. In 2004, the Dutch parliament passed legislation requiring teachers at all levels (primary and secondary) to be "not only qualified, but competent" and subsequently identified six key competencies that all teachers would be expected to meet (2006). These competencies suggest that a Dutch teacher needs to be able to do the following: (1) create a pleasant, safe, and effective classroom environment; (2) support children's personal development by helping the students become independent and responsible (in Dutch, this is referred to as "pedagog"); (3) demonstrate substantial knowledge of their subject and appropriate teaching methods; (4) thoughtfully organize curriculum supporting student learning; (5) collaborate not only with colleagues but also contribute to a well-functioning school organization); (6) collaborate with those outside the school (i.e. parents or guardians, colleagues in educational and youth welfare institutions) who are also responsible for student well-being and development; and finally, (7) reflect and develop their own strengths and weaknesses as professionals over the long term. These competencies are tied to accreditation of teacher preparation programs—faculty are required to demonstrate the ways in which their program enables students to develop these competencies. As a consequence, many teacher programs have reformulated their criteria according to these requirements, although different programs have developed particular interpretations and specific emphases.

Most recently, in 2007, the committee "Teachers" was installed by the government with the task of identifying measures that would both address the pressing teacher shortages and improve the quality of teaching. In a 2008 report, the committee suggested raising salaries and further advised that schools should involve teachers more comprehensively in decision-making about both organizational and educational issues. Subsequently, the committee suggested strengthening the position of teaching as a profession by creating more opportunities and incentives for teacher professionalization. They also called for initiatives to improve the quality of teacher education, informed by, among others, a comparison of the Dutch approach of teacher education with international developments and standards.

The Dutch approach to teacher preparation

It is within this context of debates about education and educational reforms, and heightened policy efforts to create more support for teaching as a profession, and in turn, to draw more qualified individuals into teaching, that we discuss teacher education and the features of teacher preparation programs in the Netherlands.

Various routes to teaching qualifications

In the Dutch system for higher education, a distinction is made between, on the one hand, higher professional education which is provided by universities for applied sciences and, on the other hand, academic education provided by·research universities. The teacher education programs provided by the universities for applied sciences[5] prepare students for teaching in primary education, vocational education and secondary education, except for the higher classes of higher general secondary education (HAVO) and pre-university education (VWO). These four-year programs are aimed at students with no background in the discipline, such as students directly out of high school. Graduates hold a *second level teaching qualification*.

The research universities provide a teacher education program lasting one year, that prepares students for teaching in the higher classes of higher general secondary education (HAVO) and pre-university education (VWO). These programs are aimed at students who already hold a master's in the discipline related to the school subject. As a consequence, they do not focus on disciplinary preparation in the content, but on methods of teaching the subject, and general pedagogy. The graduates of these programs receive a *first level teaching qualification*, which allows them to teach in all classes of secondary and vocational education.

Recruitment

The Netherlands has a national stipend system for students in higher education. Students who enter any of the teacher education programs are provided with a loan to pay for their expenses, which will be converted into a gift if they finish their exams in time. If they take more time to complete their program than is expected, or fail their exams, the loan will not be converted into a gift. While this may serve as a strong incentive to enter higher education in general, whether teaching itself is a career choice depends upon the availability of other options in their subject area, as well as the demand for teachers in particular subject areas.[6]

Due to the increasing concerns about teacher shortages, there have been recent efforts to attract more academically qualified individuals into teaching through designing special pathways into teaching as well as to recruit older entrants, such as those who might be interested in a career change or mid-career switch to teaching (Ministry for Education, Science and Culture 1999a, 1999b; see also Tigchelaar & Korthagen, 2004). While there have not been many large-scale initiatives to recruit teachers from minority groups, there are some organizations that attempt to bring students from racially and ethnically diverse groups into higher education in general, and some have focused upon students who wish to become teachers (e.g., ECHO, 2009). An additional initiative involves a special teacher education course that was started for undergraduate students at a number of research universities with the aim of interesting them in an early stage of their academic career in teaching in secondary education. This course takes six months.

After finishing the program successfully and passing their bachelor's exam, the undergraduate students obtain a special teaching certificate allowing them to teach the subject they study in the lower grades of secondary education in the Netherlands.

One key feature of post-master teacher preparation at the research universities is that currently many students complete the clinical part of the program with a teaching job for which they are paid a regular salary, while a smaller number of them complete the program as apprentices. A minority of these students with paid jobs already are full-time teachers and already have a teaching certificate, but seek additional certification, for instance, to teach another subject, or to teach in upper secondary education.

Selection

In the universities for applied sciences, teacher education programs that prepare students for teaching in primary or in secondary education are four-year graduate programs at the bachelor level. In contrast to the student teachers in research universities who start teacher education after gaining a master's, teacher education students in higher professional education enter directly from high school without prior disciplinary study at this level. Primary teacher education programmes are also open to students who have completed their vocational education. Indeed, a range of students, with varying levels of academic experiences, enter teacher preparation at the primary level.

There are no additional selection procedures upon entering teacher education. However, due to concern in society regarding the quality of teachers, emphasis on students' skills in Dutch language and arithmetics has been increasing. In 2008, a national test of (basic) Dutch language skills and arithmetics was introduced for students in primary teacher education. Student teachers are required to pass this test before the end of the first year, if they wish to continue their study in primary teaching.

Teacher educators

Most Dutch teacher educators either have a background as teachers themselves, have a background in educational research, or both. Some continue to do some educational research while teaching in teacher education, but many are primarily responsible for teaching future teachers, and not conducting research in education. Teacher educators have organized themselves into the Dutch Association for Teacher Educators. Apart from organizing an annual conference and publishing a quarterly journal for teacher educators, together with the Flemish Association for Teacher Educators, this association also manages a professional register for teacher educators. Teacher educators can apply to be included on the professional register by passing a professional development process and through peer assessment (cf. Koster & Dengerink, 2008).

Teacher preparation programs

While there is no universal "Dutch approach to teacher education," Dutch teacher educators do their work within a common framework and a shared vision of teaching and learning. In this next section, we briefly present the vision that many teacher education programs share. Subsequently, we will provide an overview of how teacher preparation is carried out using examples from, on the one hand, the post-master's one-year teacher education program of Leiden University, an example of a teacher education program at a research university that prepares teachers for secondary schools, and, on the other hand, the four-year bachelor's program of the Amsterdam School of Education, which is part of the Hogeschool van Amsterdam University of applied sciences, which prepares both secondary and primary teachers.

Visions in teacher preparation

Studies of exemplary teacher education programs in the US suggest that having a clear vision is a critical element in those programs (Darling-Hammond, 2000, 2006; Hammerness & Darling-Hammond, 2002; Hammerness, 2006). In these programs, an articulated vision of the role teachers could be playing with their students, their school and society undergirds the curriculum, shapes the clinical work, and provides a larger purpose for their activities (Darling-Hammond, 2006; Hammerness *et al.*, 2005). Indeed, these studies suggest that a shared and well-developed vision may be a key element that contributes to the coherence of a program—knitting together the curriculum, clinical work and student teachers' opportunities to learn, in turn, promoting and developing shared ideas about teaching and learning. Program visions, however, may differ across types of programs and pathways. For instance, work on vision in the United States documents at least three different types of visions that contribute to very different teacher preparation experiences: (1) a vision of service that conceives of teaching as only one of many opportunities to "give back" or contribute to society; (2) a vision of social justice that conceives of teaching as a direct means of addressing social inequities; and (3) a vision of practice that focuses upon teaching as means to improve and develop student learning (Hammerness, under review). This work also found that these programs emphasized one or more of these visions, to a greater or lesser extent—and the nature of that emphasis had an impact upon how the candidates in the programs conceived of teaching as well as upon their career decisions. However, as Kennedy (2006) has pointed out, it has been extremely difficult for most programs, at least in the US, to come together around such a vision.[7]

Yet a look at the Dutch teacher education allows us to better understand a set of programs that appear, to some extent, to be guided by a common vision. While Dutch teacher education programs naturally have variations in their curriculum and differ in some areas (some more substantially than others), the degree to which these programs are built around a vision of teaching as a professional practice emerges as an important feature.

The vision of the programs

Most teacher education programs, such as the ones in Amsterdam and Leiden, share a vision of teaching as a profession that has a knowledge base in research on teaching and learning, and a set of practices that can be learned over time. As their ultimate goal they see helping student teachers develop into professionals who are not only able to create a positive and safe learning environment in their classrooms, supporting the active learning of their students, but who also take responsibility for their own learning and professional development throughout their career. Teacher education programs are built upon a conception of the most powerful teaching as that which is in the service of improving student learning and development according to the present-day educational research (cf. Bransford, Brown, & Cocking, 2000). Subsequently, this research serves as the starting point for helping student teachers understand the learning processes of students in primary and secondary education—and that pupils learn best through opportunities to practice, authentic learning experiences, and ongoing assessment. Furthermore, it is emphasized that this focus on students as active learners should be mirrored in teacher education itself. In teacher education, therefore, student teachers should be active learners, should reflect on their experiences and learning process, and should have opportunities to develop over time.

Efforts to bridge theory and practice

Bringing aspects of reality shock into the program

Within Dutch teacher education programs, bridging the gap between theory and practice is regarded as one of the major challenges affecting the ability of teacher education to achieve this vision. Much pioneering work has been done at Utrecht University, where teacher educators have a long tradition aimed at helping student teachers learn from practice while at the same time building a knowledge base that is firmly based on theory regarding teaching and learning (cf. Koetsier & Wubbels, 1995; Korthagen *et al.*, 2001; Ticghelaar & Korthagen, 2004). They have developed an approach that Korthagen and his colleagues referred to as a *realistic approach to teacher education* (Korthagen *et al.*, 2001). A key idea undergirding this approach is to bring relevant theory to bear upon the particular concerns that new teachers have as they begin to practice teaching. By doing so, aspects of the reality shock are incorporated into the teacher education program (Koetsier & Wubbels, 1995; Stokking *et al.*, 2003). In this way, student teachers can be carefully supervised at the time when they are trying to cope with the practice shock by both teacher educators and supervising teachers at the schools. To ensure that the practice shock actually takes place in the program, a part of the program must be arranged in such a way that it resembles the working situation of the beginning teacher. This part of the practical component of the teacher education program should be characterized by "insecurity, complexity, a need for independent and responsible action, and a substantial work load" (Koetsier and Wubbels, 1995, p. 335). The role of teacher educators and supervising teachers in these programs is to create a safe learning environment for the student teachers in which they can become aware of their learning needs, find useful learning experiences, and reflect on their experiences.

"Rules of thumb" at Leiden University

This realistic approach deeply informs the one-year post-master's teacher preparation program at Leiden University. In meetings and in their on-line logs, students are asked to share their concerns with their fellow students and their supervisors at least once a week. Supervisors can provide theory at the right moments, i.e. when the student has a need for it to better understand and analyze his or her own experiences. An additional approach was developed in Leiden to encourage new teachers to make explicit what they have learned from practice. Students are prompted to make explicit what they have learned from their successes (in the classroom) by articulating them as *rules of thumb*. Then they are asked to examine and compare these emerging rules of thumb with theory regarding teaching and learning that they encounter at the university. Subsequently, they are helped to build on, validate and extend their repertoire of rules of thumb and their perceptions of teaching and learning. In this process, teacher educators at Leiden argue that students discover what they regard as important in teaching and learning and the consequences this has for their own perception of their own role as a teacher (Janssen, de Hullu, & Tigelaar, 2008).

"Authentic learning" at the Amsterdam School of Education

In the four-year bachelor's program at the Amsterdam School of Education, teacher educators have found the notion of *authentic learning* particularly helpful in addressing the gap between theory and practice. The faculty define authentic learning as learning that is linked to real, everyday teaching contexts and experiences. To that end, the faculty aim to make the content of the curriculum and the activities students undertake directly related to student teachers' current (and future) classroom teaching. Teacher educators work to create (as early as possible) an environment for students that mirrors professional practices (Terwindt & Wielenga, 2000). The notion of authentic learning is translated into two types of activities: institution-based projects which are designed to be strongly connected to tasks that teachers have to perform in the school, and school-based professional practice, in which student teachers have to gradually take on more and more teaching responsibility and to carry out relatively complex tasks that fit in with the objectives of the school.

For example, one school-based professional practice occurs during their first teaching practice periods, when primary education students prepare (and perform with pupils) a theatrical introduction to a new picture book. In this activity they have to draw upon some of the key content from the drama module they have taken at the university. In this way they start as teaching assistants in their first year. And for example, one institution-based project occurs during their second practice period, student teachers may create an institution-based project called the "Book of the Neighborhood" in which students focus on the local neighborhood setting of their practice school and the possibilities that it may or may not offer as a learning environment for pupils. Students are also asked to design activities for pupils and guidelines for teachers, relating the activities to the formal curriculum in the school.

To be able to do this work well, students are provided with the knowledge base and skills they need, through course modules focusing on educational and disciplinary theory and on skills training. During the four-year curriculum at the Amsterdam School of Education, students are prompted to take responsibility for their personal learning process through activities and assignments (such as the internships and the Book of the Neighborhood) that require reflection that needs to be documented in their portfolio, and by increasing the complexity of and responsibility for their clinical work. The learning of student teachers is seen as an active and social process, in which students have to give meaning to their experiences and to connect them to their personal identity. To support this process, much attention is given to the development of metacognitive reflection skills, which focus on self-knowledge and the development of a professional identity. During this process, the competencies of a qualified teacher are used as a frame of reference for students, which in turn, guides their learning.

Curriculum

Teacher education in the Netherlands reflects a strong emphasis upon combining clinical work and coursework. Because the one-year post-master's programs at the research universities and the four-year bachelor's programs at the universities of applied sciences are fairly different, we discuss them separately. Yet at the same time, the shared vision of teaching and teacher preparation, along with the intention of linking practical work and coursework in order to address issues of reality shock, represent clear throughlines for all programs.

Program for teacher education at the research universities

The teacher education programs at the research universities take one year of full-time study (beginning in August/September or January), either as a one-year course, or as part of a two-year course, in which it is combined with another master's degree. Tailor-made programs are available for students who, by training or through work experience, already have some of the competences needed for a career in teaching. Upon graduation, the students have obtained a Master of Science/Art in teaching their subject, which allows them to teach at all levels of secondary education.

Program structure

In the one-year program at Leiden University, for instance, the program begins with a one-week introduction at the university in which students are prepared for their first teaching experiences by teaching them a number of basic skills, but immediately after that introduction, students start teaching at schools for half of the week and will continue to do so until the end of the program. The other half of the week they prepare and take classes at the university. Students take these classes in small groups (organized, for instance, by school site placement, level of experience in teaching or subject), and take course modules taught by one or two teacher educators. At both universities, these module sessions as well as any other relevant meetings are all scheduled on one day of the week—allowing, as much as possible, for students to experience the "real" day-to-day life of a teacher by being in schools the majority of the week (and also preventing conflicts with school schedules).

Rather than being organized into typical teacher preparation courses such as foundation courses or methods courses,[8] the modules offered in these group sessions are designed to help the new teachers develop their skills, abilities, and understanding of six roles that are considered to represent the core areas of teachers' knowledge and development. These roles are designed to be consistent with the 2006 report articulating teachers' competencies. At Leiden University, the roles are described as: subject teacher, classroom manager, expert in adolescent psychology,[9] member of the school organization, colleague, and professional. The teacher education faculty contend that becoming a professional teacher depends upon developing in all these six areas, and furthermore, that through the program as well as beyond it a teacher should be able to take responsibility for his or her own professional development in each of the roles. From the beginning of the program, students are provided with rubrics that articulate competence in each of these roles from insufficient to excellent, so that they can track and evaluate their own progress in each arena (see the Appendix for a copy of the rubric for the role of classroom manager). This articulation of roles—and the emphasis upon students' own responsibility for their development—reflect the program vision of teachers as professionals, who themselves, are active learners.

At Leiden University, students take course modules that are designed to build their understanding of these teacher roles. These role modules are taught sequentially, although they sometimes partly overlap. Depending upon the topic, the modules are taught either by teacher educators or by specialists on the faculty (for instance, the modules on subject teacher are taught by disciplinary specialists).

The order of the role modules is designed to be consistent with research findings regarding the concerns of new teachers. For instance, because research consistently suggests that beginning teachers regard student discipline as their most serious challenge (Evertson & Weinstein, 2006; LePage *et al.*, 2005), the faculty in these programs argue that this implies that one of the first learning needs of student teachers, is how to create and maintain a positive and orderly working atmosphere in their classrooms.

The classroom manager module

For this reason, the role module for classroom manager is one of the first to be taught. As with all modules in the programs, it begins with an introduction to the relevant theory in a lecture by a specialist in this field. For practical reasons, this lecture is given to all the students from all the groups. Faculty argue that they present the theory in such a way that students can use it as a frame of reference, or "language" to think and talk about their experiences in their own classrooms. For instance, in the classroom manager role module, teacher educators introduce the notion that teachers and pupils are part of a larger social system, in which their respective behaviors influence one another (van Tartwijk *et al.*, 2009). In the lecture, students watch video clips of teachers at work in their classes, and take notes on them and then plot the various interpersonal messages (both verbal and non-verbal) they observe in terms of different dimensions introduced by the faculty.

Teacher educators from Leiden believe that working with videos is important, because they feel that student teachers, who have just started teaching, are eager to see and discuss other teachers' teaching strategies. They want the student teachers to understand through analyzing teachers' interpersonal teacher behavior that the disciplinary skill is not something mythical that teachers "have or don't have," but can be traced back to the teacher's behavioral repertoire, which can be learned with experience (as most teachers do) and deliberate practice (Ericsson, 2006). Finally, research findings are presented about the links between the teacher–student relationship and variables such as the working atmosphere in the classroom, student cognitive outcomes and motivation, and teacher experience. A reader is available in which theory that is presented in the lecture is summarized, and relevant literature for further reading is suggested. Following the lecture, in their classroom manager module, the students engage in a series of role-playing exercises around specific activities and incidents that might happen in classrooms. This role-playing provides a means for students to rehearse and test out possible responses to difficult management situations before they face them in the classroom. Opportunities like these role-playing activities echo what Grossman and her colleagues (2009a) have termed "approximations of practice;" they argue such activities should be considered as a core set of activities on which stronger teacher preparation can be built (Grossman *et al.*, 2009b).

In addition to considering these roles in their group modules, students have opportunities to develop each role through particular assignments—all of which are eventually collected and turned in as a final, culminating portfolio demonstrating their development as teachers. For example, in order for students to have opportunities to address and develop their skills as a classroom manager, the students are asked to record video clips of their own teaching in their placement schools and to administer a questionnaire to their pupils that is intended to gather feedback on the teachers' interpersonal approach.[10] Student teachers themselves also complete the questionnaire to estimate how they think their own students will answer the questions. Student teachers compare the data gathered with data on both average and "best" Dutch teachers, and with their own self-perceptions. They analyze significant differences between students' perceptions, self-perceptions, and average and ideal perceptions, and try to explain the results by carefully examining the video recordings. Results of these analyses are discussed with their fellow students and with teacher educators. The reports, the questionnaire results, and a selection of relevant video snippets are included in the student portfolios. If students and teacher educators feel that student teachers need additional help with their development in this role, students can also work on their behavioral repertoire in some dedicated skills training in small groups with other students who need similar additional support. This kind of assignment reflects the vision of these programs of teachers as active learners who can analyze their own practice, learn from practice, and take responsibility for their own professional development.

As another example, in order for students to develop their skills and abilities in teaching the subject, as a subject teacher, the students are asked to develop lesson plans several times using the theory that they encounter in their small groups, and they then must implement these plans in their placement schools. Student teachers are asked to analyze their plans and reflect upon their implementation (including examples of feedback and artifacts showing how the plans were carried out) in a dedicated section of their portfolio.

A portfolio built around teacher roles

Indeed, the portfolio (built on the six teacher roles) serves as a means of informal assessment throughout the program as well as a culminating assessment at the end. The portfolio and the plans are discussed in an individual meeting with the student's supervisor at three points during the program. Each time, the student is asked to reflect on all the information in the portfolio that has been collected thus far, using the six teacher roles as the basis for reflection, and formulate a personal development plan for future development (either in the remainder of the program, or upon graduation, depending upon the timing of the meeting). Faculty contend that the portfolio reinforces the program vision—that student teachers should be responsible for their own growth and development and the portfolio serves as a means for them to begin to construct their own development while still in the program.

Higher professional education: the curriculum at the Universities of the Applied Sciences

In higher professional education, teacher education programs focus both on the acquisition of the knowledge and skills of the discipline to be taught, and on the acquisition of the general and specific knowledge or skills of the teaching profession. The faculty work to treat these topics in parallel throughout the curriculum and at intervals integrated in tasks and assignments. As a result, the curriculum consists roughly of four different elements: disciplinary study (40%), professional study (25%), teaching practice through internships (25%) and support and supervision in what the faculty have termed Metawork (10%). As in the teacher preparation at the research universities, the topics are offered in modules.

Within the teacher education programs of the Amsterdam School of Education, a total of about 40% of the curriculum is dedicated to study of disciplinary content and to teaching the discipline (pedagogical content knowledge, focusing for instance, on learning specific complex disciplinary concepts, or alternative approaches to teaching mathematics). The disciplinary content is based on the knowledge bases that have been nationally defined for each of the school subjects. For primary school teachers this disciplinary content is focused on all subjects that are in the primary school curriculum. For secondary school teachers, the knowledge base is focused on one specific school subject.

"Professional study"

A quarter of the curriculum is dedicated to what the faculty have termed professional study which includes the study of topics including classroom management, methods of assessment, teaching in multicultural classrooms, and educational use of ICT. Part of this professional study involves students in creating institution-based projects which we referred to before and that are designed to connect the theoretical principles promoted by the university with the experiences students are having in schools. For instance, in a project focused upon understanding culture and communication in the classroom, students work to better understand the challenges of diversity in society and the role of language in learning. During the project, the faculty provide lectures that are intended to help student teachers develop some background knowledge on different cultures, and the role of language in classrooms and intercultural communication. These lectures then serve as the basis for the student teachers to design lessons with a specific focus on language use and inclusive approaches in teaching and to write small case studies focusing on dilemmas in multicultural schools. The project ends with an event where students present the multicultural landscape of schools in Amsterdam, sharing the outcomes of their case studies. Teacher educators support students by giving feedback and by modeling inclusive approaches in their teaching.

Another example of such an institution-based project is an assignment in the third year in which primary education students are required to develop their understanding of special education needs and inclusive education. The faculty provide lectures that focus upon the specific structures and policies regarding children with special needs in the Dutch educational system, the theory of multiple intelligence, and concepts and models for adaptive teaching. Building upon this background information, students then have to develop a series of lessons, using the concept of multiple intelligence. They are also required to write a case study of one child with special educational needs and to examine the often very complicated professional and bureaucratic support structures that exist around that child. The culmination of the project is a video of the lessons the student developed, and a paper that summarizes and reflects upon the case study of the child.

Learning in school settings

As in the teacher education programs at the research universities, learning within a school setting is an important element at the Amsterdam School of Education. For this reason, approximately 25% of the curriculum is dedicated to internships and the final independent teaching practice. In their first two years, all student teachers are in schools for one day a week in which they work on their assignments, observe and teach lessons. In the third year, students are in schools every week for either one day and a half (for primary education teachers) or two days (for secondary education). In the fourth and final year all student teachers are full time at a school for half a year or three days a week during the whole year. In this last year, students have a special Teacher-in-Training contract and have to perform as an independent teacher with full responsibilities (with the mentor giving support at a distance). During this internship, students are considered as a full member of the school staff and are sometimes paid a salary by the school.

The progression of student teachers' clinical work is motivated by three underlying principles: First, connected to the concept of authentic learning, the curriculum begins immediately in the first year with internships, so that students have the opportunity to start developing an identity as a teacher right from the start— as well as to relate the content of the curriculum to the reality of the teaching profession in schools. Second, this design allows for the gradual increase of complexity and responsibility in the tasks that student teachers perform, so that over time, the students take on more and more classroom teaching work and activities. Third, it allows students in their final year—in which they are working under the "Teacher in Training" contract—to be supported by faculty and to remain closely linked to the university, as they take on the work of a full-time teacher. The faculty feel that this design in particular helps reduce the practice shock that may otherwise result from a gap between teacher education and the start of the profession.

The preparation for the teaching profession in the program is centered around seven competences that are nationally defined and embedded in the law on the teaching professions as the Dutch standards for teachers: interpersonal competence, pedagogical competence, subject knowledge and methodological competence, organizational competence, competence for collaboration with colleagues, competence for collaboration with the working environment, and competence for reflection and development. These seven competences, which are translated into competence requirements and indicators, are used as a frame of reference by staff members to design the activities within the different parts of the curriculum (e.g. the tasks during the internships) and by students to reflect on their professional development.

Metawork courses to develop reflective thinking

This process of reflection by the students is designed to be addressed in the program by a curriculum structure that the faculty call "Metawork". Metawork consists of frequent meetings with supervisors at the Amsterdam School of Education, which occur throughout all four years and is specifically focused upon the development of the student teachers' professional identity and their ideas about teaching and education. During Metawork, students are supported to prepare their portfolios, which play an important role in the assessment that takes place at the end of the first year (formative), third year (summative) and fourth year (summative). Part of Metawork is also focused on the development of metacognitive reflection skills. These metacognitive skills are developed in a number of ways in the program. For instance, students are invited to select an experience at their practice school, and to discuss and reflect upon their role and actions as a teacher. A student teacher might, for example, focus on a classroom situation in which bullying occurred, describing the concrete situation and the measures that the student teacher took to end the situation and to address pupils (or by providing a video of the situation). This event would enable the student teacher to reflect upon what a teacher should do in order to create a safe learning environment—a key part of pedagogical competence as defined by the program. The student teacher would also be asked to describe any intervention he or she made, and to include, if possible, feedback from a mentor and a reflection from the students involved. The student teacher would be asked to connect the experience to theory on social behavior, interaction theory and theory on bullying as well as to reflect upon the way he or she acted in their role as a teacher in such a situation.

Within Metawork, students teachers are also asked to videotape themselves in the classroom, in order to discuss their teaching with their mentor and fellow students, and to reflect on the way in which these videos show competent performance as a teacher, relating their teaching to the national competences for teachers and to theory that is presented during the courses within the curriculum. These kinds of reflections are documented in their personal portfolio and supported by evidence (such as curriculum plans, and pupil assessments) that demonstrate the classroom teaching of the student teacher.

Clinical sites

The Dutch teacher education programs have been designed to provide student teachers with substantial experiences teaching in schools throughout their programs. Most of them feature an alternating cycle of teaching and coursework each week. In the school the student teachers typically are responsible for all the tasks of a beginning teacher and are part of the school community: they prepare and teach lessons, correct and assess student work, have meetings with colleagues, and participate in social events at the school.

Both in Leiden and in Amsterdam, the teacher preparation programs do not simply place student teachers in any school with an opening, but rather place them in specific schools that have additional resources for coaching student teachers on the job and commit themselves to providing student teachers with adequate learning opportunities. At these "opleidingsscholen" (training schools) a teacher is available who supervises the student teachers at the schools and who is regarded as a school-based teacher educator. This school-based teacher educator discusses the progress the student teacher is making together with the university-based supervisor, and takes part in the assessment of the student teacher. Usually, this school-based teacher educator has a number of colleagues who are teaching the same subject as the student teacher and who also coach the student teacher. Leiden University, for example, works with approximately 40 opleidingsscholen. The Amsterdam School of Education works with approximately 100 opleidingsscholen for primary education and 40 opleidingsscholen for secondary education. Opleidingsscholen can apply for subsidies for their teacher education activities at the Ministry of Education, Culture and Sciences and the schools can also take advantage of professional development opportunities offered to their school faculty by the university-based teacher education institute. Recently, school-based teacher educators have been organizing themselves into the Dutch Association for Teacher Educators. One of their first initiatives has been to establish a registration trajectory for school-based teacher educators as part of the professional register for teacher educators. In addition, they have called for developing competence standards for teacher educators, in light of the critical role they play in preparing new teachers (Snoek & van der Sanden, 2005).

Conclusion

Dutch teacher educators face similar challenges as those currently facing teacher educators in other European countries and the US; in particular, they are under pressure to respond to increasing demands to prepare more teachers in more effective ways. Dutch teacher educators in the programs we describe have attempted to respond to these important concerns by designing preparation that they feel is reflective of a vision of teachers as professionals, who are focused and intent upon developing their pupils' capacities to think and learn, and who can support students in reaching their potential.

Yet the key features of these programs—the shared vision; the concern to acknowledge and support teachers through the "reality shock"; the design of learning opportunities around teachers' early concerns; the aim to tightly link coursework and teaching practice—may be relevant not only because they are distinctive elements but also because there is some initial evidence that some of these features can have an impact upon new teachers' learning. While work on the impact of the features of teacher preparation programs is relatively new—as it is in the United States (Boyd *et al.*, 2006, 2008)—initial longitudinal research suggests that several of these Dutch design features appeared to be particularly effective in supporting new teachers' conceptual development and competence in the classroom (Brouwer & Korthagen, 2005). In particular, Brouwer and Korthagen (2005) found that three features of the "realistic" programs they studied were particularly effective—(1) the alternation of student teaching and college coursework; (2) the gradual increase in the "complexity" of teaching for student teachers (i.e. observing, teaching parts of lessons; teaching one or two lessons, teaching lessons in a series); and (3) the close cooperation of student teaching groups, supervisors and cooperating teachers—and were significantly associated with student teachers' increasing competence in the classroom.

The design of teacher preparation in the Netherlands also leads to a larger question about the more particular structural or curricular features that may have the most powerful impact upon new teachers' learning and development. In particular, the attempts in the Netherlands to develop a coherent curriculum around a shared vision reflect an understanding that these features may matter in preparing teachers, an area which may be worth investigating across other pathways and programs in comparative studies. In a number of countries, the challenge of providing even closer links between theory and practice is most prominent in the thinking and efforts of teacher educators, and the Netherlands has identified some promising directions.

Acknowledgments

We wish to thank Els Laroes (IVLOS Institute of Education, Utrecht University), Ietje Veldman, Nico Verloop and Willem van der Wolk (ICLON, Leiden University Graduate School of Teaching), for their careful review and feedback regarding this chapter. However, the responsibility for the final manuscript rests with the authors.

Appendix

Table 3.1 Sample rubric from Leiden University for the role of classroom manager

	Insufficient	Sufficient	Satisfactory	Excellent
Providing guidance and structure	Very often the teacher is not successful in providing sufficient guidance and structure	The teacher can provide sufficient guidance and structure. However, the teacher sometimes fails to do so	The teacher can provide sufficient guidance and structure, but sometimes it does take some effort	Providing guidance and structure is easy for the teacher and comes across naturally
Providing and enforcing rules	Although the rules about what is and what isn't acceptable in the classroom are emphasized, the teacher is often hesitant when correcting students is necessary. Sometimes corrections come out of the blue and are overdone	The teacher is clear about what is and what isn't acceptable in the classroom. The teacher corrects students when necessary, although sometimes in a hesitant manner	The teacher is clear about what is and what isn't acceptable in the classroom. The teacher corrects students when necessary without overdoing it	It is obvious for everyone what is and what isn't acceptable in the classroom. The teacher corrects students when necessary. Corrections are well-timed and balanced. These corrections are hardly noticed by the other students
Helping and understanding students	The teacher is often tense when dealing with students	The teacher communicates in a friendly manner with the students and tries to help and understand them	The teacher shows care for and interest in the students. He notices problems and takes appropriate action	The teacher shows care for and interest in the students. He notices problems at an early stage and takes appropriate action

Give/provide Freedom	The students can decide themselves what they do	The teacher is open to suggestions	The teacher takes the wishes and needs of the students into consideration	The teacher takes the wishes and needs of the students into consideration and gives them the responsibility to work as they propose
Working climate	In this teacher's classroom the working climate is not positive. The atmosphere is often cantankerous. In general the lessons proceed in a messy way	In this teacher's classroom the working climate is safe. It often takes a while before the students are concentrating on the lesson. The lessons are sometimes a bit messy	In this teacher's classroom the working climate is safe. In general, the lessons are conducted in a well-structured way	In this teacher's classroom the working climate is safe. In general, the lessons are conducted in a well-structured way and the students are concentrating on their work, which does not imply that there is no room for anything else

Chapter 4

Teacher training, education or learning by doing in the UK

John MacBeath

A sometimes disunited kingdom

To describe teacher education in the UK offers a peculiar challenge as the united-ness of the United Kingdom is not always apparent. The four countries which comprise the UK all have their own parliaments, their own laws and differing education systems. Nor is cross-border travel always easy for teachers because teaching qualifications accepted in one country are not always acceptable in another. Curriculum and assessment are not cut from the same cloth and there are differing assumptions as to age-related tasks and what are described in England as 'Key Stages' (7, 11, 14, 16 and 18). Structural differences play a significant role in teacher education and professional development. Highly selective grammar schools and elitist independent schools (paradoxically named 'public schools') are an integral part of the English landscape together with a growing plethora of comprehensive secondary schools, Specialist Schools and Academies cheek by jowl with the long-standing tradition of church schools.

While Wales and Scotland have chosen to have one single system of compre-hensive schools, closer to a North American model, Northern Ireland has more in common with England, retaining its selective grammar schools. As in England in areas where grammar schools still exist, children in Northern Ireland sit the eleven plus transfer test, the results of which determine which school they will go to, and very possibly their educational and vocational future as well.

Northern Ireland is, however, close to Scotland in respect to denominational schools. The 'Catholic tradition' is strong in both countries, particularly in the West of Scotland, a very close geographical neighbour to Northern Ireland, once a joined landmass now separated by only a short stretch of water. Like their near neighbours, Scottish children from Roman Catholic families attend primary and secondary denominational schools in which religious education is both a prevailing school ethos and a compulsory part of the curriculum. No separation of church and state there, as religious education is also compulsory in 'non-denominational' schools.

Language too is a signal differentiating factor. In Wales, for example, Welsh-speaking schools are in high demand with English-speaking schools struggling to attract customers. While less strong than in Wales, in the two other Gaelic countries (Northern Ireland and Scotland), the Irish and the Gaelic languages are enjoying a renaissance.

Many other cultural and structural differences and historical legacies provide the backdrop to any discussion of teaching and teacher education and virtually every generalisation about the UK has to be attended by a caveat.

Who wants to be a teacher?

Teaching has historically been a respected profession and something that proud parents wanted for their children. While no longer enjoying that same cultural esteem, the voluntary out-of-hours work undertaken by teachers has proved to be something of a disincentive to teacher recruitment (Galton & MacBeath, 2008). In a 2005 survey by the Trades Union Congress in Britain, which produced a league table of unpaid hours by occupation, teachers topped the pole by a significant margin – over eleven and half hours unpaid per week, two hours more than corporate managers and senior civil servants who jointly took second place.

Long unpaid hours are simply an expected part of the job and teachers only began to complain when they found their evenings and weekends encroached on by marking, preparation and keeping up with the latest government demand. Time 'on task', however, was only a piece in the jigsaw of growing dissatisfaction. Three Cambridge University studies between 2002 and 2006 (Galton & MacBeath, 2002; MacBeath & Galton, 2004, 2008) found the top five dissatisfiers to be deteriorating student discipline, lack of time for discussion and reflection, large class sizes, too many national initiatives and an overloaded unmanageable curriculum.

> I have lived and taught through a period where we were respected as professionals and if asked we would do whatever was requested. Now heavy accountability has replaced this. I have excellent examination results, the pupils love my lessons and write to me after leaving describing what they ended up doing and thank me but I now hate the job and am considering leaving for a career in entomology.
>
> (Science teacher, 21 years experience)

The theme 'a thankless task' with an adverse effect on personal and family life was constantly reiterated among teachers for whom the extra demanded of them was a bridge too far. 'I'm leaving the profession I love because I want my life back' (Teacher, 7 years experience).

While a government spokesman announced that an eight-year long decline in teacher recruitment had now come to end, 'bucking the trend', a November 2009 survey by the National Foundation for Educational Research (NFER, 2009) found that three out of four local education authorities in England were experiencing a teacher shortage, with 18% of those polled saying the problem had reached crisis levels. Of the 73% of English local authorities who said their schools were struggling to find suitably qualified staff, half said the shortage was either moderate or severe. While the government was adamant that the problem was mainly confined to London and the South-East of the country, in fact other parts of England, and Wales and Scotland also reported difficulties (Northern Ireland reported no such problems). Union leaders said the survey findings justified their claim that the teacher shortage had become acute. Mathematics and modern languages teachers were hardest to find, so prompting the government of offer 'Golden hellos', awarded at the start of a second year of teaching and after successful completion of the induction period. Awards range from £2,500 in most subjects to £5,000 for mathematics and science. More contentious was the introduction of performance-related pay, giving 'good' teachers (as determined by their head-teachers) an immediate £2,000 salary increment.

Entry routes and providers

The term 'providers' is used by government in the UK to denote those places validated to prepare teachers, the word training itself a matter for ideological debate. In England it is ITT (Initial Teacher Training), in Scotland and Northern Ireland ITE (Initial Teacher Education). While in the three Gaelic countries providers are limited to a relatively small number of universities, England has pursued a much more market-driven path. Prospective candidates can choose among an almost bewildering array of agencies and routes into teaching. The Training and Development Agency website (http://www.tda.gov.uk/) informs them, 'No two courses of initial teacher training are the same' – largely because no two ITT providers are the same. Universities, colleges and schools all display varying characteristics, strengths and entry requirements, not to mention course content and structure. Applicants are then directed to a comparison site where they can compare providers as rated by Office for Standards in Education (Ofsted) inspectors.

'League tables' have proved to be something of an addiction in England, with schools, universities and teacher education providers rated and ranked. In Scotland, Wales and Northern Ireland publication of 'performance tables' (as they were politically correctly referred to) were withdrawn in 2007. Of the four UK countries, England has gone furthest in making education more of an open market, trying to make access easier, sidestepping the traditional requirement of a university pre-service course and opening up providing agencies to a wider entrepreneurial market. School-based training schemes allow entrants to start teaching immediately with the support of experienced teachers complemented by seminars and lectures which deal with curriculum, assessment and classroom management.

The School Centred Initial Teacher Training programme (SCITT) generally lasting for one year full-time, is run by consortia of schools and colleges (primary, middle and secondary years) in all parts of England and up to the Welsh border, using some Welsh schools as part of their programme although SCITT does not operate in Wales. All SCITT courses lead to Qualified Teacher Status (QTS). Many, though not all, also award the Postgraduate Certificate in Education (PGCE) validated by a higher education institution. Entry requirement to these programmes is a UK degree or a recognised equivalent qualification. If it is entry to secondary teacher education, the degree has to relate to the subject to be taught or, in the case of primary, to expertise in the core subjects of the National Curriculum. Pre-training courses are, however, provided for primary teachers to get their knowledge up to the required level.

Direct on-the-job training is also available through the Graduate Teacher Programme (GTP), in Wales as well as England, allowing graduates, often job changers, to gain unqualified teacher status. GTP graduates are employed by a school and earn a salary of around £15,000 a year. To be eligible for the GTP, an applicant must have the equivalent of a UK Bachelor's degree and GCSE (General Certificate of Education school-leaving qualification) grade C or above in Mathematics and English (a somewhat modest standard which the Conservative Shadow Minster of Education promised to raise if the Conservatives were elected).

The traditional route into graduate teaching through a full-time course at a university remains alongside the 'arrivistes'. The PGCE takes place over one academic year. Part-time and distance learning PGCE courses are normally taken over two years. The full- and part-time programmes are designed for people with sufficient subject knowledge at degree level so that the focus of the course is on pedagogy rather than the subject content. A two-year PGCE (Conversion Course) is available for applicants who need to update their relevant subject knowledge. Conversion courses tend, however, to only be available in shortage secondary subjects.

Primary school trainees spend at least 18 weeks on school placements, secondary trainee placements last at least 24 weeks. These are intended to be shallow end experiences with trainees spending time observing, co-teaching and being mentored, gradually being given a class with the teacher present, observing and following up with helpful formative comment. Practice does not, however, always follow the ideal. Student teachers may still find themselves thrown in at the deep end, left alone with a class or covering a class for an absent teacher. While this is against the code of practice, students teachers often welcome the chance to take a class on their own, enjoying the opportunity to be a 'real teacher' with all the challenges that entails. School placements usually take the form of partnership between a higher education institution and local schools with university staff visiting, supporting and assessing student teachers' practice, ideally with the student, the teacher (or mentor) and the university teacher engaged in a form of collaborative assessment and forward planning.

The PGCE remains the gold standard post graduate route in Scotland, now renamed the PGDE (Post Graduate Diploma), offering a route to a Master's degree. As in England, post-graduate courses are complemented by two-year part-time and distance courses, offered at three Scottish universities and the UK-wide Open University. Something similar obtains in Wales but only one university offers the PGDE while the others all offer the PGCE. Prospective teachers fluent in Welsh may opt to take their teacher training through the medium of Welsh and undertake their practical teaching experience in a Welsh-medium school. A Welsh-medium Incentive Scheme provides financial and linguistic support to students who need additional confidence and competence training to help them teach their secondary subject through the medium of Welsh. In Northern Ireland, as in Scotland, Initial Teacher Education (ITE) is preferred to the English ITT, and post-graduate PGCE courses take place in one of five universities, with part-time and distance learning offered by the Open University.

Universities continue to offer four-year undergraduate programmes, which may be BEd, BA, MA or PGCE. These admit young people on completion of school if they have achieved satisfactory grades at GCSE (the General Certificate of Secondary Education). The PGCE qualification usually involves half of the four-year programme time being spent in schools with the rest of the time in university divided among school curriculum subjects and psychology, educational studies and pedagogy.

Continuing to learn

Practitioner Professional Development (PPD) is the term used to refer to teacher education as an ongoing process, more commonly known as Continuing Professional Development (CPD). Where once teachers trained and were then seen as fully qualified to teach until retirement, the front-end pre-service is now regarded as only the initial stage in professional learning. It was a Conservative Minister, Kenneth Baker, who introduced what are still widely known, two decades later, as 'Baker Days', the entitlement of teachers to five days of professional development per year. These may be school-based, offered by universities or by other private agencies keen to exploit what is a large and growing entrepreneurial market.

The new developing market in Continuing Professional Development has not gone down well with university providers, many of whom are unwilling to tailor their programmes to the delivery of government policies. They lament lost opportunities to help teachers to theorise their practice and to take a more critical stance to received wisdom. As Furlong wrote in 2003:

> Despite 10 years of almost constant revolution, with wave upon wave of reform, during that time, almost every aspect of the shape and purposes of teacher education has been transformed. But in that process. those in higher education – who traditionally might have been expected to lead such debate – have been marginalized and silenced.
>
> (2003, p. 23)

Nonetheless, universities continue to provide professional development for prac-tising teachers. While differing considerably in style, content and academic credit from one higher education institution to another, they tend to take the form of a ladder of qualifications – from the Certificate of Professional Studies (CfPS), to the Post-graduate Diploma of Educational Studies in turn leading to a Master of Education degree (MEd).

A new rung on the ladder: the Chartered Teacher

The ladder is also a common feature of Continuing Professional Development in Wales and in Scotland but in both places with the addition of the Chartered Teacher route. This was created to reward and retain excellent teachers in the class-room rather than have them following the promotion pathway into administration. The 'significant financial incentive' promised by government was simply a bonus for teachers whose preferred choice was to exercise leadership at classroom level rather than whole school level. In the *Standards for Chartered Teacher* guidelines in Scotland, the distinguishing quality of the role is described in these terms:

> In every sphere of his or her work the Chartered Teacher will be reviewing practice, searching for improvements, turning to reading and research for fresh insights, and relating these to the classroom and the school. He or she will bring to his or her work more sophisticated forms of critical scrutiny, demonstrate a heightened capacity for self-evaluation, and a marked disposi-tion to be innovative and to improvise.
>
> (Scottish Executive, 2002, p. 5)

The Chartered Teacher programme is made up of 12 modules, each module involving around 150 hours of study. The modules are provided through univer-sities with continuous assessment rather than through formal exams. Completion of the Chartered Teacher Programme leads to the award of a Master's degree. Moving up the qualifications ladder by undertaking further post-graduate study is a growing trend in the UK and in 2008 the Labour Government floated the idea of a government-sponsored Master's degree for all teachers. Not to be outdone, the Conservatives argued for tougher minimum standards for entry to teacher training.

Keeping up with the Finns

This shift in raising standards at a time of teacher shortage is an interesting one, explained in part by studying the success of high performing school systems in Singapore, South Korea, Hong Kong and Finland, where entry to teaching is highly selective. The 2008 Government White Paper, *21st Century Schools* (DCSF, 2008) proposed a new licence to teach, renewable every five years, together with legislation which would require all new teachers to undertake a Master's degree in teaching and learning. This was seen by many commentators as marking a watershed in government thinking and policy. 'After 30 years of policy that has been driven by a mistrust of teachers, this could signal a new age for education policy', suggested a BBC report in July 2009.

The watershed marks both the rethinking of teacher professional status and the rebuilding of trust which had been progressively eroded over more than a decade. This was particularly significant in respect of an inspection regime, introduced by the Thatcher Government to put an end to 'producer interest', in which, it was claimed, those in higher education had managed the system of teacher education in their own interests. Conservative Ministers were determined not to be 'in thrall to the prejudices of academics' (Baker, 1993, p. 198). Together with the introduction of a centrally determined curriculum, new agencies were established to determine the initial teacher training curriculum and to establish teachers' conditions of service. The manner of determining school budgets was now to be a matter for central government rather than the local authority.

The period from the early 1980s onward had witnessed a steady growth in government micro-management of what happens in the classroom through a National Curriculum which mandated not only content but mode of 'delivery'. It was described by one academic, Campbell (1993), as a dream at conception that had become a nightmare at delivery.

Education, education, education?

The Labour Government, elected in 1997 to reverse the Tory years of assault on the education establishment, came in with a promise that their three priorities would be education, education, education. The euphoria among teachers that greeted the election of New Labour is captured in this description of a visit by a teacher educator to a school on the morning after the election:

> We went back to the staffroom and there was a party going on – the head had brought in a case of champagne and everybody in the school was there. There was no thought that anybody in that school would have voted Tory, no thought whatsoever. A glass of champagne was thrust into my hand and a nice bagel with smoked salmon and cream cheese! And the break was extended by half an hour. I also think the kids had a can of Coke and a Kit-Kat each, or something like that.
>
> (Mary Bousted, in Bangs *et al.*, 2010)

The euphoria turned out to be short-lived as within six weeks the Secretary of State for Education had continued and even strengthened the Conservative policy of 'naming' and 'shaming' underperforming schools. Mary Bousted recalls the shock at hearing a Secretary of State declaring, 'Kids in inner city schools fail because the teachers have no expectations.' Her words – 'I thought that was a shameful thing for a Labour Minister to say' – spoke for many in the profession.

The war on teachers

The 'war on teachers'[1] was to prove a continuous thread from the Thatcher to the Blair Government. Headlines such as 'Inspector Attacks Woolly Teachers' (*Daily Telegraph*, 27 January 1995) and demands that the government should 'Sack these Failed Teachers Now' (*Evening Standard*, 5 February 1996) were to continue to figure large under the Labour Government. The anti-teacher rhetoric did not diminish under New Labour, one of whose first acts was to retain the Chief Inspector of Schools, Chris Woodhead, and the Office of Standards in Education (Ofsted). As he saw it, Woodhead was tasked with 'a responsibility to expose failure' and he was, ten years on, unapologetic as to 'the trauma of failure', arguing that shock, and shaking up, were the catalyst needed to tackle the deep-seated problems of failing schools and failing teachers. He adds: '"Prickly, confrontational, arrogant, incapable of working with anyone". Yes that is me. But it is what the Chief Inspector has to be if Ofsted is to maintain any semblance of independence' (2002, p. 108).

Estelle Morris, Minister for Education under the Blair Government, while distancing herself from some of New Labour's policies, pointed to the political imperative needed to convince the public that Old Labour was dead and buried:

> I think naming and shaming of schools gave two clear messages; in the eyes of the public politically it put it on the side of the users of the services, not the producers of the services; and secondly it gave the message to the teaching profession that we weren't the same Labour Party as last time we came into power but we would have a different focus.
>
> (Interview, August 2009, in Bangs *et al.*, 2010)

Despite Estelle Morris' espousal of the political rationale for the naming and shaming strategy, as a former teacher herself she also acknowledged the pressures on teachers which, she agreed, the incoming Labour Government, did not under-stand. As she said in an interview in late 2009, 'I don't think that, unless you've done it, anybody knows the nature of the pressure in the classroom.'

Redesigning teacher education

The Labour Government was to continue the Conservatives' redesign of teacher education (or 'training' as the Conservatives preferred to call it), no longer to be determined by 'producer interest' but by 'quangos' (quasi-autonomous govern-ment organisations) such as the Teacher Training Agency (the TTA) and the QCA (the Qualifications and Curriculum Authority) established to oversee entry to the profession, qualifications, curriculum and professional standards. Adding to these monitoring and validation bodies Ofsted ensured that little would escape 'the big cats prowling the education landscape' (Learmonth, 2000).

The National Curriculum and its associated national tests were to continue seamlessly from one government to the next with central prescription reaching its height in 1998 with the National Strategies, introduced to provide teachers with virtually minute-by-minute instructions as to the 'delivery' of numeracy and literacy lessons. While increasing pressure was brought to bear on teachers to adopt interactive whole class teaching as the main pedagogic strategy likely to raise student performance, a recent review by Cordingley *et al.* (2003, p. 15) claim that this has merely resulted in 'a rash of lessons characterised by fast and furious close questioning and superficial answers rather than extended dialogue'.

The word 'delivery' is a significant indicator of government thinking about the intermediary role of teachers between policy prescription and children's learning. Among teacher educators this was construed as an attempt to de-professionalise teaching by challenging teacher autonomy, encouraging a restricted rather than extended notions of professionalism (Galton, 2007).

The implications for teacher education were far-reaching. At the very centre of teacher education there had to be a focus on government strategies, less theory and more practice, implementation rather than reading and reflection, less challenge and more compliance.

One consequence of this, as illustrated by the nature of new programmes in England, is that student teachers now spend far more time in schools during their initial teacher preparation programmes than they did a decade ago (two-thirds for prospective secondary school teachers). At the same time, higher education institutions have to pay schools up to one quarter of their gross income for their contribution, with the result that the staffing structure of many university schools of education has been destabilised.

Taking the foot off the fast pedal

A belated recognition of the adverse effects on teacher morale and recruitment problems together with the impact of PISA (Programme for International Student Assessment) has led to signs that the level of micro-management is now being reduced. Successive reviews of the National Curriculum have progressively curtailed the amount of prescription and allowed more flexibility in the approach to the numeracy and literacy strategies, National tests for 14-year-olds were abandoned in 2009 and Ministers even allowed a question to hang over the future of tests at age 11 which have so distorted the final year of primary school. Even the creation of a consumer market through league tables and parental choice was being rethought in light of the widening gap between the highest and lowest achieving schools.

Reporting in July 2009, the BBC Education Correspondent, Mike Baker, described the last three decades as ones that had witnessed a move from high autonomy and low accountability to its polar opposite low autonomy and high accountability but with a new emerging trend – high autonomy and high accountability. He concludes:

So schools and teachers should be trusted more: trusted to devise their own curriculum, their own teaching styles, and their own forms of assessment. But the price of that freedom is strong accountability. But an accountability that is more intelligent than the rather crude measures we have had until now, which have distorted school behaviours.

In the past half a decade, school inspection has gradually and progressively moved away from the punitive approach of Ofsted to a lighter touch and proportional review (intervention in proportion to school success) with school self-evaluation at the centre focused on the quality of the school's own approach to improvement.

A new relationship with schools

In England, the government's promise in *A New Relationship with Schools* (DfES, 2005) was an explicit recognition that the old relationship had done more to damage than to improve schools. A substantial body of evidence gathered over the previous decade had charted a detrimental effect on improvement. A 1998 study by Cullingford and Daniels reported an adverse effect on examination performance for a sample of schools while Rosenthal's (2001, p. 16) study in the following year found 'significant negative effects of Ofsted visits on school exam performance in the year of the inspection', diverting resources, teacher energy and student effort from teaching and learning to tactical measures to raise performance.

Employment of inspection consultants and rehearsal for the forthcoming event had become an increasingly common feature of school life. A report by the University of Brunel (Jones *et al.*, 1999) referred to 'anticipatory dread', impairing normal school development work and effectiveness of teaching, an impact on a school which, it was claimed, could last for over a year. Such reactions are to be expected in systems where inspection carries high stakes consequences for teachers.

There are some who will argue that this was needed in an era of teaching and learning which covered the whole spectrum from the sublime to the ridiculous but it was the indiscriminate nature of the attack on the profession that finally convinced government that it needed to repair the ruins of a demoralised teaching force.

Endorsing inspection as 'a vital part of the education system' was, nonetheless considered essential, as a Government Select Committee called for 'less sterile controversies', 'less heat and more light' and 'mature debate' on the strengths and weaknesses of the inspection system. It called for 'the development of a professional dialogue between inspectors and teachers' to improve morale and rekindle confidence in the teaching profession, advocating an increase in the numbers of serving teachers who train as Ofsted inspectors, complemented by Lay Inspectors.

Successive Chief Inspectors have brought a different perspective to the role, marked by a willingness to work positively with teacher and teacher unions. In

2006, Maurice Smith reasserted the place and value of dialogue between teachers and inspection teams together with shorter inspection visits:

> Weeks of anxious pre-inspection preparation and sprucing up are a thing of the past. We want teachers and pupils to concentrate on teaching and learning, not on preparing for inspections, and we want to see the school in its normal state, as it is from week to week through the year, not as it wants to be seen . . . These are short, sharp inspections, by small teams. The days when a dozen inspectors would camp in a school for a week are past.
>
> (Ofsted, 2006)

A 2007 report by the NFER (McCrone, Rudd, & Blenkinsop, 2007) found that three-quarters of the schools surveyed said that the new form of inspection had already contributed to improvement and 85% of schools agreed that the new inspection system was likely to contribute to school improvement in the future. Some 66% completely agreed with Ofsted's recommendations for improvement and 92% of respondents thought the recommendations were helpful.

William Atkinson, head of an inner-city London school, speaking in interview in 2009, welcomed the new regime as teachers 'haven't had time to be psyched out, feeling miserable week after week, their weekend's been ruined, the temperature just rising and rising' (interview, October 22, 2009, in Bangs *et al.*, 2010).

Shorter inspections are only a part of the solution. Some of the positive endorsement is due to a less confrontational Ofsted regime that has helped to restore teachers' confidence, says Mick Waters (former Director of the QCA). 'I think overall some of the morale in the later people in the profession is better than it was a few years ago' (cited in Bangs *et al.*, 2010), something he puts down to a more open attitude among Her Majesty's Inspectorate with whom he worked closely while at the QCA.

Teaching as a subversive activity

When Neil Postman and Charles Weingartner wrote their book of the above title, it was not a rebels' charter but a treatise on the place of teaching as intellectual subversion. It was an argument for the place of dialogue and a quest for meaning. Good teachers have always practised subversion and when ill-informed policies tried to stifle that creative dissatisfaction, teachers found a way round what Michael Barber (2007) has called 'uninformed prescription'.

In Giroux's terminology, they rise above the 'grand narrative' and take hold of practice, although rarely individually and generally in a context where there is collegial resilience and self-confidence in the direction of travel:

> There is no grand narrative that can speak for us all. Teachers must take responsibility for the knowledge they organise, produce, mediate and

translate into practice. If not, there is a danger that they come to be seen as simply the technical intervening medium through which knowledge is transmitted to students, erasing themselves in an uncritical reproduction of received wisdom.

(Giroux, 1992, p. 45)

There is encouraging evidence of teachers working collaboratively across the borderlands of their own subject, beyond their own classrooms and their own schools. One such strategy in secondary schools is departmental pairing, an activity which takes teachers out of their immediate frame of reference, both exposing their own practice to their colleagues in different disciplines as well as learning from them. So, for example, the English department may be paired with the Mathematics department, Music with P.E, Science with History. This may take the form of a weak–strong pairing, an asymmetrical relationship in which one department has most to learn from another, or it may be construed as a more equal relationship in which the learning exchange takes place on a more reciprocal basis. The external support of a critical friend can offer added value to the process, helping to scaffold and guide the process.

Another example of exchange of practice is the Learning Wall. These wall displays, located in public spaces or in staffrooms, provide a meeting point of good ideas, offered by teachers to their colleagues, and in some instances contributed by pupils too. In a Hertfordshire secondary school, David Frost describes the powerful impact on practice when teachers use sticky Post-its to share observations, questions and breakthrough practices. As he reports, 'These classroom observations therefore became the catalyst for cross-cutting conversation about teaching and learning' (2005, p. 22).

These schools exemplify what Wenger (1999) terms 'communities of practice', teachers together creating knowledge and building systemic capacity. Opening up of practice to colleagues whose intentions are to learn rather to judge, removes, or at least attenuates, anxiety and pressure. It both rests on and engenders trust. When there is a measure of professional trust, it is possible for there to be mutual support, a relationship in which people experience a genuine intention on the part of the other to help without a hidden agenda, without a sense that support comes with caveats and some form of payback, It is what Elmore (2005) calls 'internal accountability', and its necessary correlate is a form of self-evaluation that is genuinely embedded in teachers' thinking and day-to-day practice.

The evidence is persuasive. Teachers become better teachers when they talk about their own learning and share their own learning difficulties. Teachers, like their students, have 'special needs'. They are rarely polymaths. They are typically highly specialised in some areas but with yawning knowledge gaps in others. Their knowledge of the world is necessarily limited if still growing. The bravest among them model for their students what they don't know as well as what they do know. They exhibit what Guy Claxton (2006) calls 'confident uncertainty'. They encourage questions to which they don't know the answer, not only in the expanding realm of human knowledge but in relation to pedagogy, in which realm there are always new insights to be had.

This has been a continuous theme in Ann Lieberman's work in the United States and resonates with ongoing work in the UK. With her colleague Linda Friedrich, she writes of teacher leadership which comes into its own when teachers have the space and support to learn from one another: 'We knew that the social practices that participating teachers engage in—such as honoring teacher knowledge, guiding reflection on teaching through reflection on learning, and turning ownership over to learners—are a key part of their leadership' (Lieberman & Friedrich, 2007).

Schools need friends

The paradigm of teachers confident in their own learning with a sense of professional authority and welcoming of challenge is not easily accommodated within a hierarchical system of external accountability in the form of targets, tests and inspections. It steps outside the long-standing expectations of what a teacher is and should be. As we have found from a number of studies (MacBeath & Mortimore, 2001; James *et al.*, 2007; MacBeath & Dempster, 2008), the courage to break with traditional expectations benefits hugely from the support of a fellow traveller, a critical friend, an informed outsider who assists through questioning, reflecting back and providing another viewpoint, prompting honest reflection and reappraisal. The Icelanders have a term for this – the visitor's eye view. It refers to that unique perspective offered by the fresh eye, untrammelled by habits of seeing, able to perceive what is significant in the commonplace. It helps to see anew insights yet to come rather than the extension of insights gone by. It may be challenging and uncomfortable, yet helping to reframe and enhance practice.

The key lies in the nature of the 'passport' carried by the external visitor, whether it invites a defensive posture, a guarded response or an open welcome. Friendship implies trust and advocacy, as a prelude to provocative questioning, constructive critique, and alternative perspectives. As Brighouse and Woods (1999) describe the role, it is interpretive and catalytic, helping shape outcomes but never determining them, alerting teachers individually and collectively to issues often only half-perceived. It is best exercised when there are no hidden agendas, no differential power bases, nor premised on accountability rather than improvement (Swaffield, 2007).

While colleagues from universities or other agencies can play this role, teachers within the same school or from other partnership schools can also offer such a service. The role is not, however, one that is simply slipped into. It is subtle and complex and requires the hand of critical friendship of its own. As David Bridges warns:

> 'Understanding' needs always to be replaced by 'understandings'. Members of the same community will, notwithstanding this identity, have different

understandings of the community's experience. Not only that, but any one individual will, at different times and places and for different purposes construct different understandings of the same experience or social situation. Any attempt to understand the other, therefore, has to be interpreted in terms of a collection of understandings engaging with another collection of understandings – and this is an encounter in which the differences between insider and outsider understandings become very blurred.

(2007, p. 1)

He is careful not to claim the superiority or exclusivity of insider understanding but rather to argue that understanding is simply richer and fuller by virtue of the extent of the insider's engagement with an outsider perspective.

William Atkinson, head-teacher of the Phoenix School in London, extends the insider/outsider model to inspection, in which teachers take charge of both internal and external evaluation and Her Majesty's Inspectors (HMI) play an overseeing and quality assurance role. He argues that not only would practising teachers (trained to bring a rigorous critical eye to neighbouring schools) add credibility to the process, but that 'there are tremendous staff development opportunities for those doing it' (interview, October 22, 2009, cited in Bangs *et al.*, 2010).

There is an obvious logic to such an approach, one which builds professional capacity both from within and across schools. It offers an alternative to the one-off training session and the dependency engendered by external judgements of quality and impatient injunctions to improve. When there is intelligent accountability and the critical support of a trusted adviser, schools are likely to respond more positively to external pressure. They are better able to take a critical stance to prevailing orthodoxies and inert ideas and to resist the pressures of competitive attainment.

Conclusion

The argument for school-based pre-service teacher education rests on an assumption that schools which admit student teachers are genuine learning communities. In such schools what milieu could be better for the novice teacher? In schools which welcome the external eye of critical friends, teacher education no longer plays a reproductive function but a transformational one. Student teachers are most likely to thrive and grow in schools where leadership does not rest at the apex of the pyramid but is widely exercised. Their agency is enhanced in environments where leadership is emergent, shared and spontaneous, not always an individual activity but embedded in collective action and in networks. In learning and growing schools, configurations or patterns of leadership are manifested 'in varying combinations and degrees at times individual, at times in couplings and partners, triads, quartets, networks, formal and informal teams and other groupings of temporary, semi-enduring or enduring status' (Waterhouse *et al.*, 2008).

Such developments do not diminish, but rather enhance, the role of universities in teacher education as there is much to do before schools arrive at the ideal, possibly idealistic, scenario depicted above. Although front-end graduate programmes are likely to continue much in their present form for the immediate future, university staff in all four UK countries will have to be proactive in exploring alternative routes and creative partnerships with schools, with local authorities and with government agencies.

Chapter 5

Hong Kong

Professional preparation and development of teachers in a market economy

Janet Draper

Background: a rapidly changing context

Hong Kong's performance in international educational test comparison has been consistently high. In the face of global change, no system can stay static and like many other places Hong Kong has initiated major educational reform to protect its international competitiveness in many spheres. To understand Hong Kong's current educational situation and the changing nature of teacher education and teacher development, it is helpful, and possibly necessary, to look back. Hong Kong is now a packed modern urban space, a major high tech place with many high tech jobs, but its development has been extremely rapid. Its population grew from 2 million in the early 1960s to 7 million in 2011, with a surge in population with many immigrants from mainland China in the late 1960s and early 1970s, mirroring a similar influx in the period following 1949. This huge increase in population required extensive housing development, the building and resourcing of schools and the finding of teachers to teach in them, along with the expansion of other public services. Classrooms were designed for the formal teaching of 40 students in a class. In spite of many difficulties, universal primary education was introduced in 1972 and nine-year compulsory education in 1978.

Education for all

The education system expanded to match population growth in the face of major economic changes. The economy changed significantly from a major manufacturing and shipping centre to its current role as a logistics and financial centre. Much manufacturing has now moved over the border into Mainland China and the educational needs of Hong Kong have changed significantly. Not only have population numbers grown but the needs of employers and expectations of education have changed radically. In line with the impact of globalisation elsewhere (Darling-Hammond & Bransford, 2005), the expansion has thus not been simply 'more of the same' for a very rapidly increasing school-aged population, but rather a need for more of 'something different'.

From a highly elitist post-war system there have been significant shifts in access to educational opportunity over the past fifty years. Following universal primary and then secondary education in the 1970s, in 1980 there were places for the highest performing 40% of form three students to take up senior secondary education. There was major competition for these places and educational opportunity and success have been consistently highly valued. While education was doubtless appreciated for its own sake, its instrumental significance was also very important in its capacity to open doors to restricted further opportunity. Teachers were experts, and highly respected, following the pattern of traditional Confucian education. Learning was passive, competitive, involved intensive study and much of it was by rote. Students were generally well behaved, especially in the more prestigious schools. Education was the province of the elite and held the promise of security in the face of major social and political upheavals. The highly competitive environment fed the development of private tutorial support and tutorial colleges, a 'shadow' system of education (Bray, 2007) as families sought to ensure their children made the best possible progress towards good jobs and security. These attitudes and associated motivations may go some way towards explaining the high performance of Hong Kong students in international tests. There was, and continues to be, intense competition between schools, and numbers gaining places at university have been used, as elsewhere, as an indicator of school success. Demand greatly outstripped the supply of places and historically many students from Hong Kong have sought both upper secondary and tertiary education abroad, particularly in the UK, the USA, Canada and Australia (Ma, 1999). The availability of senior secondary school places for all who are 'willing and able' was finally achieved in 2009. Now that access to schools is wider, student numbers are larger and students more diverse, the challenges of teaching are changing though planned intakes to higher education places are virtually unchanged. This change may have implications for international performance comparison scores, since entry to senior secondary has in the past been highly selective.

All these developments, universal primary then secondary education, high numbers of immigrant families and students and, subsequently, the changing needs of employment in a more globalised world have impacted on what is expected of schools, teachers and of teacher education.

Although the performance of Hong Kong school students in international comparisons has been high, the Asian financial crisis of the late 1990s raised major concerns in the society about the appropriateness of the school curriculum and the examination-orientated teaching and assessment. Major reforms have been put in place in an attempt to move from an elitist system to one which raises the education level of the population as a whole, from a traditional system to one which can better meet the competitive demands of a globalised world.

Educational reform

In 1982, an international review group reviewed education in Hong Kong (the Llewellyn Report) and suggested that while the government department was an effective administrative body, it did not take a strategic view of the system. The Education Commission was therefore established in February1984 to review education and make recommendations for its development. The Education Commission comprises a range of educators and community representatives, mainly from the business sector. Its first report, the Education Commission Report (ECR1) was published in October 1984.

The Education Commission report of 2000, *Learning for Life, Learning through Life*, recommended a set of major reforms to curriculum, assessment, school structure and teacher development. Curriculum reform has introduced a new integrated, wide-ranging and more process-orientated Key Learning Area of Liberal Studies in the New Senior Secondary curriculum, which, combined with English Language, Chinese Language and Mathematics, forms the core of upper secondary schooling. Other traditional subjects have become electives and there will be much greater choice for students from a wide range of electives, applied learning opportunities and other learning experiences. Assessment is shifting from a focus on summative assessment to determine later options to assessment intended to support learning, and a new examination structure allows for a wide range of choice, coupled with a new element of school-based assessment. The secondary school structure has been trimmed from three years of junior secondary and four of upper secondary for those who could access it to three years plus three years. This has been accompanied by a change in higher education with a standard undergraduate degree programme becoming four rather than three years. Hence the reforms are frequently referred to as 334 (for a summary of progress with the reform, see http://www.e-c.edu.hk/eng/reform/progress004_pdf_eng.htm).

While the reforms focused on many aspects of education, in the context of this chapter, they have shaped teachers' professional development in several ways: ensuring familiarity with the new curriculum and assessment regime, a need to meet new expectations of teachers and teaching, a scheme for the induction of beginning teachers and the confirmation of the assumption that continuing professional development (CPD) is part of every teacher's work and obligations. The reforms have altered the pedagogical focus of initial teacher education as it prepares new teachers for the new arrangements. Arguably, however, an even greater impact has been on CPD for those already teaching who find themselves under pressure to alter their pedagogy to match the new requirements but continue to be responsible for large classes. In addition, many teachers have found their subject expertise in less demand, and some have been deployed into the refreshed area of Liberal Studies with its focus on process rather than specific content.

Learning for Life, Learning through Life emphasised quality education and the importance of lifelong learning to support the development of Hong Kong people to the fullest and to sustain international competitiveness in a fast-changing globalised world. These changes are not of course confined to Hong Kong but are similar to those taking place in many systems, including in Asia, for example, in Singapore (Singapore Ministry of Education, 2009), but they are in sharp contrast to the previous focus on examinations and identifying the elite. Hong Kong's report (Education Commission, 2000) recognised that the competitive elitist system had 'undercut social equity and divided society' (p. 39) and that new arrangements were needed.

In Hong Kong, there was a new commitment to develop a system for all, moving beyond elitist education by offering more choice for all, improved access to educational opportunities and opportunities to 'think, explore and create' (Education Commission, 2000, p. 29) which were seen as lacking. It was proposed that the focus of education should move from the content knowledge which had characterised Hong Kong education in the past, and which had stood it in good stead in international comparisons, to learning to learn which was seen as essential to future human and economic progress in the longer term.

> The curriculum should . . . become more flexible, diversified and integrated. Through more flexible timetabling, the use of more diverse teaching materials, the integration of all round learning activities both inside and outside the classroom, inspiring teaching methods as well as diversified assessment mechanisms, students will become more proactive in their learning and they will 'learn how to learn'.
>
> (Education Commission, 2000, p. 9)

This represented a major shift away from the traditional Confucian approach to learning (Louie, 1984) towards an approach which focused on the acquisition of independent cognitive skills for learning through changing the focus of education, including the role of assessment and the development of thinking skills and creativity. In a very examination-orientated society and one where, until 2009, there was restricted entry to the higher levels of secondary education, the focus had been on formal student performance to the exclusion of other areas of development. This had, unsurprisingly, generated tensions for teachers, many of whom were committed to a wider set of goals for the educational process.

The new curriculum has brought an emphasis on whole person education with its wider set of educational outcomes. This means that pastoral and associated counselling roles may become as central to the acknowledged role and commitments of teachers in Hong Kong as subject and pedagogical expertise. Teachers had reported they spent considerable time talking with students and parents about students' difficulties, in the light of concerns about low grades closing off future opportunities, and this had been reflected in research on parental and student expectations of teachers (Cheng, Tam, & Tsui, 2002). The focus on the whole person could bring greater congruence between the expectations of teachers and the community's assumptions about what constitute relevant student learning outcomes.

Inevitably, the shifting curriculum with a greater emphasis on whole person education has made a wide range of new demands on all teachers and CPD has become central to the change process. Teaching in Hong Kong is currently characterised by large classes of around 40 students who are taught in rooms which mainly have just sufficient space to accommodate the numbers in the class. Average secondary class size was recorded as 37.5 in 2005/6 (Education Commission, 2006b). Teaching strategies have been mainly highly skilled whole class teaching strategies with little differentiation in standard classes. The demands of learning to learn, including a focus on creative and critical thinking, attention to diversity, active and independent learning and reflection on assessment for learning represent and require a significant move away from didactic to more facilitative strategies for teachers in the classroom. Such changes in practice do not come easily and as class sizes have begun to reduce in primary schools, this has been accompanied by a range of in-service offerings to help teachers exploit the learning opportunities afforded by smaller classes.

Morris (2004), however, has warned that, in practice, the policy-making elite continue to regard teaching as a technical knowledge transfer task, focused on content-based examinations, and that while the reforms represented a significant shift to a more learner-centred focus, this was not fully reflected in their implementation.

Becoming a teacher in Hong Kong

Concerns about the supply, and the cost, of teachers have been very real in a rapidly expanding system and there has been a reluctance to set hurdles for entry so high that insufficient teachers are available. There has been a continuing tension between ensuring there are sufficient teachers and enhancing the quality of teaching. This tension was particularly evident when many educated Hong Kong residents left the territory to live in other countries, for example, Canada and Australia, in order to obtain a passport as an insurance against concerns about the return of Hong Kong to China in 1997. From the mid-1980s, the supply of teachers was under threat from the approaching 'hand-over' of Hong Kong to the People's Republic of China, which was formally acknowledged in 1984 with the signing of a Joint Declaration and planned to take place in 1997. Sweeting reports that towards the end of 1987 there was a brain drain of some of the better educated members of the population who moved elsewhere in order to obtain foreign passports:

> as a form of insurance against the possible effects of the Chinese resumption of sovereignty over Hong Kong . . . the outflow of well qualified, often relatively young people from Hong Kong including increasing numbers of teachers and of newly qualified graduates soon had a marked impact both on the schools and the recruitment of student teachers . . . opportunities for employment as teachers without professional qualifications were increasing.
>
> (2004, p. 366)

The desire to have an exit strategy available strengthened following the Tiananmen Square incident in China in 1989. Concerns about supply led to hurdles for entering teachers being set aside by employers.

In Hong Kong, therefore, it was, and remains, the case that teachers who are graduates may teach without a professional qualification in teaching. However, they must have government permission to teach by applying for a school-specific 'permit' to teach, hence they are termed '*permitted* teachers'. The permit is not transferable between schools and must be sought again if the teacher seeks to move elsewhere. There is an expectation, with no time limit, that these teachers will obtain a professional qualification. Those who complete a professional qualification may become fully *registered* teachers with the government, a status which belongs to them and is transferable between schools. With approximately 50,000 teachers, around 3000 permits were issued over each of the last three years (2008–2011) and a roughly similar number of new teachers became registered. The numbers, however, are not directly comparable since, as noted above, permits are school-specific, and permitted teachers moving school must apply anew.

Professional qualification, and the right to register, require completion of a programme of initial teacher education. Initial teacher education in Hong Kong is offered through five main routes, four of which are pre-service and one in-service.

Higher education institutions are the providers of professional qualifications in teaching and they work in partnership with schools which offer placements.

The four *pre-service* routes are:

1   Bachelor of Education (four years at present, moving to five in 2012; mainly primary).
2   Double degrees: a combination of a Bachelor's degree in a subject and a Bachelor's degree in education (hence 'double degree') taken concurrently. (Four years at present, moving to five in 2012: mainly secondary.) One degree focuses on the chosen major, for example, English, while the other focuses on teacher education, for example, in the teaching of English.
3   Diploma in Education which is taken concurrently over two years with the final year of a Bachelor's degree split into two years. (Four years in total at present, moving to five in 2012: leading to a Bachelor's degree with a teaching qualification.)
4   Full-time Postgraduate Diploma in Education for graduates (one year) (PGDE): focused on teacher education.

The *in-service* programme is a two-year part-time PGDE taken by those working in schools during the day and focused on teacher education. These teachers have to contend with a standard teaching load plus evening study, usually as they begin their career in teaching. Some choose to delay the start of their PGDE, or suspend their programme registration, for a year or two until they have their teaching work more under control and/or are clear they wish to pursue a teaching career. The taught elements of the programme are similar to the full-time pre-service programmes although, naturally, the starting point and pedagogy reflect the different needs and experiences of the students.

Reflecting the concerns about supply noted above, from 1985/86 to 1992 the proportion of post-graduate places which were part-time in-service rose from 25% to 84%, while overall yearly intake numbers stayed around 800–1000 (Sweeting, 2004). In 1992, the Education Commission Report 5 suggested a career-long path for teacher development: that all teachers should be professionally trained and that beyond that, all teachers should be encouraged to continuously improve their teaching. A government statement in 1997 (Tung, 1997), as Hong Kong was 'handed back' to the People's Republic of China, proposed that all new teachers should be both graduates and professionally qualified. It was expected following 1997 that demand for the in-service route would fall away and that all new teachers would enter by the pre-service routes but this has not occurred.

Quotas set by government for the different routes, however, continue to give significant preference to the part-time route. Many train while they teach, and prefer to do so if they can, perhaps because demand for jobs outstrips supply and also because they are paid while they undergo training. Graduates who apply for the pre-service full-time PGDE route often also apply for teaching posts. If successful, they transfer to the part-time in-service route. Government quotas for places on the different programmes reinforce this (Table 5.1).

In addition to the issue of professional qualifications and in spite of the stated desire for a graduate profession, not all posts in schools are posts for graduates. Schools have both graduate and non-graduate posts. While government policy on graduate posts on schools was originally intended to raise the status of the profession, it is now the case that more graduates work in schools than there are

Table 5.1 Intake quotas for student teacher places on the range of programs offered in Hong Kong

Programme	2009/10	2010/11	2011/12	Three-year total
Undergraduate primary (BEd and double degree)	600	650	650	1900
Undergraduate secondary (BEd and double degree)	100	100	150	350
Full-time PGDE primary	100	200	200	500
Full-time PGDE secondary	200	200	100	500
Part-time PGDE secondary	1300	1250	1300	3850

Note: Most primary teachers qualify through the undergraduate BEd route. Since the late 1980s, most secondary teachers have qualified through the part-time PGDE route.

graduate posts available. Since 2009/2010, the proportions have been 85% in secondary schools and 50% in primary (EDB, 2009) but over 90% of teachers in both sectors are graduates. There continue to be insufficient graduate posts for the proportion of graduates in teaching, and many graduates, especially in primary schools, hold non-graduate lower paid posts.

The context and content of professional preparation

Those entering teaching may take their initial teacher education as pre-service undergraduates or postgraduates or in-service postgraduates. The undergraduate routes include both wider general and degree-specific courses for their aim is to achieve a degree as well as to produce professionally qualified teachers. The shorter PGDE routes, as elsewhere, focus on the professional preparation of graduates.

Teacher education (locally termed teacher training) is located firmly in Higher Education Institutions (HEIs or tertiary institutions), of which all but one of those preparing teachers are universities. Li and Kwo (2004), drawing on Leung (2003), argued that there was no professional consensus over the content and balance of different elements in teacher education (for example, subject knowledge, pedagogical skills and practice, general conceptual understanding). All include placement in schools, with balance of placement in programmes being at the discretion of the programme providers, the higher education institutions. Generally in pre-service programmes placement occupies around 10–12 weeks in total.

There are currently no centrally set specific guidelines which must be complied with in terms of length and content of course, content and length of placement and other dimensions which are tightly prescribed in some other systems, and there is no set of common standards to be achieved. The tertiary institutions which provide initial teacher education have considerable autonomy in designing their programmes and they have the trust of government that effective preparation will be offered. Universities are self-accrediting and the accreditation of programmes by the academic institutions is the assurance of quality. Programmes are taught by staff who are mainly, but not exclusively, experienced teachers who have changed career into teacher education. It is interesting to note that high levels of performance in international tests can be achieved without high levels of central prescription for initial teacher education.

Perhaps because of the absence of central prescription, programmes vary across institutions in their design, although all are of similar length for the same type of programme. All Hong Kong programmes include pedagogical, subject and professional discipline knowledge and skills and placement experience, and most are underpinned by the concept of the reflective practitioner. These elements are combined in different ways, for example, some integrate discipline underpinnings in professional studies courses while others cover these separately, for example, with distinct educational psychology and philosophy courses. Programmes incorporate new developments in pedagogical focus, and in curriculum and assessment. Assessment is conducted in multiple ways including examinations (especially for undergraduate routes), essay-type assignments, individual and group projects and presentations and reflective journals and portfolios. Beyond these commonalities, conceptions of teaching developed within different institutions provide a framework for the programmes on offer. At Hong Kong Baptist University, for example, the model of four Pillars of Education was developed to underpin programmes of teacher education. The pillars represent four distinct roles which teachers play and for which teacher education should provide learning opportunities. The roles are:

- social and autonomous individual
- facilitator of learning
- educational innovator
- professional educator.

This structure underpins the courses which constitute the core of the programme, and it shapes the elective courses on offer.

Although there is no set of common requirements, a competency framework (Advisory Committee on Teacher Education and Qualifications, ACTEQ, 2003) which was developed to underpin post-qualification CPD is beginning to be referenced for consideration. As part of the implementation of reform, the ACTEQ drew up a set of generic teacher competencies for all, comprising four domains of professional competence, underpinned by six core values and incorporating three levels of competent performance. For the first time, expectations of teachers' professional competence were made explicit. The four domains of practice – teaching and learning, student development, school development and professional relationships and services – were intended to capture the full breadth of the teacher role. Each domain has further sub-areas. The framework allows for different levels of development: threshold, competent and accomplished and avoids labels such as expert. For each domain and sub-area and for each level, descriptors of practice have been elaborated which acknowledge and highlight the complexity of the teaching role. These are intended to make clear statements about what may be expected of whom. The competencies do not, however, stand as an isolated structure. Underpinning them are six core values: belief that students can learn; love and care for students; respect for diversity; commitment and dedication to the profession; collaboration and team spirit, and passion for continuous learning and excellence which together make a further statement about what is expected. The entire framework sits within a context which formally focuses on whole person education and there is a considerable emphasis on the broad range of competencies expected of a teacher in order to enable children and young people to develop as whole rounded people, in line with the reforms. It is a liberal but demanding account of the work of teachers and incorporates many elements with which most educators would comfortably concur. It remains to be seen, however, whether the framework has an impact on the expectations of other stakeholders, especially parents and employers or whether the very competitive focus on exam results crowds out other concerns. The continuing high demand for the 'shadow' provision of tutorial colleges suggests there is a way to go before the wider outcomes of education embodied in the reforms are fully acknowledged.

The competency framework is beginning to be used to frame school placement and its assessment. For example, students at the University of Hong Kong are expected to be familiar with both the Teachers' Competency Framework and the Code of Practice for teachers, prior to going on school placement (Hong Kong University, 2011).

All students undergo placement in schools which is structured in different ways but generally includes observation and familiarisation prior to taking up significant teaching responsibility; support or mentoring by teacher colleagues; and supervision and assessment by programme tutors from the relevant tertiary institution. Students must receive satisfactory reports from their placement schools. At the Chinese University of Hong Kong, the intended learning outcomes for school placement/teaching practice state that students will:

- Demonstrate a competence in the core teaching skills.
- Integrate and apply pedagogical content knowledge in practice.
- Apply concepts of reflective practice to real classroom situations.
- Develop appropriate attitudes and values of a qualified teacher.

(Chinese University of Hong Kong, 2008)

Professional training costs are partly covered by the government which sets a quota for paid places for all entry routes. Students pay fees. Those who study full-time pay fees which are in line with undergraduate and postgraduate fee structures; there is no subsidy and no stipend. Those who study part-time in the evening and work as teachers or teaching assistants during the day pay a pro-rata fee and fund their studies from their work.

Professionalism and professionalisation

In spite of the stated preference for teachers being professionally qualified, the predominance of the in-service initial teacher education route means that students in schools are regularly taught by those who have not been trained to teach. This clearly raises questions about the extent to which teaching is regarded in Hong Kong as a profession, with its own specialist body of knowledge and skills beyond subject knowledge

Eligibility to teach has heretofore been a matter of qualifications, with the Government Department of Education (under various titles over time but now the Education Bureau, EDB) overseeing regulations and entry to teaching as

either a 'permitted' teacher or a registered teacher. Although a professional qualification is necessary in order to register, the fact that those with a degree in a
subject may teach as a graduate provided they are permitted to do so by the EDB
implies a focus on subject knowledge rather than pedagogy. This concentration
on academic knowledge rather than pedagogical or professional knowledge and
skills has been a feature of the system and while the main route into secondary
teaching remains the in-service PGDE, this is unlikely to change. Those who
train while they teach will teach for at least two years before they are fully professionally equipped as beginning teachers.

Unlike many other systems, there is no post-qualifying assessment/certification
process for those who undergo pre-service training, to establish that they can
handle the wide range of responsibilities of teaching through confirmatory
evidence of competence. The professional teaching qualification is regarded as an
indicator of competence in itself, albeit untested with a full teaching load and a
full set of wider responsibilities for those who have followed the pre-service route.
However, most first and subsequent early career posts are time-limited contracts
and schools have the option, in a context where the demand for teaching jobs is
generally greater than the supply of posts, not to renew contracts if performance
is perceived as lacking. Hence, the market in the form of schools (principals) and
parents (through feedback to schools) decides who teaches.

Continuing teacher development

Teacher development was seen as essential to the successful implementation of
the reforms. While the concept of CPD and teacher commitment to improvement have been assumed for some time, the expectation was quantified in 2003
when ACTEQ recommended that all teachers, regardless of their post, should
engage in 150 hours of CPD over a three-year period. The area of teacher development received attention and included the development of induction arrangements for beginning teachers as well as a broader definition of CPD for all
teachers.

The new induction scheme for beginning teachers

Research on the experiences of beginning teachers in Hong Kong (Draper &
Forrester, 2009; Forrester & Draper, 2005) suggested that while some were
very well supported in their schools as they began their teaching career, others
had little support or recognition of their needs as novices. 'To enhance the
professionalism of the teaching force, there is a need to establish an effective
teacher induction scheme, in addition to good quality initial teacher education
and CPD for serving teachers' (Cheung Pak Hong, Chairman of ACTEQ: see
http://www.acteq.hk/category.asp?lang=en&cid=297&pid=39).

ACTEQ oversaw the developments in induction for beginning teachers who
had undertaken pre-service teacher education. The new HK induction scheme

was intended to empower rather than regulate schools and beginning teachers. The scheme, launched in 2008, drew on the competency framework which ACTEQ developed as the basis for CPD and, following the identification of a range of needs and concerns of beginning teachers, it developed a 'tool kit' to support new teachers and meet their needs for development through articulating the ways in which schools might develop their own support systems (ACTEQ, 2008). It also offered staff development support, a network for sharing and the dissemination of research and good practice. Mentoring is expected, but not funded, and schools determine what will be provided. Some schools had already developed support systems for new teachers and were encouraged to continue to develop their own practice. This lack of prescription to a common process may seem surprising when some systems have been very directive in order to ensure equity for new teachers, but it is important to remember the rather fragmented and very diverse nature of Hong Kong schools which have different sponsoring bodies and funding arrangements.

It is expected that there is considerable autonomy for schools to make a range of arrangements for teachers. There is considerable room for manoeuvre for school principals in how staff are deployed and in matters relating to staff generally, but much less autonomy over what is taught and how schools should be staffed. Issues related to management of staff are handled at school level and there is considerable variation in culture, climate and process.

The scheme is school-based and assumes a mentor is identified to work with each new teacher. Key players in induction are identified as the school management committee, the principal, beginning teacher themselves, their mentors and heads of subject groups ('panel heads'). A number of activities are suggested, including mutual observation of lessons with pre- and post-observation discussion and the process is firmly on development rather than proving competence. Furthermore, administrative arrangements are highlighted, and it is suggested schools can help by, for example, timetabling mutual free periods for discussions between teachers and mentors and allocating work space (individual work stations in large staff work rooms) which is close enough to be convenient for discussion and support. Beginning teachers are encouraged to reflect on the effectiveness of their teaching and its impact on student learning and to express their philosophy of education. Schools are strongly encouraged to support new teachers, but there is no formal requirement for them to do so and no mechanism of accountability. Unlike some other systems (for example, Scotland), there are no specific resources allocated to provide mentor support, since it was assumed by ACTEQ that as part of teacher professionalism, such support would be offered. 'It is a mark of professionalism for more experienced members of the school community to support new ones through sharing practices and expertise.' There is little recognition that new teachers may be able to contribute as well as to learn.

The absence of specific resources also means that, unlike some other induction schemes, for example, Scotland and England, new teachers in Hong Kong begin with a full workload. During induction new teachers are expected to complete 360 periods of teaching or 210 hours, and of these periods two-thirds should be in their key learning area. It is thus assumed that teachers teach outside their subject specialism. The absence of formal assessment and certification enables the system to focus on development rather than proof of competence and while the demands on new teachers are high, they also have scope for developing their own style.

Progress with the reforms and teacher development

Seven key areas of reform were identified in ECR7: curriculum reform, assessment mechanisms, language education, support for schools, professional development, student admission systems, and an increase in post-secondary opportunities. Progress with the implementation was reported regularly in 2002, 2003 and 2004 and a major report in 2006 documented progress with the reform measures for each stage of education (Education Commission, 2006a). In this report, under curriculum reform, teachers' professional development and training are highlighted as a major area where specific provision has been and will be further offered to school heads and teachers and in-service programmes have been provided on changes in curriculum, assessment practice and culture. In addition, a network of schools was set up in the area of gifted education.

To meet the continuing demands of the reforms, in the 2006 report, professional development for principals and teachers on the New Secondary School curriculum was to be provided, along with the enhancement of professional development programmes for heads and teachers on curriculum reform, the planning and implementation of whole school curriculum, strategies to cater for learner diversity (for inclusive policies, if not practices are in place), and the use of diversified modes of assessment for improving student learning. There would also be training on the 'infusion of creativity and critical thinking' in the key learning areas and in gifted education. Much of this professional development is offered in the form of system-designed commissioned CPD.

Professional development has been regarded as a major plank of the reform and ACTEQ was charged with making proposals for its implementation. Three reports on professional development have been produced to date (ACTEQ, 2003, 2006, 2009) and the view in the 2009 report is that overall 'considerable progress has been made and the impetus has been sustained' (2009, p. 35).

Bolam's analysis of CPD in England (2000) suggested that, while CPD might be related to any or all of system, school and/or individual teachers, the majority of CPD provision actually focused on system needs. Day and Sachs (2004) reported similar findings in the US, and evidence to the McCrone Inquiry (Scottish Office, 2000) on teachers' work in Scotland again revealed this pattern, that CPD tended to focus on topics related directly to policy change and was not differentiated by teacher need.

Types of professional development

The provision of professional development in Hong Kong falls into four main areas:

1   Highly focused courses contracted by the EDB, where content is spelt out hour by hour for those who run them, which are commonly higher education institutions. The learning process in these therefore is highly orientated to system needs rather than to teacher needs, and allows for little or no accommodation to current level of teacher development or of individual teacher need. The focus is on timetabled time and directed learning rather than space for experienced professionals to think and reflect, and, perhaps rather incongruously, mirrors the type of teaching and learning strategy which the reforms for teaching and learning in school are intended to change.

2   Qualifications and awards offered by the higher education institutions beyond initial teacher education, which include a range of postgraduate diplomas, master's and doctoral work which vary in the balance they achieve between purely academic and academic professional orientation.

3   School-based development opportunities. Schools have three development days per year and vary in how they use this time. Some offer highly structured sessions for all staff with outside speakers while some offer more varied and individualised or group-orientated provision.

4   Individual personal and professional development.

The process of these professional development activities varies, in Bolam's terms, from highly system-orientated to more school-orientated. Analyses of CPD undertaken by and for ACTEQ (ACTEQ, 2009; Chan & Lee, 2009) suggest that, as in many systems, teachers experience great difficulty finding time for CPD which is principally undertaken in the evening and at weekends. While some day release arrangements are made for EDB-commissioned courses (type 1), schools have proved reluctant to release teachers, especially at short notice, and the prevailing culture is that CPD is undertaken outside work time. This implies individual rather than a system focus in terms of responsibility, but the CPD provision itself is system focused. In consequence, many teachers resource their own CPD in both time and funds, even though it may be contributing to a major system reform programme.

Models of effective CPD

On CPD process, a series of systematic reviews of CPD research (EPPI, 2003, 2005a, 2005b) suggested that sustained and collaborative teacher-need related CPD was more likely to be effective. Corcoran (2006) has also identified elements which are more likely to enable effective CPD and which share some characteristics with the EPPI findings. Corcoran's model includes the focus of CPD (on individual teacher as well as school and system CPD, focusing CPD on knowledge of learning and teaching) as well as the process of CPD (the encouragement of site-based CPD initiatives, enhancing understanding and conceptual development not just details of practice (tips), using a constructivist model of learning and encouraging engagement with colleagues, treating teachers as adult learners and respecting their experience, accessible CPD which includes enough time and support to explore and follow up learning). Chan and Lee (2009) used the Corcoran model to review CPD experiences of Hong Kong teachers and concluded that at the policy level the policy framework offered by ACTEQ reflected the principles of CPD which was likely to be effective.

Implementation, however, is another matter and a good policy is no guarantee that effective CPD will follow.

Effective CPD?

Much CPD provision in Hong Kong has been highly specific commissioned courses on a one-size-fits-all model. This is not surprising in a system where very skilled whole class teaching in schools is the norm, but it begs questions about the extent to which the needs of all teachers may be met at different points of their development. In addition, in an era of reform and with a long hours work culture and substantial administrative elements in their work, Hong Kong teachers, in common with many teachers elsewhere, find it difficult to find time for CPD. There is some evidence that teachers' CPD choices in Hong Kong are strongly influenced by availability and scheduling issues (ACTEQ, 2009; Draper, Chan, & Cheung, 2008), with structured courses and seminars being more common than school sharing and more informal forms of CPD, in part because they are more clearly recognised and more easily counted. In spite of the enthusiasm of ACTEQ and others for the development of effective learning communities, the more formal forms of CPD undertaken are less likely to lead to this outcome.

ACTEQ (2009) also reported that the availability of financial and resources support was an important factor for two-thirds of teachers in choosing CPD experiences and urged schools to develop strategies to support teacher CPD. Three- quarters of teachers said finding time was an issue. However, comparative research with the Chinese Mainland (Wu & Kwo, 2003) and Macao suggested that working conditions in Hong Kong and Macao compared unfavourably and teachers had less time to focus on CPD than their mainland counterparts.

Professional development: resources and collaboration

Given that all teachers are now recommended to complete a minimum of 150 hours of CPD over three years, it is not surprising that some teachers reported that meeting CPD requirements was also a significant factor in their choices. CPD appears to represent, for at least some, yet another task to be done rather than an opportunity for interesting learning. ACTEQ as a body has made little reference to costs of CPD except to state 'teachers should be prepared to bear the cost, in whole or in part, of engaging in CPD, as an investment in their own professional development and career advancement' (2003, p. 16), and again 'teachers should be encouraged to exploit the potential of different learning modes including self-directed learning which can be undertaken flexibly in their own time and at their own pace' (ACTEQ, 2009, p. 34). At the same time ACTEQ has suggested that CPD should be focused on the school context (2009, p. 2) and collaborative and that schools and the whole teaching force should seek to develop as learning communities (2009, p. 35). However, the pattern of teachers' careers reflects contractual constraints and most teachers stay in one school throughout their careers. This probably exacerbates the 'colleagues as rivals' phenomenon (Ball, 1987; Burns & Stalker, 1961) and is unlikely to help collaborative practice for work and development.

When teachers seek collaboration, other contextual factors may make collaboration across schools and the creation of wider learning communities more difficult. A study on CPD for information technology in schools reported that:

> Despite the evidence that a collaborative culture is emerging and taking root in school, some teachers expressed that the collaboration and experience sharing among schools have been deteriorating. This could be attributed to the rising competition among schools, especially those situated within the same district, as a result of the declining student enrolment in recent years.
>
> (Joint Consultation Service Team, 2007)

Conclusion

In Hong Kong, the provision of education has expanded rapidly and the success of its students in international comparison tests has been striking. The progress made to cater for the educational needs of a fast-growing population has been remarkable. Motivation for education is high, commitment to educational success is dominant and vigorous, and they have been strongly reinforced by limited access to university education and good career prospects following school. The move from a manufacturing base to a knowledge economy in a competitive globalising world has made major new demands, and systems are being developed to begin to address the new need for a more highly educated population, to offer extended educational opportunity for all rather than simply for the elite. Progress is being made at the younger end on the thorny issue of class size. Elsewhere in schools large class sizes continue to drive large, albeit highly skilled, whole class teaching, making it more difficult to meet the individual learning needs which are at the heart of the reform goals. The needs of the system for expert and continually developing teachers are recognised but there are tensions between the current pedagogical experience and the expertise of the existing teacher workforce and the future educational needs of the society.

Changes in both initial teacher education and teachers' CPD are underway and will continue. However, there is scope for greater progress to be achieved than seems likely with the incremental change and the modes of CPD which are currently in use. More radical thinking, perhaps about teacher preparation and job design, could potentially yield greater benefits. The ease of entry to teaching without a professional qualification undermines the status of teachers and teaching as a profession and therefore it seems likely that teaching will be less attractive to a goodly number of the best graduates.

The perception that teacher development is at the heart and indeed is the engine of education reform is not reflected in a recognition that effective CPD depends on teachers' time, funds and energy. Furthermore the conception that CPD is for individual professional and career benefit sits uncomfortably with the recognition that the community as a whole benefits from better teaching. Yet teachers themselves, schools, initial teacher education and CPD carry the major burden in trying to achieve the ambitious goals of the reforms.

Once a barrier to progress is acknowledged in the Hong Kong system, there is clear evidence that ameliorative action follows, though, as elsewhere, there is always concern about the costs of resourcing development. Further recognition of the needs of teachers may be necessary in order to take forward fully the reforms to which the system is committed and to maintain high performance and competitive success in international comparisons.

Acknowledgments

I am very grateful to Dr Raymond Chan, Tony Lai, Dr Sandy Li and Dr K.C. Tang for their assistance in commenting on an earlier draft of the manuscript and their wise advice.

Chapter 6

Building capacity for sustained school improvement

Ben Levin

This chapter describes the approach adopted in Ontario, Canada, since 2003 that has resulted in significant improvements in student outcomes and improved educator morale—a rarely found combination. Building capacity was the central element of this strategy.

Context

Ontario has about 2 million children in its publicly-funded education system, which is organized into four sets of locally-elected school boards with overlapping boundaries, reflecting Canada's constitutional requirement for public support of minority language and Catholic schools. Some 31 English public school boards serve about 1.3 million students; 29 English Catholic boards serve about 560,000 students; 8 French Catholic boards have some 60,000 students and 4 French public boards have 13,000 students. School boards range in size from a few hundred students to about 250,000 students in the Toronto District School Board—one of the largest in North America. In total, there are nearly 5000 schools extending across a huge geographic area—Ontario is 415,000 square miles, or about the size of the combined states of North and South Carolina, Tennessee, Mississippi, Alabama, Florida, Georgia and Louisiana, or somewhat larger than France, Germany, Denmark, Belgium and the Netherlands put together.

The population is about 80% urban with most people living in the very south of the province. The six largest school districts have about a third of all the students in the province. However, many Ontario schools are small, with the average elementary school enrolling about 350 students and the average secondary school having fewer than 1000. Ontario also has a very diverse enrolment, with 27% of the population born outside of Canada (one-third of whom have arrived in the past 10 years), and 20% visible minorities. The Greater Toronto Area, which has nearly 40% of the province's population, is one of the most diverse urban areas in the world and receives more than 125,000 new immigrants each year.

The provincial government provides 100% of the funding to school boards using a formula that is always controversial, but attempts to allocate money on a combination of per pupil or school amounts and elements that recognize differing needs across the province (Levin & Naylor, 2007).

Ontario's 120,000 teachers are organized into four unions that roughly correspond to the four school systems. Most of the 70,000 support staff—caretakers, secretaries, maintenance staff, education assistants and professional support workers such as social workers—are also unionized. School principals and superintendents must have specific Ontario qualifications. These, as well as teacher qualifications, are controlled under law by the Ontario College of Teachers, which is governed by its own Council, elected primarily by teachers.

Improvement comes

Education in Ontario has all the challenges one might anticipate—large urban areas and very remote rural areas; significant urban and rural poverty levels; high levels of population diversity and many English as a Second Language (ESL) students; areas with sharply dropping enrolment and others with rapid growth.

In 2003, the Ontario education system was in trouble. The government in office from 1995 to 2003 had alienated teachers by accusing them of being lazy, imposing a multiple choice test prior to certification, cutting funding to schools, removing some bargaining protections, and imposing a new curriculum, all very rapidly. Measures of student achievement were static or, in the case of high school graduation rates, apparently declining. Morale in schools was low and bargaining disputes, including work to rule and strikes, were frequent. Teachers were leaving the profession in droves, and increasing numbers of students were moving from public schools to private schools.

In 2003, Ontario elected a new government that made the rebuilding of public education one of its very highest priorities. A new Premier and Minister of Education came into office with a strong commitment to rebuilding positive relationships with the profession as a key element in improving student outcomes. They had an ambitious agenda for change, centered on better outcomes for students, and strongly influenced by Fullan's work on change, improvement and capacity building.

By 2007, education in Ontario was in a very different situation. All measures of student achievement were increasing, teacher attrition had dropped dramatically, and growth in private schooling had stopped. That trajectory has continued through 2010. The proportion of students reaching the province's (high) standard in literacy and numeracy has increased from about 55% to 70%, while the proportion below the basic competence level has fallen from 10% to 5%. The percentage of very low performing elementary schools has fallen by three-quarters. The proportion of the age cohort graduating from high school in a timely way has gone from 68% to 81%.

At the same time, teacher morale in Ontario has improved dramatically. The number of teachers leaving the profession in their first five years has fallen to below 10%, which is probably an appropriate rate. The average age of retirement has increased by more than two years as teachers decide to stay longer (and this happened before the economic crisis of 2008).

How did this happen? Change of that magnitude is never the result of a single factor; it requires a comprehensive, powerful and sustained strategy. In Ontario, the key elements were:

- strong, positive political leadership from the Premier and the Minister of Education, backed with funding, legislation and other supports as required;
- a clear agenda, with simple, powerful goals that could engage the public and the profession;
- strong positive engagement of the education sector to build their ownership and commitment to the strategy;
- a central focus on capacity-building; increasing the ability of people in schools to deliver good results.

Ontario's change process focused on a small number of key goals while still paying attention to a broad range of student outcomes. The overall approach has been respectful of professional knowledge and practice. Change strategies are comprehensive with an emphasis not only on professional capacity-building and strong leadership, but also on targeted resources and effective engagement of parents and the broader community. A substantial effort has been made to make main elements of change coherent and aligned at the provincial, district and school level. Key partners—the provincial Ministry of Education, school boards, schools, and provincial and local organizations of teachers, principals, and other partners—work together even though they do not agree on every aspect of the changes.

These central elements were supported by a whole range of other aspects, such as a focus on reducing achievement gaps, stronger leadership development, labor peace and stability through long-term collective agreements with teachers, reconfiguration of the work of the Ontario Ministry of Education, and others. The full strategy is described in Levin (2008).

All these elements are essential for system-wide progress, but the focus of this chapter is on the element that is most often neglected in large-scale education reforms in many places—that is, increasing the capacity of educators and schools to improve student outcomes. So often in education our reforms focus on governance, or finance, or choice, or curriculum standards—on almost anything other than what matters most, which is how learners are supported every day in classrooms and schools. And there is no way to change the experience of learners in schools without changing what the adults—teachers and others—do around them (Elmore, 2004; Levin & Fullan, 2008).

The Ontario capacity-building strategy was itself complex and evolved over time. It was also developed differently in the elementary and secondary sectors. What follows, then, is a simplified account, centered around five key elements that are the focus of this chapter:

1   Work with the sector and build on existing good practice.
2   Push improved practices but avoid "mandating" as much as possible. Respect teacher professionalism without agreeing that "every teacher has his or her own way."
3   Maintain the focus on a broad curriculum and higher order skills; do not support efforts to teach to tests or narrow the curriculum.
4   Focus on the school and district as the locus of change rather than the individual teacher.
5   Build the infrastructure (supports, policy, resources) necessary to achieve widespread changes in practice.

Work with the sector and build on good practice

Two of the key people in the Ontario strategy—Michael Fullan as senior advisor to the Premier and Minister, and Ben Levin as Deputy Minister (Head of the Provincial Ministry of Education), had been involved a few years earlier in evaluating England's National Literacy and Numeracy Strategy (Earl *et al.*, 2003; Stannard & Huxford, 2006; Barber, 2007). We saw in the English strategy both some very good elements and some things that we regarded as mistakes. The chief mistake, in our view, was the failure to engage the teaching profession in the reforms. Many teachers, especially the most capable, saw the reforms as something done to them that made their jobs worse. In our view, a successful strategy has to engage educators, and especially the most skillful and energetic ones, so that they become local leaders rather than resistors.

A positive approach of this kind was not only desirable in a political sense. We were confident that almost everything that needed to be done in our schools was being done somewhere among Ontario's nearly 5000 schools. If we could find and share good practices, we could have an organic process of improvement led by educators, which is necessary for sustainability.

So in Ontario, one major component of our work has been to find and recognize outstanding practice across the province by schools and by districts. For example:

- Our Literacy and Numeracy Strategy has identified 'Lighthouse Schools' which are achieving results better than anticipated given their demographics. These schools are publicized and given additional funds to share their good practices with other schools.
- The Ontario Focused Intervention Program provides additional support and advice to struggling or coasting schools, which are then networked with similar schools with more success in other districts for mutual learning.
- Ontario has funded Student Success Leaders in every district to lead the effort to improve high school graduation rates. These leaders meet regularly to share their learning.

- We funded learning projects in a wide range of schools in our first couple of years for schools and districts to experiment with various approaches to improvement. Over two or three years, the number of new projects was steadily reduced in favor of wider implementation of those found to be most effective.
- Ontario's directors of education (chief superintendents) created, with Ministry of Education support, a network of 20 districts that wanted to work together to improve outcomes for Aboriginal students. Ontario's directors of education led a major effort, financed by the Ministry, to strengthen the capacity of teachers to work with more diverse students, thereby reducing rates of referral to special education (Rees-Potter & Kasian, 2006; van Roosmalen, 2007).

Many similar examples could be cited. In all these areas, the Ministry of Education leads but does not prescribe. It is leaders in the system who provide much of the spark, leading to much wider take-up of ideas. As a group of teachers said to me, after moving their school from 18% success to 71% in three years, "Now we know that any school could do this, because there is nothing remarkable about us. We will never go back to teaching the way we used to." Now that is sustainable change! In that school, and many others showing rapid improvement, what made the difference was the teachers' collective commitment to learning from and helping each other, to using the best available research evidence to guide their practice, and to using data from students on a regular basis to guide their own work.

At the same time, we wanted to avoid the typical education approach of endless pilot projects that last as long as they are funded, and then disappear with no impact on the larger system. The goal of experimentation is to learn, and to use what we learn across the system, an approach that has been sadly lacking in education in many places.

In support of that wider learning, what the Ministry does do is change its policies and practices to support what we learn from effective schools or districts to encourage its wider use. For example, a number of Ontario secondary schools were using something they called "credit recovery" to help students recover course credits without having to redo the entire course. However, this was "illegal" in that it was not recognized in Ministry policy and funding. After a process of discussion with all partners, including the teacher unions, the Ministry changed its policies to encourage and support credit recovery in all schools as one part of improving graduation rates.

Push improved practices but avoid "mandating" and respect teacher professionalism

Reformers are often frustrated in schools by the difficulty of getting widespread adoption of practices that they regard as obviously desirable. The typical solution to this problem is to make such practices compulsory through policy, evaluation, inspection or other means. We tried to avoid that approach, because we believe it is demotivating for good educators and therefore ineffective. At the same time, we explicitly rejected the idea that every teacher or every school must find its own way and that there cannot be standard practices in education. In fact, it is precisely the right combination of standard practices and individual judgment that makes a profession. In every profession there are things that all members of the profession do, without having to think about them, because they are known to be desirable practices. Far from reducing autonomy, this increases the ability of professionals to focus their effort and judgment where it is most needed—on exceptions and unusual circumstances where the standard practices do not work.

Schooling has been strangely resistant to this view of professionalism. There are very few areas where the teaching profession (unlike others) has adopted particular practices as being pretty much universally desirable, even where we have compelling evidence of their value. Use of formative assessment would be an example, as would student engagement through choice of work.

In Ontario, we tried very hard to avoid prescribing practice, but to rely instead on widespread dissemination of good practice led by respected educators. We were able to get quite high levels of adoption in this way. For example, virtually all Ontario elementary schools now use "data walls" to display student progress and encourage staff discussion of issues and strategies for improvement. Data walls are not mandatory; they are used because teachers value them.

What we did require was an organized planning process for improvement, eventually organized through the Ontario School Effectiveness Framework (www. edu.gov.on.ca/eng/literacynumeracy/framework.html). Even here, districts and schools are freely able to adapt the tool to their own needs and style, as long as they have a process that pays real attention to better outcomes and reduced gaps in achievement. We accept Reeves' dictum (2006) that the prettiness of the plan is inversely proportional to its effectiveness.

In 2010, the Ministry has supported "teaching-learning critical pathway" work, in which schools and districts across the province define areas of interest for improvement and work on using data and student feedback to develop and embed "big ideas" in their daily instructional practice.

Research should play an important part in improving education practice. We have increasing knowledge about effective practice in many areas, not least of which is early reading instruction. So one element in our strategy was to increase the use of research across Ontario schools. The Ministry took a number of steps to do this, including embedding research elements in all our major strategies, giving public profile to high quality research and researchers, and developing and implementing an education research strategy (Campbell & Fulford, 2009) to increase capacity and strengthen partnerships among researchers, school districts and schools. As one example, the annual Ontario Education Research Symposium, which brings together all the partners, started in 2005 and is now one of the most oversubscribed events in the annual education calendar, always having to turn away participants to maintain a reasonable size. It has now been replicated by several universities at a regional level, a further sign of success and impact.

Another part of our effort was to engage Ontario's four teacher unions (plus a fifth umbrella professional teacher organization) in the improvement effort. Our view is that strong teacher unions are essential to strong education systems, and that the idea that success lies in reducing the union role is misguided; virtually all high performing education systems in the world also have strong and effective teacher unions, because this is a key part of attracting and keeping good people in education. Further, in our view the primary responsibility for building positive relationships lies with management but too many districts write the union off as a problem rather than making the sustained efforts needed to build trust. This is not to adopt a naïve view that there will be some harmonious era in which labor–management conflict vanishes. It is to say that with effort one can build relationships that support a good education agenda.

Teacher unions were engaged in all areas of our policy and strategy development. We sought their views regularly and—as with credit recovery—invited them to have a major role in setting out the conditions for some of our policies. In addition, the Ministry provided the unions with substantial funding to offer professional development sessions to teachers as a way of recognizing and strengthening the role of unions in promoting good professional practice. As one example, the federations developed the "teacher leader learning program," which encouraged teacher leaders in and across schools to engage with leading experts and each other to strengthen teaching practices.

The success of these efforts is illustrated by the ubiquitous presence in Ontario of the Ministry's three central goals of improving student outcomes, reducing gaps in those outcomes, and increasing public confidence in public education. Although these goals were never mandated, they are widely referenced by schools and districts in their own plans and have become a mantra across the province.

Maintain the focus on a broad curriculum and higher order skills; do not support efforts to teach to tests or narrow the curriculum

A main criticism of much education reform has been that it pushes teachers to teach to the test and results in a narrow and impoverished curriculum. Although Ontario did have a focus on literacy and numeracy, we set out from the start to support a rich and diverse curriculum, understanding that this was, in fact, the best way to get better achievement in literacy and numeracy. Ontario leaders have said consistently that our goal is not simply to improve test scores; it is to strengthen students' real skills and to increase their motivation as learners.

Ontario did not reallocate time from other subjects to literacy and numeracy. We did not change our curricular emphases on areas such as science, social science and the arts. Indeed, this broad focus was given additional emphasis when, as a result of collective bargaining in 2005, about 2000 specialist teachers were added to elementary school staffs to enrich teaching in areas such as art, music and physical education while also providing more preparation and professional learning time for classroom teachers. Daily physical activity is a requirement in Ontario elementary schools, and teachers have been provided with a range of resources to show how physical activity can support other school goals as well (including, for some teachers, their own level of physical fitness). Ontario also supported a character education initiative that gave broad latitude to schools and districts to work on various aspects of non-academic character goals—again, without requiring the adoption of any particular program.

It is also noteworthy that the results of Ontario's provincial achievement tests over the past few years have consistently shown that students are strongest on so-called basic skills and have most room for improvement on higher order skills such as comprehension and number sense. These latter skills cannot be developed through drill or test taking practice. The teaching and learning practices required to improve student performance are entirely consistent with the kind of pedagogy that strong teachers support, involving rich and engaging teaching for meaning.

Focus on the school and district as the locus of change rather than the individual teacher

Our theory of improvement identifies schools as the main place where improvement happens, with districts playing a vital supporting role. We addressed this focus in several ways.

First, every school and every district created a leadership team for literacy and numeracy in elementary schools and a leadership team for student success in secondary schools. Each school or district determined who would be on these teams, which were to create and support the local strategy for improvement. Simply having a group of people in a school focused on the key goals is itself a vital step, although it is often ignored in change efforts, where the principal is presumed to be able to do everything alone.

Our extensive professional development efforts also focused extensively on schools and districts. We tried to avoid one-shot workshops in favor of various kinds of school and district-based development efforts, including coaching, mentoring and other strategies. Although the Ministry often proposed approaches, we were always open to a school or district that wanted to try it another way in light of their circumstances. As one example, the province created two extra professional development days in the school calendar, and required that they be used to support the provincial strategy. Districts, in consultation with the Ministry, decided how best to use those days to support their own goals and strategies.

As noted earlier, we also created many opportunities for district and school leaders to meet with others to share their learning. We created a new data tool, Ontario Statistical Neighbors, to allow schools to find other similar schools. A school can locate other schools in the province with similar demographics and compare its performance to theirs, then reach out for advice and support to schools that seem to be more successful.

Another important element was support for improved leadership across the system. The Ministry, working closely with a range of existing organizations such as principal and superintendent groups, developed a leadership strategy (www.edu. gov.on.ca/eng/policyfunding/leadership/actionPlan.html). The strategy is closely aligned to the broader improvement strategy and is intended to help all our leaders focus on the core mission and get better at it. The leadership strategy also has a strong element of networking and self-direction. For example, the "Leading Student Achievement: Our Principal Purpose" project is a joint effort with Ontario's three associations of school principals to create networks of principals across the province to share good practices and research findings on improving student success.

Yet another support for the district role has been work to help districts improve their administrative operations such as transportation or human resources or capital management. The goal here is again to share best practices, including those from other sectors, so that education leaders can spend less time on administrative tasks and more on leading teaching and learning.

One sidelight to this strategy is that Ontario has made no significant effort to address initial teacher education, choosing instead to focus almost entirely on working with existing schools and their teachers.

Initial teacher education in Ontario occurs primarily through the province's 11 faculties of education and is mainly a one-year (eight month) program, though there are also some concurrent four-year programs and some two-year Master's programs leading to certification. (Note: the government has just announced that it will implement a two year initial teacher education program.) Both teacher certification and the regulation and quality control of programs take place through the Ontario College of Teachers. Universities do have autonomy over their own programs, but in order to be certified in Ontario, graduates must meet requirements for certification set by the College; these include appropriate subject area background, breadth of study especially for elementary teachers, significant practicum time in schools and other requirements as determined by the College. In addition to Ontario universities, some foreign universities offer teacher education programs in Ontario or just across the U.S. border; these programs are not supported by Ontario government funding (as are the other 11 universities) but their graduates are eligible for Ontario certification if they meet the requirements.

Prior to 2004, due to high teacher turnover, Ontario added additional spaces to university teacher education, but since 2008 the province has had a significant surplus of teachers (even though many new positions have been created) and these additional spaces have been removed from the system.

There are three reasons why we chose not to give significant attention to changing initial teacher education:

- Ontario already has a sufficient overall supply of new teachers, and our new teachers are, by and large, capable and well educated. Our system partners

did not identify a shortage of teacher talent as an issue with the exception of remote regions or some specialized subject areas (such as the worldwide challenge around science and mathematics teachers; OECD, 2005).

- Our view is that schools will change new teachers far more than new teachers will change schools. If school practices do not change, then all the changes in the world in initial teacher education will not matter. If schools change their practices, then initial teacher education will adjust in part, and new teachers will adjust fully when they enter the schools.

- It is very difficult to change initial teacher education, which is provided by highly autonomous universities and regulated by an independent College of Teachers. Our reading of the research on previous attempts to reform initial teacher education did not give us confidence that the results would be worth the time and effort.

Of course, initial teacher education could be better. But given limited resources, we felt the right choice was to invest in schools rather than in initial teacher education.

We did, however, introduce an induction program for all new teachers, providing first year teachers with extra release time, targeted professional development, and mentoring, all based on a careful analysis of the literature and on a series of pilot projects.

Build the infrastructure (supports, policy, resources) necessary to achieve widespread changes in practice

One of the central lessons we took away from the English experience is that changing a large system with many thousands of people requires a dedicated, significant infrastructure. Although the observation seems trite, it is rarely practiced. Many systems seem to think they can change practice with a new set of standards or curriculum, a test, and a few days of in-service. That is foolish.

Ontario built a very significant infrastructure to support our priorities. For both our literacy and numeracy strategy and our high school student success strategy we created special purpose organizations led by outstanding educators seconded from the education system. At the start it was necessary to have two separate units with separate leadership simply in order to get things moving. More recently, the two strategies have been merged into a single unit in the Ministry and are gradually melding more of their work, helping to improve coherence and alignment in the education system.

These structures work in a very interactive way with schools and districts, providing both pressure and support. For example, the Ministry's student achievement officers work closely with district leaders to review school improvement plans, to share research, to plan effective professional learning, or to support networking of teachers and school leaders. Ministry staff will also challenge school or board plans where they feel that these are not sufficiently specific or well-grounded in the evidence. Over time, districts have grown to welcome and appreciate this critical friend role that helps them do their own work with greater clarity and ambition.

Supporting improvement took many forms. Helping districts and schools set reasonable and ambitious goals and work towards them was one major element. Providing extensive professional development opportunities was another. A third was to set up and support learning networks across the province to share good practices (and mistakes). Another element involved providing resources of various kinds, from curriculum support documents to web casts to DVDs of good practice, many of which are now very widely used.

As noted earlier, the Ministry also made appropriate policy changes to support improvement efforts. In secondary schools we increased the use of cooperative education and began to recognize "dual credits" to support wider use of these innovative practices. For elementary schools, as a result of teacher concerns, the provincial tests in grades 3 and 6 language and mathematics, which are closely linked to the Ontario curriculum, were changed in 2005 to take less time and give quicker results to schools. Although many teachers continue to have concerns about provincial testing, this is now a rather minor issue in Ontario education because of the increased support for improved teaching and learning including using a range of student achievement data to support school improvement.

Ontario also used collective bargaining to advance its capacity-building agenda. We recognize that strong teacher unions are important to strong public education. Two main examples—the addition of many more specialists in elementary art, music or language and the creation of "student success teachers" in all secondary schools—have already been mentioned. These efforts were another instance of engaging the interests of teachers and their unions with the improvement agenda; as suggested by Leithwood (2006), there is much more compatibility in these two agendas than is often realized.

This change in the work of the Ministry was not a small thing. Most Ministries of Education (and the author has worked with many of them around the world) are not organized to support improvement in schools. They are set up to make and enforce rules, to distribute funding, and to solve administrative or political problems. Those are important functions, but they are not at all the same as leading improvement.

Changing the work of the Ontario Ministry from being about rules and compliance to being about results and improvement was itself a major effort. It meant some changes in leadership, but even more changes in the culture of the organization. The wonderful part of this work is that many Ministry staff saw it as a welcome change, even as we and they struggled to understand how to make it work. Good people want to do good work; a key task of managers is to enable them to do so by supporting the right practices and structures, and getting rid of or at least minimizing the others.

Much of the public debate about education revolves around money, with constant arguments about whether there is enough. Ontario has committed significant new resources to education since 2003. Per pupil expenditure has grown by about 30%, mostly related to improved compensation and working conditions for teachers, including a large cost to fulfill the government's commitment to reduce class sizes in 90% of primary classrooms to 20 or fewer students.

Yet in another way it does not take a huge amount of money to move a system. Some new resources are like the drops of oil that lubricate the machinery, but, as every engineer knows, too much oil can be almost as bad as too little. In fact, the incremental cost of our major strategies for literacy and numeracy and for high school student success were approximately 1% more spending in each sector. The main drivers of the 30% increase were the costs of collective bargaining changes, price increases in areas such as fuel and utilities, and a large program of improving school buildings. We continue to believe (Grubb, 2009; Levin & Naylor, 2007) that there are many opportunities to use resources more effectively.

Conclusion

All those involved, in the Ministry and in school boards, speak with pride of what has been accomplished in the past few years in Ontario education. The province gets 50–80 delegations a year from around the world to look at what we have done. We have had positive reviews recently from U.S. Chief State School Officers, from the Gates Foundation, and from international experts such as Richard Elmore. There is much of which to be proud.

At the same time, nobody in Ontario can be complacent. Our levels of student achievement have risen, but they are not yet nearly high enough. Some of our achievement gaps are smaller, but they are still too big. We do not know how far we can progress, but we do know that we are not yet at any apparent limit.

Continued progress rests on continued political commitment and leadership but even more on effort by many thousands of people, like those teachers who will never return to their previous practices. In organizing that effort, building capacity is the single most important element.

In all of this work the goal has been and remains the right combination of pressure and support; to help our talented professionals get better at the work they want to do. In Ontario, we have invested heavily in what Michael Fullan (2010) calls "collective capacity building" because it is a strategy that builds both expertise and common commitment.

One never gets this balance exactly right, but various sources of evidence suggest that the vast majority of Ontario's teachers and school leaders feel that the province is on the right track in terms of education. When people come together at the provincial level, the energy and enthusiasm are palpable. As noted, our attrition rates for early and late career teachers have dropped sharply. And although it is a highly unscientific measure, I have had many, many educators tell me in the past few years that they are having the best time in their careers as they get to work on the things they really care about, with the sense that the system as a whole is focused on helping all of us do better, not blaming people for what has not yet been achieved. That is capacity-building in action!

Chapter 7

Rethinking teacher education in Australia

The teacher quality reforms

Diane Mayer, Raymond Pecheone, and Nicole Merino

Teacher education in Australia: an overview

In Australia, teachers are prepared for teaching through multiple study pathways in university settings including: (1) four-year undergraduate Bachelor of Education degrees; (2) four-year double degrees comprising a degree in the subject discipline area and a degree in education; and (3) one-year Graduate Diploma in Education programs after an initial three-year Bachelor's degree in the discipline area. In addition, two-year graduate level Master of Teaching programs after a Bachelor's degree in the discipline area have become popular pathways into teaching in recent years. Four-year undergraduate Bachelor of Education degrees are often the preferred pathway for school leavers preparing to teach primary (elementary) years, while the graduate entry or 'end-on' programs are often the preferred pathways for those preparing to teach in secondary schools.

Teacher education programs usually comprise professional studies, curriculum studies and professional experiences or practicum. The four-year undergraduate courses also include discipline study in relevant teaching areas. Primary teachers teach a range of subjects in primary schools including mathematics, English, the arts, science, humanities, health and physical education, technology, and teaching languages other than English. All pre-service primary teachers are prepared to teach across these subjects, while secondary pre-service teachers usually prepare to teach two subject areas.

Practicum experience

All teacher education programs include professional experience or practicum which includes a series of supervised experiences in schools comprising 12–20 weeks in total, depending on the length of the teacher preparation program. The practicum program is structured developmentally to support learning to teach and includes a variety of placement schools. The experiences vary in length of time in schools and comprise days per week as well as week-long blocks in the later phases of the program. They are linked to the on-campus component of the program and occur in all years of the teacher education program. The

Commonwealth Government[1] provides funding to Higher Education Institutions for practicum supervision who then contract directly with individual schools for the provision of supervision of pre-service teachers. An Industrial Award, the Australian Higher Education Practice Teaching Supervision Award 1990, provides guidelines for the eligibility of teachers for practicum supervision as well as the rates for payment for supervising in all Australian States and Territories.

Entry into teacher education

Entry into teacher education programs is managed by state- or territory-based tertiary entrance centres including the Victorian Tertiary Admissions Centre (VTAC), the Queensland Tertiary Admissions Centre (QTAC), the South Australian Tertiary Admissions Centre (SATAC), the Tertiary Institutions Service Centre (TISC) in Western Australia, and the Universities Admissions Centre (UAC) in New South Wales and the Australian Capital Territory. The University of Tasmania manages applications in Tasmania and Charles Darwin University manages applications in the Northern Territory. These tertiary entrance centres administer applications for places in tertiary courses at universities, Technical and Further Education (TAFE) institutions and sometimes independent tertiary colleges in that state. They are funded by the participating institutions and the processing fees are paid by the applicants. The centres receive and forward applications and supporting documentation to the institutions and after institutions make their selection decisions, the centres send offer letters to successful applicants on the institutions' behalf. In addition, they usually manage the calculation and issuing of tertiary entrance scores for high school leavers. Tertiary entrance scores are a major determinant in selection for higher education courses but applicants are also required to have a solid foundation in secondary school English and mathematics. The procedures by which tertiary entrance scores are calculated vary in each state/territory but this usually involves the determination of a single score that reflects achievement in some combination of state-based test and school-based assessments that have been moderated across the state.

Professional regulation

Entry into the profession and ongoing certification of those in the profession ('registration' in Australian terminology) have traditionally been the responsibility of the states and territories. State/territory teacher registration boards determine the conditions for teacher employment and qualification requirements. Teachers must be registered (usually provisionally) before applying for employment. There are seven teacher registration boards: the Queensland College of Teachers, the New South Wales Institute of Teachers, the Victorian Institute of Teaching, the Teachers Registration Board of Tasmania, the Teachers Registration Board of South Australia, the Western Australian College of Teaching and the

Northern Territory Teachers Registration Board. They have governing councils or boards comprising representation from employers, schools, unions, and universities. Teacher education programs are developed by teacher educators in universities and accredited by the relevant registration board in order for graduates to be eligible for teacher registration in that state/territory. Accreditation of a teacher education program usually involves a committee making a judgment about whether the program will prepare graduates able to demonstrate competent professional knowledge and practice in relation to the registration authority's professional standards for graduating teachers. While it varies slightly from jurisdiction to jurisdiction, there are usually categories of registration including provisional registration upon graduation from an approved teacher education program and then full registration after a period of 12–18 months, during which time the beginning teacher must provide evidence that they have achieved the standards of professional practice required for full registration. This time usually involves an induction program including school-based mentoring and workshops and other professional learning opportunities. Induction programs are usually state- or employer-run and mentors are sometimes given classroom release time to carry out their mentoring role, but are not usually paid extra for that role. Ongoing registration throughout the career of a teacher is usually dependent on demonstration of ongoing professional learning.

Funding for teacher education

The Australian higher education system is small by comparison with other countries, with 39 universities, of which 37 are public institutions and two are private. Teacher education is offered in the Schools or Faculties of Education in 34 of the public universities across the country.

Funding from the Commonwealth Government is provided to higher education providers through annually negotiated funding agreements specifying the number of student places that will be funded in discipline clusters. However, a recent change in legislation has 'uncapped' undergraduate places. From 2012, public universities will be able to determine the number of students they enrol in bachelor degrees and will receive funding for these students. The funding rate per place for each cluster is set in legislation and amended in each year's budget. For 2012, the Commonwealth contribution amount for a place in a funding cluster is as shown in Table 7.1.

Most students are Commonwealth supported. They are required to pay a part of the cost of tuition, called the 'student contribution', while the Commonwealth pays the balance. Student contributions can be paid 'up front', but many are 'deferred'. These contributions are paid to the university by the Commonwealth on behalf of the students, who defer payment of their contribution as part of a Higher Education Loan Programme (HELP). The Commonwealth's Department of Education, Science and Training (DEST) and the Australian Taxation Office (ATO) jointly administer HELP. In addition, qualified students may be entitled

Table 7.1 Commonwealth Grant Scheme funding cluster amounts

Item	Funding cluster	Commonwealth contribution amount (AUD)
1	Law, Accounting, Administration, Economics, Commerce	$1,861
2	Humanities	$5,168
3	Mathematics, Statistics, Behavioural Science, Social Studies, Computing, Built Environment, Other Health	$9,142
4	Education	$9,512
5	Clinical Psychology, Allied Health, Foreign Languages, Visual and Performing Arts	$11,243
6	Nursing	$12,552
7	Engineering, Science, Surveying	$15,983
8	Dentistry, Medicine, Veterinary Science, Agriculture	$20,284

to Youth Allowance or Austudy Payments which are means and assets tested. Further assistance is also available in the form of scholarships.

The teacher quality reforms

Historically, schools and teachers' work have been the jurisdiction of the states/territories and higher education has been the jurisdiction of the Commonwealth. This has sometimes created a 'push–pull' tension of sorts since all taxes are collected federally and then distributed to states to fund and manage the P-12 schooling sector, while funds are distributed directly to universities as described above. In education, this means that the funding and related policies for teacher education are the jurisdiction of the Commonwealth, while the funding and related policies for the schooling system within which the graduates will work as teachers are the jurisdiction of the state. When the political party in government at the federal level has different policies from the political party leading the state government, tensions can and do occur.

In recent years the Commonwealth has made moves to increase its influence over schooling and teachers' work mostly in the name of greater accountability to the tax-paying public. Most recently, the Australian Government announced the *Smarter Schools – Improving Teacher Quality National Partnership* (TQNP) program to be funded by the Commonwealth at $550 million over five years. The broad goals of the TQNP program are to attract, prepare, place, develop and retain quality teachers and school leaders in schools, and to improve the quality of teaching including improving teachers' skills and knowledge of teaching Aboriginal and/or Torres Strait Islander students. Areas for reform include:

- attracting the best graduates to teaching through additional pathways;
- improving the quality of teacher education;
- developing national standards and teacher registration;
- improving retention by rewarding quality teachers and school leaders.[2]

These reforms are discussed in the following sections. To varying degrees, these reforms are in response to a number of political agendas currently gaining attention in Australia.

The political landscape of teacher education in Australia

Like many so-called developed countries, teacher education in Australia is currently being positioned as a 'policy problem'. As Marilyn Cochran-Smith reminds us, teacher education in the US was first positioned as a 'training problem', then as a 'learning problem', and more recently as a 'policy problem' (Cochran-Smith & Fries, 2005). A similar framing is evident in Canada, the UK and Australia. Peter Grimmett (2009) also analyses this positioning of teacher education in relation to its governance structures in three phases:

1   Phase 1 (1960–1980): teacher education as training under government control.
2   Phase 2 (1980–2000): teacher education as learning to teach under institutional governance.
3   Phase 3 (1990–2010): teacher education as policy in a governance context of professional self-regulation and deregulation.

In Australia, the 1980s and early 1990s were characterized by a focus on the preparation of a professional teaching workforce wherein teacher education was informed by research that aimed to illuminate the professional knowledge base of teaching and teacher education. Terms like 'teacher training' were rejected in favor of 'teacher education' and 'learning to teach', and 'reflective practice' became a major focus in the teacher education. Teacher education students were engaged in activities that helped them reflect on their pre-existent beliefs and the effects of their professional practice for all students. In the main, teacher education was self-governed by the institution responsible for the delivery of the teacher preparation program. Teacher educators had programmatic control over the way they prepared teachers and to a large extent influenced the political agendas related to professional learning and professional practice.

However, a sharper focus on 'quality assurance' and 'outcomes' emerged in the 1990s, and since the early 2000s, teacher education governance has been characterized by an increasingly intense focus on outcomes, particularly student learning outcomes and whether or not teacher education makes a difference to student learning in classrooms. Most recently, it has been argued that the most appropriate policies and practices for teacher education should be decided according to empirical evidence about their value-addedness in relation to student achievement as measured by standardized tests. As a result, the policy debates around teacher education governance have become increasingly polarized, posing on the one hand, the deregulation and marketization of university-based professional training (often in tandem with calls for increased centralized control of curriculum and pedagogy), against a defence of professionalism grounded in the academy. Those promoting deregulation argue there is little valid evidence to support the value-addedness of teacher education as it is currently practised, and argue instead for regulatory standards and performance indicators in lieu of traditional teacher education pathways. Those calling for increased professionalization argue for policies and practices that promote professional self-regulation and semi-autonomy.

In this contested context, politicians, bureaucrats, the business community, members of the community and even members of the teaching profession, are increasingly asking questions about the professional preparation of teachers, including: What is the value of teacher education? What should beginning teachers know and be able to do? How can judgments be made about what beginning teachers know and are able to do? This section examines each of these questions in turn and discusses the emerging national debates, policies and actions that are responding to the questions.

What is the value of teacher education? The deregulation and professionalization debates

Historically, all teachers in Australia have been prepared through what might be called (in North American parlance) 'traditional pathways' including study in university Faculties or Schools of Education in programs accredited by the state legislated authority for teacher registration. However, following the situation in the US, a recent wave of criticism of teacher education has invited consideration of 'alternative' pathways into teaching. While not quite at the position where traditional routes to teacher certification via teacher education programs in schools and colleges of education are being seen as 'barriers to becoming a teacher among otherwise highly qualified individuals' (US Department of Education, 2004, p. 2), such a view is gaining some attention in the Australian political landscape.

Many within the academy and the teaching profession are alarmed at what they see as a deskilling and deprofessionalization of teachers and their work. Like colleagues in the US (for example, Darling-Hammond, 2000; Wilson *et al.*, 2001), Australian teacher educators argue that qualified and registered teachers are more effective than un- and underqualified teachers in terms of student achievement. They argue for a focus on the professionalization of teaching and posit that the basis for reform should be policy investment in the quality of teachers through teacher education, registration and recruitment practices, and professional development, not by bypassing with teacher education. They argue for 'professional accountability' where a self-regulated teaching profession would take collective responsibility for ensuring that all those permitted to teach are well prepared, have and use all available knowledge to inform professional practice and maintain a primary commitment to clients (i.e., students and the public). Such a professional accountability model represents a 'policy bargain' the profession makes with society, whereby greater (self-) regulation of teachers is guaranteed in exchange for deregulation of teaching (Darling-Hammond, 1989; Mayer, 2005).

Like the US, teacher education governance in Australia is increasingly being characterized by a focus on outcomes, particularly student learning outcomes and whether or not teacher education makes a difference to student learning in classrooms. Various inquiries into teacher education have recommended large-scale research projects investigating the value of teacher education. One example is the Victorian Parliament's inquiry into teacher education in 2004 that recommended:

> *Recommendation 2.7:* That the Victorian Government undertake a major research project for the long-term evaluation of teacher education. This project should include a comprehensive data and collection management system that links pre-service teacher profiles and various teacher education courses to recruitment, retention and advancement within the profession. This evaluation should compare outcomes for various structures and approaches to teacher education.
>
> *Recommendation 2.8:* That the Victorian Government pursue through MCEETYA[3] a longitudinal study into the long-term effectiveness of various approaches to teacher education in terms of student outcomes.
>
> (Education and Training Committee, 2005, pp. 66–7)

However, as yet, no such large-scale studies are underway across Australia. This is not surprising, because as in the US:

> Major (research) grants are rare in the field of teacher education, and as a result teacher educators often study their own teaching and their own programs, producing a wide variety of studies that include many small scale and unconnected studies of practice.
>
> (Mayer, 2006, p. 6)

While such studies may provide a useful research base for informing teacher education programs and practice, a significant gap remains for high quality, larger-scale research into teacher education. There is a great need in Australia for national competitive large grants to support such research.

Within this context, the Commonwealth Government has attempted to take increasing control over teacher preparation as indicated in the TQNP reforms areas noted above.

Teach for Australia: selecting outstanding graduates

One significant recent addition to the teacher preparation context in Australia as a result of TQNP activity is 'Teach for Australia', a program not unlike Teach First in the UK and Teach for America in the US. Teach for Australia commenced in 2010 and aims to recruit and select outstanding university graduates from all disciplines who have distinguished academic performance, leadership experience, and communication and empathy skills to teach in socio-economically disadvantaged secondary schools. These Teach for Australia Associates complete an intensive 6-week teacher training program and then teach for two years during which they are supported by mentors and work with business partners who will provide leadership support and business coaching. The University of Melbourne has been awarded the contract by the Commonwealth Government to develop and deliver the content for the Associates' training, which is being delivered through a combination of intense on-campus blocks of study and self-paced coursework study over their first two years of teaching. At the end of the two years, the Associates will graduate with a Postgraduate Diploma in Teaching and be qualified to teach at secondary schools anywhere in Australia. Full course costs for the Postgraduate Diploma in Teaching are funded for Teach for Australia Associates by the Commonwealth Government.

Australian Institute for Teaching and School Leadership: quality teaching and school leadership

In 2005 the Commonwealth government established *Teaching Australia* to be 'a strong unifying body acting in the interests of teachers and school leaders, drawing the profession together to promote quality teaching and school leadership for the good of all Australians'. Even though Teaching Australia initially explored the development a national system of teacher education accreditation, it subsequently focussed most of its attention on establishing a national recognition system for highly accomplished teachers and school leaders (Mayer, 2009). However, in 2010, the *Australian Institute for Teaching and School Leadership* (AITSL) was established to replace Teaching Australia. AITSL has a specific brief to support the NQTP reform agenda and provide a significant national role in setting and using professional standards, providing national professional learning activities, research to improve pedagogy and school leadership, and activities to celebrate good practice in schools.

National accreditation of teacher education:

The Ministerial Council for Education, Early Childhood Development and Youth Affairs (MCEEDYA) which comprises state, territory, the Australian Government and New Zealand ministers with responsibility for the portfolios of school education, early childhood development and youth affairs, has supported AITSL's development of an Australia-wide accreditation of programs for the professional preparation of teachers.

Not that this is a new move in Australia. As far back as the mid-1990s, the Australian Council of Deans of Education supported a national framework. In July 1996, funding was approved, under the federally funded Projects of National Significance Program, for a project to develop national standards and guidelines for initial teacher education in Australia. The Australian Council of Deans of Education managed the project and produced a comprehensive report that recommended National Standards and Guidelines for Initial Teacher Education be used as criteria for the accreditation or approval of initial teacher education programs (Australian Council of Deans of Education, 1998). Then, in June 2005, the newly established Teaching Australia commissioned the Australian Council for Educational Research (ACER) to conduct a project to provide advice on developing a national system for the accreditation of pre-service teacher education programs (Ingvarson *et al.*, 2006). In addition, in 2007, the Australian Parliament's House of Representatives Standing Committee on Education and Vocational Training recommended that:

> Once the national system of accreditation has been established, the Australian Government should require universities in receipt of Commonwealth funding to have their teacher education courses accredited by the national accreditation body.
>
> (House of Representatives Standing Committee on Education and Vocational Training, 2007, p. xv)

In 2011, the MCEECDYA endorsed new national professional standards (Australian Institute for Teaching and School Leadership, 2011a) and new processes for accrediting initial teacher education programs (Australian Institute for Teaching and School Leadership, 2011b). Accreditations and re-accreditations will be undertaken under the new national system for programs to be delivered in 2013 or later. Program accreditation will continue to be undertaken by the relevant state and territory authorities, however they will now do this using the new national graduate teacher standards and program standards, and using the endorsed national accreditation processes. The new regulation includes some significant changes for teacher education providers. Most significant for this chapter is the increased emphasis on outcomes and teacher education providers providing evidence that graduates can demonstrate professional knowledge, practice and engagement as outlined in the new national graduate standards.

What should beginning teachers know and be able to do? The professional standards debate

Professional accountability and a self-regulated profession demand explication of what it is teachers know and do. But teaching is complex and therefore recognizing and naming quality teaching are complex. Challenging curriculum expectations and more diverse learners mean that teachers have to be more sophisticated in their understanding of the effects of context and learner variability on teaching and learning. Instead of implementing set routines, teachers need to become ever more skilful in their ability to evaluate teaching situations and develop teaching responses that can be effective under different circumstances: teaching is intellectual work requiring professional judgement. Despite these challenges, sets of professional standards for teaching have been developed in Australia and a number of countries in an attempt to describe effective professional practice at various junctures in a teaching career (for example, beginning or new teacher, fully qualified teacher, accomplished teacher, and teacher leader). These standards seek to capture the nuances associated with teaching in different subject areas and grade levels as well as in different school systems and contexts.

Professional standards for teaching

In Australia, there has been rampant growth in the development and implementation of professional standards for teaching, but these have often been unrelated to each other and used in differing and unrelated ways. State teacher registration authorities have each developed their own version of professional standards for graduates from teacher education programs and also standards for more competent professional practice linked to ongoing registration. In addition, state and territory education jurisdictions have created generic teaching standards (e.g., The State of Queensland, 2005) against which they make employment and career stage decisions, while the Commonwealth Government created a national standards framework in 2003 through what was then called the Ministerial Council on Education Employment Training and Youth Affairs (MEETYA, the predecessor of MEEDYA) (Ministerial Council on Education Employment Training and Youth Affairs, 2003) In addition, Teaching Australia developed standards for school leadership and advanced teaching (Teaching Australia, 2008), and subject associations developed standards for accomplished teaching in English language and literacy, mathematics, science, and geography, e.g. Australian Association of Mathematics Teachers, 2006; Australian Science Teachers Association, 2002; Standards for Teachers of English Language and Literacy in Australia (STELLA), 2002).

So, while statements of professional standards are intended to create a shared and public 'language of practice' that describe how the specialized knowledge of teaching is used in practice and also be a vehicle for assessing and judging professional activity (Yinger & Hendricks-Lee, 2000), the standards landscape is somewhat fragmented and uncoordinated. Many constituencies within the profession have attempted to articulate effective professional knowledge and practice at various junctures along the professional learning continuum and related career transition points, and to control and regulate their slice of the profession.

With the establishment of AITSL, the Commonwealth has introduced a common set of professional standards to be used across the country. The Graduate and Proficient levels of these standards will be used for teacher registration purposes in determining provisional registration after completion of an accredited teacher education program and full registration after a period on induction into the profession. These levels have quickly been included in the new national system for accreditation of initial teacher education (Australian Institute for Teaching and School Leadership, 2011b). However, because of the related industrial issues, the Highly Accomplished and Lead levels of the standards and how they might be used, are the subject of much ongoing discussion and debate across the country.

Thus, Australia's TQNP agenda is designed to provide nationally agreed and consistent requirements and principles to guide reform in the areas of teacher registration, accreditation of pre-service teacher education courses and accreditation of teachers at the graduate, competent, highly accomplished and lead teacher levels. It is also designed to inform professional learning and performance appraisal. The expectation is that these reforms will support mobility of the teaching workforce and increase public confidence in the professionalism of teachers by providing a nationally agreed quality assurance mechanism. It remains to be seen whether each constituent's goals, agendas and ownership priorities will allow this national focus to happen.

How can judgments be made about what beginning teachers know and are able to do? The teacher testing and performance assessment debates

'Guaranteeing the competence' of the members of the teaching profession involves 'the profession' not only defining professional standards of practice, but also using them to regulate entry into the profession and ongoing registration. As discussed above, entry to the profession in Australia is currently regulated by state agencies which use input models to make decisions about teacher registration. Judgments are made about the quality of a teacher education program usually by paper review involving a panel of stakeholders deciding on the likelihood that the program will prepare a competent beginning teacher. Then, employers and teacher registration authorities use proxies like completion of an accredited teacher education program, grades in university subjects or practicum evaluations and observations of teaching to make a judgment about a graduating teacher's level of professional knowledge and practice – about their readiness to teach.

The area of teacher accountability and judging teacher competence is gaining close attention in Australia within the TQNP policy context. Taking note of forms of teacher accountability evident in the US and the UK, increasing consideration is being given to the use of student results in standardized testing schemes to make judgments about teacher competence.

Standardized tests and teacher accountability

Australia does not have a history of national standardized testing of student learning, but in 2008, the National Assessment Program – Literacy and Numeracy (NAPLAN) commenced with all students in Years 3, 5, 7 and 9 across Australia being assessed annually using national tests in Reading, Writing, Language Conventions (Spelling, Grammar and Punctuation) and Numeracy. The Commonwealth government has recently established its *My School* website which has caused great controversy amid concerns it will allow schools to be ranked in league tables. The website provides profiles of almost 10,000 Australian schools that can be searched by the school's location, sector, or name. It provides statistical and contextual information, as well as NAPLAN results that can be compared with those of statistically similar schools across Australia. There are concerns within the profession that teachers will be judged according to the NAPLAN results of the students they teach without consideration of the great range of variables that impact student learning. Much professional and public debate including industrial action is occurring across the country.

In addition to prompting much heated discussion within the profession and the wider community in relation to concerns about how NAPLAN data might be used and interpreted, it is clear that these national assessments of student learning have already begun to impact teacher education policy and practice. For example, following poor Queensland results in NAPLAN in 2008, Geoff Masters, Chief Executive Officer of the Australian Council for Educational Research, was engaged to review Queensland's curriculum and educational standards for primary schools. The report (Masters, 2009) contained five key recommendations aimed at improving the performance of Queensland primary schools in literacy, numeracy and science, including one recommendation targeting pre-service teacher education. It recommended:

> That all aspiring primary teachers be required to demonstrate through test performances, as a condition of registration, that they meet threshold levels of knowledge about the teaching of literacy, numeracy and science and have sound levels of content knowledge in these areas.

The other recommendations referred to ongoing professional learning, training of specialist teachers, the introduction of standardized science tests in Years 4, 6, 8 and 10 and improved school leadership. All recommendations were supported by the Queensland government. Teacher tests were developed and trialled in Queensland in 2010 and introduced across the state in 2011. Interestingly, considerations of pre-service or graduating teacher tests were ultimately rejected (after much national debate) in the new national accreditation system (Australian Institute for Teaching and School Leadership, 2011b).

Rewarding accomplished teaching

For some time in Australia, there has been growing support for recognizing and rewarding accomplished teaching, usually founded in a desire to enhance the status of the profession and acknowledge, retain and sometimes financially reward highly accomplished teachers. The Business Council of Australia called for 'a new national certification system that recognizes excellent teachers and provides the basis for a new career path for the profession'. This is to be accompanied by 'a new remuneration structure that rewards excellent teachers' and underpinned by 'a comprehensive strategy that supports teachers to continue to learn' (The Business Council of Australia, 2008, p. 2). Some jurisdictions across the country are trialling various approaches to recognizing and rewarding highly accomplished teachers usually employing a portfolio-based approach for their judgments.

Judging teacher performance authentically

Following examples in the US, authentic assessments of the actual professional practice of teachers in the workplace, incorporating multiple measures and focussing on judging the impact of teachers on student learning, are being explored in Australia.

Current research of teacher influence suggests, beyond class size and configuration, teachers have a strong influence on student learning outcomes (Rivkin *et al.*, 2005; Rockoff, 2004; Sanders & Rivers, 1996). Teacher personalities, level of education, and types of training have all been independent variables in the examination of student learning outcomes. Other characteristics including academic success, subject matter expertise, and classroom experience, have also been found to contribute to teacher impact in the classroom (Darling-Hammond, 2000; Rice, 2003). Further, teacher influences seem to carry over time and impact student learning beyond current year of instruction.

Examination of teacher effectiveness, however, is often focused on a single variable as the indicator of student success. In a review of research on teacher impact, several studies suggest that teachers' academic success provides strong indicators of teacher effectiveness. However, other studies point to teaching aptitude, content expertise, or intelligence as marker of teacher impact on student learning (for a complete review, see Darling-Hammond & Youngs, 2002). Teacher preparation courses have also been found to relate to student achievement. Teachers who took courses on content-specific pedagogy were found to have a large effect on student learning; more so than increased content knowledge alone (Monk, 1994). Goldhaber and Brewer (2000) found that teachers who were certified, compared to those who were not, had students with higher test scores on the subject matter in which the teacher's certification was held, regardless of subject matter experience.

The research above identifies several characteristics (including teaching ability, subject matter expertise, and content pedagogy) are important when measuring teaching impact on student learning. When measuring factors that lead to teacher effectiveness, one should not single out any one factor as the sole contributor to the impact a teacher has on student learning. Although there is a lack of research examining multiple measures of teacher effectiveness, the research is clear that there are multiple factors involved when considering teachers' effect on student learning.

Considering the factors identified above as indicators of teacher effectiveness, features of teacher preparation seem to be a means to experience most of those factors. Research indicates that type of preparation matters when examining teacher impact on student learning. Those teachers prepared to use feedback to further students' learning have helped increase student achievement (Black & Wiliam, 1998). Further, programs that use materials during learning to create a less abstract learning environment have produced teachers that increase their students' achievement (Wenglinsky, 2003). An increased focus on working with students with multiple needs, the length of the program, and the ability of pre-service teachers to have immediate practice with the concepts learned during coursework may all positively affect teachers' self-efficacy for teaching and influence student achievement.

Therefore, evaluation of teachers on multiple measures is important when considering teacher impact on student learning. Any single measure could diminish or exaggerate the impact a teacher has on student achievement. Although useful for linking specific programmatic feature to teacher outcomes, value-added measures often restrict our ability to infer results to other regions or other classroom compositions. In order to assure high quality evaluation of teachers, classroom performance and content-specific knowledge should be considered when measuring teaching impact. Locally-developed performance assessments provide high quality evaluation of teachers that focuses on higher order thinking and content-specific knowledge.

Performance assessment: current state of the field in teacher education in Australia

A variety of approaches are used by universities in Australia to assess novice teachers. The three most common means of collecting evidence on the quality of teaching are: (1) observation protocols that include evaluation scales developed by teacher educators, linked to professional standards for beginning teaching; (2) portfolios documenting pre-service teachers' professional knowledge and reflection on their professional practice; and (3) teacher and/or student work samples. The strength of these university-based approaches to pre-service teacher assessment is that they are primarily designed to be used in formative ways to support teacher learning, and attempt to provide information about specific strengths and weaknesses in pre-service teachers' professional practice that can be used to support their growth as well as inform program improvement. However, as the determination of teacher quality becomes a state and national priority and a way by which summative decisions are made about beginning teacher competence and teacher education program effectiveness, the bar for meeting standards of reliability and validity is significantly raised. Even when local assessments are authentic, thoughtfully implemented, and reflect program values, they generally do not have the psychometric properties that would allow policy-makers to have confidence in the results. Although universities already expend considerable energy and resources to assess pre-service teachers and compile lots of data on their programs, most campus-based assessments of teaching lack sufficient technical evidence of validity and reliability.

In this section, we overview program-embedded performance-based approaches to teacher evaluation that are generally in use in pre-service teacher preparation programs in Australia:

- observation-based instruments;
- on-demand performance tasks;
- portfolio assessments.

While there may be other types of performance-based assessments being used in some programs and the quality and rigor of the assessments vary, these three types represent genres that are frequently used to assess teaching in teacher preparation programs in Australia.

Observation-based assessment

Observations of pre-service teachers during the practicum experience is standard practice. Observation-based ratings instruments have a long history and have evolved over time. Throughout their history, observation forms and checklists have focused on specific behaviours that reflect the dominant view of effective teaching (Arends, 2006a). Observations of teaching, even if done infrequently, are considered to be indispensable to working with prospective teachers to develop their teaching skills as well as to evaluate their readiness to teach. Therefore, observation is often considered the single most authentic and important indicator of teacher quality. However, while many teacher education programs place great faith in their observation protocols, evidence of technical quality of the observation instruments and procedures is almost non-existent. Lack of time and resources to provide training to teacher education supervisors and cooperating teachers to achieve an acceptable level of inter-rater agreement on observation ratings instruments means that the assessment of teacher quality is primarily left up to the professional judgment of the evaluators to decide what is considered 'proficient or passing performance'. Moreover, because the information collected through observation is mostly used developmentally to identify teachers' strengths and weaknesses to guide further professional development, issues of evaluator reliability and validity are often not rigorously addressed.

An entire chapter could be written on the strengths and weaknesses of observation-based evaluation instruments. However, from an equity and policy perspective, the fact that there often seems to be little variance in final ratings received by pre-service teachers means that the assessment of pre-service teaching using observation instruments appears to be treated more as a 'rite of passage' than an objective evaluation of professional practice. Given the national focus on quality teaching, it is becoming increasingly important for any performance assessments to stand up to rigorous measures of validity and reliability. For observation protocols to serve as the basis of a state- or national-based teacher accountability measure, issues of technical quality would need to be in the forefront, including but not limited to, standardized scoring protocols, standardized training and calibration practices and standardized implementation guidelines that are uniformly applied across all institutions. Developing high quality and professionally acceptable scales of this type is extremely difficult and costly and most programs are unlikely to have the resources or capacity to do the development and research needed.

On-demand performance tasks

On-demand performance tasks present to the pre-service teachers a set of prompts that focus on specific dimensions of teaching (e.g., student assessment). They can be constructed and presented to pre-service teachers using problem-based scenarios or simulations that mimic authentic teaching situations and that do not necessarily have one correct answer (Arends, 2006b). For example, teachers may be given a topic and a description of students in a class, and prompted to describe their plans for a lesson and explain how their plans reflect the strengths and needs of students in the class. A wide range of responses could satisfactorily meet the evaluative criteria for the task. Other tasks may prompt teachers to evaluate a student work sample and describe the level of achievement and/or what kind of feedback they would provide to the student, or describe how they would handle a challenging classroom situation. Currently, on-demand performance tasks in teacher preparation programs across Australia are generally embedded in specific units of study and are used formatively to build pre-service teacher capacity to teach.

An example of a unit embedded on-demand performance task that is used by many universities is a child case study. Child case studies have a long tradition in primary teacher education and usually include narrative reports focused on building a child's developmental profile (including children with special challenges and needs). These profiles usually address the child's physical, social, emotional, and academic/cognitive development through interviews and observations of the child in a variety of contexts. This task is usually used for formative purposes:

through building this profile, pre-service teachers draw implications about the most appropriate ways to work with the child or to design curriculum and pedagogy or an intervention focused on meeting the child's educational needs.

Well-designed on-demand performance tasks prompt pre-service teachers to explain their thinking and decision-making so as to make their content knowledge, pedagogical knowledge, and pedagogical content knowledge transparent (Arends, 2006b). On-demand tasks are designed to be integral to the goals and objectives of the course and therefore are the least intrusive form of assessment. However, if on-demand performance tasks are to be used exclusively for high-stakes summative purposes (e.g., registration or graduation decisions), there are some built-in drawbacks. There is little opportunity for pre-service teachers to receive a detailed evidentiary record of why they were successful or why a performance fell short – there does not appear to be much opportunity to learn from the assessment. For pre-service teachers to truly learn about what works in the classroom, e.g. how to improve the learning of struggling students (e.g., a child case study), they must have opportunities to follow up on their plans and learn from what worked and what did not work. These experiences are not ones that a simulation can easily duplicate. Moreover, the formative focus of these performance tasks and the placement of them in specific units of study would raise some significant technical challenges (reliability/validity) that will be difficult to overcome given the autonomy university and teacher educators traditionally have in the development of curricula and course syllabi.

Portfolio assessment

Portfolio assessments are widely used in teacher preparation programs, most often as a form of 'capstone' or culminating assessment (St. Maurice & Shaw, 2004). Portfolios can be for multiple purposes and tend to fall on a continuum that can be described as low stakes to high stakes. In our discussion of portfolios, we distinguish between structured and unstructured portfolios. Structured portfolios are those that require pre-service teachers to submit specific artefacts of teaching with standardized prompts that require direct responses. These artefacts and responses are then scored in a standardized way by trained scorers using a common evaluation tool, usually a rubric. In the US, the National Board for Profession Teaching Standards portfolio is an example of a highly structured portfolio. In the construction of unstructured portfolios, what and how artefacts are selected depend on the intent of the university. For example, in a 'showcase portfolio' pre-service teachers are free to choose select artefacts that represent their 'best work'. In portfolios that are meant to be used as a tool for professional learning pre-service teachers' selection may be more scaffolded to include specific artefacts, such as a statement of teaching philosophy, a videotape of their teaching, lesson plans or units, or original curriculum materials they have developed, with accompanying reflections. While a great deal of time and effort goes into the compilation and assessment of these portfolios, they serve a primarily formative purpose.

However, if the portfolio is to be used to support a graduation or registration decision, then the design and the development of the assessment must be much more structured. Wilkerson and Lang detail the legal and psychometric issues involved in using teacher portfolios as a teacher certification assessment:

> [A teacher's portfolio] can be used as a summative evaluation tool, but to do so requires a much more structured process and a complex set of assessment strategies. The assessment component requires clear criteria, an established set of reliable and valid scoring rubrics, and extensive training for the evaluators in order to ensure fairness and reliability. These considerations can all be met, but they are often beyond the capacity or the will of a local university.
>
> (2003, pp. 94–5)

An example of a structured portfolio that has been used for high stakes decisions in California is described in the next section.

Performance Assessment for California Teachers (PACT)

Performance Assessment for California Teachers (PACT represents a multiple measures assessment used for initial teacher licensure in California and to gather evidence of content/pedagogical knowledge and higher-order thinking skills from pre-service teachers. Passing the PACT assessment is required in California to be recommended for a teaching credential. Some teacher educators in Australia are considering localized versions of a multiples measures assessment like PACT.

Since 2002, the PACT has been through seven years of development and implemented in 32 teacher education programs in California, including both traditional pre-service teacher education programs and alternative certification programs offered by school districts and a charter management organization. The assessment allows for both formative and summative assessment of pre-service teacher performance. Following specific design principles, PACT was designed to ensure an assessment focus on student learning through intentional teaching practices and the systematic collection of teaching artifacts. The design principles require that a teacher performance assessment should do the following:

- maintain the complexity of teaching;
- focus on content/pedagogy within disciplines embedded in the teacher preparation curriculum;
- examine teaching practice in relationship to student learning;
- provide analytic feedback and support;
- be both adaptive and generalizable.

Programs have used the data generated by PACT to make programmatic improvements that have resulted in enhanced preparation and pre-service teacher performance. PACT has been approved as an official performance assessment for licensing by the California Commission on Teacher Credentialing based on extensive reliability and validity studies that met rigorous standards (i.e., AERA, APA, NCME). Extensive research continues to ensure reliability and validity measurements, including an in-progress value-added study of pre-service teaching in relation to student learning in California.

Following California's model, some Faculties/Schools of Education in Australia have worked in collaboration with the state and territory employing authorities and the teacher registration boards to trial approaches to teacher performance assessment in pre-service teacher education. For example, Deakin University is collaborating with the Victorian Department of Education and Early Childhood Development (DEECD) and the Victorian Institute of Teaching (VIT) to develop and trial a capstone teacher performance assessment designed to authentically assess teacher education graduates' readiness for beginning teaching as defined by the VIT *Standards of Professional Practice for Graduating Teachers*.

Conclusion

This chapter has examined the teacher quality reforms currently being debated and enacted in Australia as responses to the political positioning of teachers and teaching in Australia and related questions about the value of teacher education, professional standards and teacher assessment. The Commonwealth Government has proposed a 'national solution' through its *Smarter Schools: Improving Teacher Quality National Partnership* (TQNP) program. This program aims to attract, prepare, place, develop and retain quality teachers and school leaders in schools, and generally improve the quality of teaching, by doing the following:

- attracting the best graduates to teaching through additional pathways;
- improving the quality of teacher education;
- developing national standards and teacher registration;
- improving retention by rewarding quality teachers and school leaders.

Drawing on the experiences of other parts of the world, the reforms include high level funding and policy support for:

- pathways into teaching that bypass traditional teacher preparation programs in universities before beginning teaching;
- national accreditation of teacher education programs and also registration of teachers;
- national professional standards for beginning teaching, highly accomplished teaching and school leadership;
- recognizing and rewarding highly accomplished teachers and school leaders;
- student learning outcomes on standardized tests as indicators of quality teaching and quality teacher education.

Progress has been made on many of these fronts, but the professional and political discussions continue. Teacher educators are struggling to be heard within a context where the traditional approaches to teacher education are being questioned and teacher education itself is seen as a 'policy problem'. As in the US, Canada and the UK, it is clear that teacher educators in Australia will have to direct their research foci and professional activity to areas where findings will speak directly to the questions being asked of teaching and teacher education. That or risk marginalization as Commonwealth funding and political energy are directed towards agendas which could end up simply bypassing teacher education as it is conducted in universities, and increasing bureaucratic control of the teaching profession across the country.

As mentioned above, funding is rare in Australian for large-scale projects in teacher education that are likely to produce more generalizable findings to influence policy deciders. However, teacher educators in Australia do have a strong history of collective action through professional groups like the Australian Council of Deans of Education, the Australian Association for Research in Education and the Australian Teacher Education Association, as a well as a range of subject-specific professional associations. Teacher educators are increasingly working towards partnering with colleagues in other universities, a range of schooling jurisdictions, and teacher registration authorities in the pursuit of professionally justifiable and rigorously researched responses to the questions being posed and the national solutions currently being proposed as part of the TQNP initiative.

It is important that teacher educators in Australia direct their research to studies examining the value of teacher education and lead national policy discussions about quality teaching within a professional accountability framework. It is important that our research is relevant to and informs the construction of national statements of quality teaching as well as the ways in which teacher education is to be accredited nationally. Moreover, it is critical that our work informs the mechanisms by which new teachers are judged as eligible for entry into the profession and the ways in which they are recognized and rewarded for reaching significant professional milestones throughout their teaching career. Failure to do so could mean further bureaucratic control and accompanying directions and directives for teacher education programs. As discussed in this chapter, one particular area for attention is the evaluation of teachers on multiple measures including the development of teacher performance assessments that provide high quality evaluation of teachers focused on the important dimensions of professional judgment and decision-making particularly in relation to content-specific knowledge.

Chapter 8

Teacher preparation and development in the United States

A changing policy landscape

Linda Darling-Hammond

The keyword for any kind of educational policy or practice in the United States is variability—and this is especially true for teacher education and development. The past twenty-five years have witnessed a remarkable amount of policy directed at teacher education in the United States—and an intense debate about whether and how various approaches to preparing and supporting teachers make a difference. A strong argument for professionalizing teaching was mounted in the mid-1980s with the report of the Carnegie Task Force on Teaching as a Profession, the Holmes Group (1986), and the founding of the National Board for Professional Teaching Standards ([NBPTS], 1989). At that time researchers, policymakers, and practitioners of teaching and teacher education argued for the centrality of expertise to effective practice and the need to build a more knowledgeable and skillful professional teaching force. A set of policy initiatives was launched to design professional standards, strengthen teacher education and certification, increase investments in induction mentoring and professional development, and transform roles for teachers (see e.g., National Commission on Teaching and America's Future [NCTAF], 1996).

Meanwhile, a competing agenda was introduced to replace the traditional elements of professions—formal preparation, licensure, certification, and accreditation—with market mechanisms that would allow more open entry to teaching and greater ease of termination through elimination of tenure and greater power in the hands of districts to hire and fire teachers with fewer constraints (see, e.g., Thomas B. Fordham Foundation, 1999). Advocates of this perspective have argued that teaching does not require highly-specialized knowledge and skill, and that such skills as there are can be learned largely on the job (e.g., Walsh, 2001). Others see in these "systematic market attacks" a neoliberal project that aims to privatize education, reduce the power of the teaching profession over its own work, and allow greater inequality in the offering of services to students (Barber, 2004; Weiner, 2007).

Particularly contentious has been the debate about whether teacher preparation and certification are related to teacher effectiveness. For example, in his Annual Report on Teacher Quality (USDOE, 2002), the U.S. Secretary of Education Rod Paige argued for the redefinition of teacher qualifications to

include little specific preparation for teaching. Stating that current teacher certification systems are "broken," and that they impose "burdensome requirements"
for education coursework comprising "the bulk of current teacher certification
regimes" (p. 8), the report suggested that certification should be redefined to
emphasize verbal ability and content knowledge and to de-emphasize requirements for education coursework, making student teaching and attendance at
schools of education optional, and eliminating "other bureaucratic hurdles"
(p. 19). Associated policy initiatives, encouraged by the federal government
under the No Child Left Behind program, have stimulated alternative certification programs and, in a few states, pathways to certification with no professional
preparation at all.

This chapter examines the different kinds of preparation and professional
learning opportunities that have emerged from these different policy perspectives. In the process, we examine the implications of an emerging standards
movement for student learning and for teaching and what has been learned about
the challenges of implementing such standards.

Framing the issues of teacher preparation and teaching quality

Because of these debates, quite a bit of research has been conducted in the United
States regarding the characteristics of teachers that are thought to make a difference for their effectiveness in promoting student learning.

Over the years, researchers have analyzed how differences in teacher characteristics, including educational background and teacher training, are related to
student learning. Various lines of research looking at teacher effectiveness since
the 1960s have suggested that many kinds of teacher knowledge and experiences
may contribute to teacher effectiveness, including teachers' general academic and
verbal ability; subject matter knowledge; knowledge about teaching and learning;
teaching experience; and the set of qualifications measured by teacher certification, which typically includes the preceding factors and others (for reviews, see
Darling-Hammond, 2000; Wilson, Floden, & Ferrini-Mundy, 2001; Rice, 2003;
Darling-Hammond & Wei, 2009). Other studies have also found that traits such
as adaptability and flexibility are also important to teacher effectiveness (for a
review, see Schalock, 1979).

During the period of time that teacher characteristics have been examined,
requirements for teaching have also evolved. Since the mid-1980s, states have
taken steps to strengthen their licensure requirements, which are now substantially stronger than they were 20 or more years ago. In most states, candidates for
teaching must now earn a minimum grade point average and/or achieve a
minimum test score on tests of basic skills, general academic ability, or general
knowledge in order to be admitted to teacher education or gain a credential. In
addition, they must generally secure a major or minor in the subject to be taught
and/or pass a content test, take specified courses in education and, sometimes,

pass a test of teaching knowledge and skill. In the course of teacher education and student teaching, candidates are typically judged on their teaching skill, professional conduct, and the appropriateness of their interactions with children.

Because of public attention to the importance of teacher quality for student learning and the unequal access U.S. students have to well-qualified teachers (see, e.g., NCTAF, 1996), the federal Congress included a provision in No Child Left Behind Act of 2002 that states should create plans to ensure that all students have access to "highly qualified" teachers, defined as teachers with full certification and demonstrated competence in the subject matter field(s) they teach (defined as completing a college major or passing a test in the field). This provision was historic, especially since the students targeted by federal legislation—students who are low-income, low-achieving, new English language learners, or identified with special education needs—have been in many communities those least likely to be served by experienced and well-prepared teachers (NCTAF, 1996).

At the same time, reflecting the differences in views among policy-makers, the law encouraged states to expand alternative certification programs, now operating in at least 47 states, and regulations later developed by the Department of Education allowed candidates who had just begun—but not yet completed—such a program to be counted as "highly qualified." Policies across the states since then have simultaneously increased expectations for traditional teacher education and certification—for example, adding subject matter requirements, pedagogical requirements, and tests—while, in many states, reduced the expectations for pre-service preparation for those undertaking alternative routes. Although they run a wide gamut of models, many alternative routes allow candidates to minimize or skip student teaching and to reduce the number and kinds of courses required. In a few states, candidates can gain a license without any pedagogical preparation if they pass a content test. Thus, the variability that characterizes U.S. education policy has increased with respect to what teachers know and can do across various states.

Pathways into teaching

The format and content of teacher education programs are shaped both by state laws and professional associations, such as accrediting bodies that approve college programs. What teachers encounter when they try to become prepared for their future profession depends on the state, college, and program in which they enroll, and the professors with whom they study. Prospective teachers take courses in the arts and sciences and in schools of education, and they spend time in schools. In general, these courses include preparation in the subject matter(s) the teacher will teach, along with courses in teaching methods or pedagogy (in some schools, content-specific and, in others, general), child or adolescent development and learning, and foundations of education—history, philosophy, and sociology of education. Most states now also require preparation in the teaching of special education students, and a growing number require preparation in the teaching of

English language learners. Some require preparation in curriculum and assessment. Requirements for student teaching range from eight weeks to as many as 30 weeks over the course of training.

Although state licensure and accreditation policies have enforced some commonalities across teacher education programs, what prospective teachers study and from whom varies from university to university. In particular, there is wide variability in the extent to which professors of teacher education are themselves well grounded in research and practice regarding teaching, and the extent to which their courses are connected to clinical work in the field. Unlike other professions where the professional curriculum is reasonably common across institutions, the enacted curriculum of teacher education in the United States is often much more idiosyncratic to programs and their professors. Students' learning experiences can be distributed widely across university departments and school sites, often with little coordination among them (Darling-Hammond & Ball, 1997).

What is considered "traditional" teacher preparation has evolved over the last century. Feiman-Nemser (1990) describes three historic traditions that have influenced approaches to teacher education: (1) the normal school tradition; (2) the liberal arts tradition; and (3) professionalization through graduate preparation and research.

Undergraduate teacher preparation

The normal school provided teachers with training during or right after high school throughout the late 19th and early 20th Centuries. It offered a practical curriculum focused directly on teaching and gradually increased in duration from one year to three. The liberal arts tradition has dominated since the 1950s, when normal schools moved into colleges and universities, and teachers undertook their preparation as part of four-year undergraduate programs leading to a Bachelor's degree, usually in education. The most prominent of these—and the largest suppliers of teachers in most states—are the schools, colleges, or departments of education within state public college systems. There are also a number of private liberal arts colleges that offer teacher education programs, which are generally much smaller.

Over the years, undergraduate teacher education has often been criticized as lacking subject matter rigor, on the one hand (Conant, 1963; Koerner, 1963), and practical relevance, on the other (Lanier & Little, 1986). However, while most U.S. teachers continue to prepare for teaching in four-year undergraduate programs, the landscape is changing. Because of many changes in state and federal rules, and expectations in state and national accreditation systems, fewer of these undergraduate degrees are now in education: most teachers graduate with a major in a content field and a minor or credential in education. Whereas the traditional model front-loaded courses and then added 8 to 10 weeks of student teaching at the end of the fourth year, contemporary programs generally have included more clinical learning opportunities throughout the program, through practicum experiences tied to courses which aim to better integrate courses with clinical work.

Post-graduate teacher preparation

In the past two decades, a host of alternatives to the traditional four-year undergraduate program have been created. The term "traditional teacher education" is often used to compare and contrast the features of university-based teacher preparation and "alternative" teacher preparation routes that are organized and run by non-university entities such as state and district internship programs or other recruiting programs that fast-track the placement of individuals into classrooms.

However, most "alternative" certification programs are actually operated by universities (Feistritzer, 2005), and they range widely in design. These alternatives have included extending undergraduate programs to five years (for example, blending undergraduate and graduate training in a five-year sequence, or creating a one-year graduate level teacher education program added on to the four-year Bachelor's degree), moving professional studies to the graduate level (e.g., one or two-year Master's degree programs offering a Master of Arts in Teaching or Masters in Education degree), and substituting on-the-job training programs (e.g., alternate route and internship programs) that offer a few weeks of summer training before a candidate becomes a teacher of record.

What Feiman-Nemser (1990) referred to as the "professionalization" approach has generally focused on graduate level preparation strategies, which have been advocated on and off for many decades, but rarely adopted on a wide scale. Graduate-level Master of Arts in Teaching programs, promoted as early as the 1930s by James Conant, president of Harvard University, and implemented in a number of elite universities during the 1960s and 1970s, were seen as more academically rigorous than undergraduate programs and as a way to attract a stronger pool of applicants (i.e., those who had already completed a liberal arts education with a specific content major). Master of Arts in Teaching (MAT) programs have been advocated in times of teacher shortages, as they open up new pools of potential recruits and can be completed in one or two years, combining educational coursework with clinical internships. Longstanding examples of this model include the graduate teacher education programs at Bank Street School of Education, Columbia University's Teachers College, Harvard University, and Stanford University.

The Educational Masters (EdM) was promoted by Henry Holmes, dean of the Harvard Graduate School of Education in the 1920s and namesake of the Holmes Group of education deans and chief academic officers from 120 research universities that organized in the 1980s. In their 1986 report, *Tomorrow's Teachers*, this group argued for the elimination of undergraduate degrees in education in favor of five-year models that convey a Bachelor's degree in a content area and a Master's degree in education (Holmes Group, 1986), and a number of their members adopted these programs in order to ensure stronger subject matter preparation and to better integrate theory and practice. They instituted early field experiences throughout the undergraduate portion of the program and to extend the amount of student teaching time to a full year in the fifth year of study. A number of research universities, such as the University of Connecticut, the University of New Hampshire, and the University of Virginia adopted the five-year preparation model during the 1980s and 1990s.

The Holmes Group also advocated for the creation of professional development schools. In these sites, new teachers learn to teach alongside more experienced teachers who plan and work together, and university and school-based faculty work collaboratively to design, implement, and conduct research about learning experiences for new and experienced teachers, as well as for students (Holmes Group, 1990). Ideally, the university program and the school develop a shared conception of good teaching that informs their joint work. Thus professional development schools (PDSs) aim to develop *school practice* as well as the *individual practice* of new teacher candidates. As of 1998, the American Association of Colleges for Teacher Education estimated that there were more than 1,000 professional schools in 47 states in operation across the country (Abdal-Haqq, 1998).

The mix of programs and pathways

Despite all the reform efforts that have been launched over the years, graduate level teacher preparation has been slow to spread. Arthur Levine's (2006) study, *Educating School Teachers*, reported that, in 2003, the nearly 1,200 schools and departments of education in the U.S. produced 106,000 teachers in undergraduate programs (61% of the total), 63,000 teachers in Master's programs (36%), and about 4,000 teachers in certificate programs (3%). However, not all of these prospective teachers enter the profession, while others who are not prepared in universities do enter. Consequently the profile of beginning teachers is somewhat different. The National Center for Education Statistics (2010) reported that, in 2008, about 20% of 160,000 first year public and private school teachers entered with a Master's degree or higher. About 3% had less than a Bachelor's degree.

One reason for the disparities in teacher production and hiring is that a number of individuals enter teaching without having completed—or sometimes even begun—a preparation program. In 2008, about 25% of newly hired beginning teachers entered without certification or on a waiver or emergency permit, which means they had not yet met certification or licensure standards regarding preparation or testing. The proportion of new, uncertified teachers is greater in the private school sector (which comprises about 10% of all U.S. students) than the public school sector, but it has remained above 10% in public schools. In addition, a growing number of teachers—by some counts as many as 15% of new entrants (variously labeled as uncertified or alternatively certified in different states)—participate in quick-entry alternative credentialing programs in which they receive a few weeks of training in the summer and then become teachers of record in the fall while they complete additional coursework, either through a university or through a district training program.

Most public school teachers who are not fully credentialed, or who enter through alternatives where they train on-the-job, teach in low-income and minority schools in poor rural and urban communities. The unequal distribution of prepared teachers in the US is largely a function of differential salaries and working conditions across districts serving more and less affluent students. These differentials are, in turn, a result of school funding systems that provide widely varying revenues to local schools. For example, high-spending states like Connecticut, Massachusetts, and New Jersey spend three times as much as low-spending states like Utah. Furthermore, within states, a three-to-one ratio between high- and low-spending districts is common. Thus, entering teachers' salaries vary substantially among wealthy and poor school districts, as do class sizes, the availability of materials and specialists, and the adequacy of facilities.

Teacher education program effects

Recent reforms in teacher education seem to have resulted in improved perceptions of the quality of teacher preparation. Since 1990, surveys of beginning teachers who experienced teacher education (Gray *et al.*, 1993; Howey & Zimpher, 1993; Kentucky Institute for Education Research, 1997; California State University, 2002a, 2002b) have found that more than 80% felt that they were well prepared for nearly all of the challenges of their work, while a somewhat smaller majority (60–70%) felt prepared to deal with the needs of special education students and those with limited English proficiency.

Veteran teachers and principals who work with current teacher preparation programs, particularly five-year programs and those that feature professional development schools, have also reported their perception that their newly-trained colleagues are much better prepared than they were some years earlier (Andrew & Schwab, 1995; Baker, 1993; Darling-Hammond, 1994; National Center for Education Statistics, 1996, Tables 73, 75).

Given the wide variability in programs and entry pathways to teaching—and the strong ideologies that shape advocacy for these different approaches—there has been great interest in examining the outcomes of different program models, ranging from retention in teaching to the measured effectiveness of program graduates.

Retention in teaching

There is some evidence that retention in teaching varies across pathways. A recent longitudinal study of graduates of Bachelor's degree programs in teacher education found that nearly 80% of those who finished university-based pre-service programs remained in teaching five years after graduation, and that the rates of leaving were more than three times greater for those who entered teaching without certification than those who entered teaching fully prepared (Henke, Chen, & Geis, 2000).

Other research has found even higher rates of entry and retention for graduates of five-year models (Andrew & Schwab, 1995; Baker, 1993; Denton & Peters, 1998), who also felt more confident in their teaching and were viewed by their supervisors as more competent. Candidates prepared in professional development schools associated with both four- and five-year teacher education programs have also shown higher rates of teacher retention (Kenreich, Hartzler-Miller, Neopolitan, & Wiltz, 2004; Hunter-Quartz, 2003). In the largest study of this issue to date, Latham and Vogt's (2007) longitudinal study of about 1,000 graduates compared the retention rates of teachers prepared in PDS programs versus traditional elementary education programs over eight years. They found that controlling for teacher background and academic qualifications, teachers prepared in PDS programs had higher rates of entry into teaching and retention in the teaching profession.

It is possible that the full year of clinical training such programs often provide may be associated with these outcomes, as several studies have found a relationship between the experience of student teaching and feelings of preparedness (California State University, 2002a, 2002b), as well as retention in teaching (Henke, Geis, Giambattista, & Knepper, 1996; Henke *et al.*, 2000; NCTAF, 2004). Meanwhile, a number of studies have found significantly lower rates of retention for recruits who entered through alternative pathways that do not offer student teaching (NCTAF, 2003; Shin, 1994).

Teacher effectiveness

While there are many kinds of alternative routes, those that bypass student teaching and offer little pre-service training also appear to have the least productive outcomes for their recruits and the students they teach. A large-scale North Carolina study found negative effects on student achievement for high school teachers who had entered teaching on the state's "lateral entry" program, an alternate route that allows entry for mid-career recruits who have subject matter background but no initial training for teaching (Clotfelter, Ladd, & Vigdor, 2007). Three other longitudinal studies, using individual-level student data from New York City and Houston, Texas, found that elementary teachers who entered teaching without full preparation—as emergency hires or alternative route candidates—were less effective than fully-prepared beginning teachers working with similar students, especially in teaching reading (Boyd, Grossman, Lankford, Loeb, & Wyckoff, 2006; Darling-Hammond, Holtzman, Gatlin, & Heilig, 2005; Kane, Rockoff, & Staiger, 2006). This was as equally true of alternate routes like the New York City Teaching Fellows and the highly selected Teach for America recruits as it was of other entrants who entered without pre-service preparation.

All three studies also found that by the third year, after the alternate route teachers had completed their required teacher education coursework for certification, there were few significant differences in their effectiveness and that of the traditionally prepared teachers. In two of the studies, students of experienced Teach for America recruits had larger gains on average in mathematics. However, 80% of the Teach for America entrants and half of other alternatively prepared teachers had left the profession, leaving questions about whether the measured effectiveness of later year recruits was because the less effective teachers had left or the ones who remained had improved their teaching performance.

The evidence is less clear that the structures of university-based teacher education programs (e.g. four year, five year, or other) by themselves predict the success of their graduates. There seem to be more and less successful programs within each of these structural alternatives. For example, a study of seven teacher education programs that graduate extraordinarily well-prepared candidates—as judged by observations of their practice, administrators who hire them, and their own sense of preparedness and self-efficacy as teachers—found successful exemplars among four-year, five-year, and graduate level programs, which suggests that program structure is not the determinative factor in predicting program success (Darling-Hammond, 2006).

However, there is evidence that teachers learn different things from different programs and feel differentially well-prepared for specific aspects of teaching (Darling-Hammond, Chung, & Frelow, 2002; Denton & Lacina, 1984), and certain structures may make it easier to institute some kinds of program features that may make a difference to candidates' preparation.

Program features that appear to matter

The seven-program study mentioned above included public and private institutions offering undergraduate and graduate programs that ranged in size from dozens to hundreds of candidates, but all produced graduates who were extraordinarily well-prepared from their first days in the classroom.[1] The research team found that, despite outward differences, the programs had common features, including:

- a common, clear vision of good teaching that permeates all coursework and clinical experiences, creating a coherent set of learning experiences;
- well-defined standards of professional practice and performance that are used to guide and evaluate coursework and clinical work;
- a strong, core curriculum, taught in the context of practice, grounded in knowledge of child and adolescent development and learning, an understanding of social and cultural contexts, curriculum, assessment, and subject matter pedagogy;
- extended clinical experiences—at least 30 weeks of supervised practicum and student teaching opportunities in each program—that are carefully chosen to support the ideas presented in simultaneous, closely interwoven coursework;

- extensive use of case methods, teacher research, performance assessments, and portfolio evaluation that apply learning to real problems of practice;
- explicit strategies to help students confront their own deep-seated beliefs and assumptions about learning and students and to learn about the experiences of people different from themselves;
- strong relationships, common knowledge, and shared beliefs among school- and university-based faculty jointly engaged in transforming teaching, schooling, and teacher education (Darling-Hammond, 2006).

These features confront many of the core dilemmas of teacher education: the strong influence of the "apprenticeship of observation" candidates bring with them from their years as students in elementary and secondary schools; the presumed divide between theory and practice; the limited personal and cultural perspectives all individuals bring to the task of teaching; and the difficult process of helping people learn to enact their intentions in complex settings. They help produce novice teachers who are able, from their first days in the classroom, to practice like many seasoned veterans, productively organizing classrooms that teach challenging content to very diverse learners with levels of skill many teachers never attain.

These findings are similar to those of a recent New York City study that evaluated the contributions to value-added student achievement in English language arts and mathematics of beginning elementary teachers from different teacher education. Several pre-service programs had much stronger outcomes than any of the other traditional or alternative routes. The researchers examined the features of these programs, and found that, in addition to strong faculty, they had:

- more coursework in content areas (e.g. math and reading) and in content-specific methods of teaching;
- a focus on helping candidates learn specific practices that they apply in classrooms where they practice teaching alongside their coursework;
- carefully-selected student teaching experiences, well-matched to the contexts in which candidates will later teach;
- opportunities to study the local district curriculum;
- a capstone project—typically a portfolio of work done in classrooms with students.

Other studies reinforce these findings. For example, many studies suggest that candidates who have more opportunity to *study and apply subject-specific teaching methods* are more effective (Begle, 1979; Druva & Anderson, 1983; Ferguson & Womack, 1993; Monk, 1994; Monk & King, 1994; Sykes *et al.*, 2006). Furthermore, teachers who have participated in targeted learning opportunities on effective teaching practices in specific content areas, with immediate opportunities to apply these practices, have produced student achievement gains that were significantly greater than those of comparison group teachers (Angrist & Lavy, 2001; Ebmeier & Good, 1979; Lawrenz & McCreath, 1988).

The *quality, duration, and timing of clinical experiences* also appear to matter. Research suggests that candidates learn more from their fieldwork and coursework when they have opportunities to connect their coursework in real time to practice opportunities in the classroom. In the pre-service context, courses that occur during or after the time candidates have been in the field appear to be more salient than front-loaded courses where theory is learned in the absence of practice (Denton, 1982; Denton, Morris, & Tooke, 1982; Henry, 1983; Ross, Hughes, & Hill, 1981; Sunal, 1980). Carefully constructed field experiences can enable new teachers to reinforce, apply, and synthesize concepts learned in coursework (Denton, 1982; Denton *et al.*, 1982; Henry, 1983; Ross *et al.*, 1981; Koerner, Rust, & Baumgartner, 2002; Sunal, 1980). For example, Denton (1982) found that teacher candidates with early field experiences performed significantly better in their methods courses than those without early field experiences.

Other work suggests that the care with which placements are chosen, the quality of practice that is modeled, and the quality and frequency of mentoring candidates receive may influence candidates' learning (Feiman-Nemser & Buchmann, 1985; Goodman, 1985; Knowles & Hoefler, 1989; Laboskey & Richert, 2002; Rodriguez & Sjostrom, 1995).

In addition, the quality and intensity of supervision, and the evaluation tools used to guide supervision, are factors that may be potentially important elements of teacher learning. The match between placements in which candidates learn to teach and their eventual teaching assignments—in terms of the type of students, grade level, and subject matter—appear to be associated with stronger teaching in the early years (Goodman, 1985; Koerner *et al.*, 2002). Some research also suggests that the duration of student teaching experiences may influence teachers' later teaching practice and self-confidence (Denton & Lacina, 1984; Denton *et al.*, 1982; Denton & Tooke, 1981–1982; Koerner *et al.*, 2002; Laboskey & Richert, 2002; Orland-Barak, 2002; Sumara & Luce-Kaplar, 1996).

Perhaps because of the presence of several of these elements, studies of highly developed professional development schools—those that have managed to create a shared practice between the school and the university curriculum—find that teachers who graduate from such programs often feel more knowledgeable and prepared to teach (Sandholtz & Dadlez, 2000; Stallings, Bossung, & Martin, 1990; Yerian & Grossman, 1997) and are rated as better prepared than other new teachers, both overall and in specific areas of teaching, ranging from classroom management and uses of technology to content area skills (Gill & Hove, 1999; Mantle-Bromley, 2002; Neubert & Binko, 1998; Shroyer, Wright, & Ramey-Gassert, 1996).

Veteran teachers working in highly-developed PDSs have reported changes in their own practice and improvements at the classroom and school levels as a result of the professional development, action research, and mentoring that are part of the PDS (Houston Consortium of Professional Development, 1996; Jett-Simpson, Pugach, & Whipp, 1992; Trachtman, 1996). And a small set of studies has documented gains in student performance and achievement tied directly to curriculum and teaching interventions resulting from the professional development and curriculum work professional development schools have undertaken with their university partners (e.g., Fischetti & Larson, 2002; Frey, 2002; Gill & Hove, 1999; Glaeser, Karge, Smith, & Weatherill, 2002; Houston *et al.*, 1995; Judge, Carrideo, & Johnson, 1995; Wiseman & Cooner, 1996).

Finally, *program standards* may matter in several ways: Recent work on the use of standards to guide teacher development and assessment suggests that the clarity and salience of standards and performance tasks against which candidates are judged—and the extent to which they represent research-based elements of teaching—may organize teacher learning in important ways (Darling-Hammond, 2006; Hammerness & Darling-Hammond, 2002). Also the rigor of the expectations the program holds for students—as seen in course expectations, clinical requirements, and whether weak candidates are counseled out of the program—may signal both aspects of selection and program quality. Finally, the extent to which the program holds itself accountable by engaging in self-study and continual improvement may be an indirect measure of program quality.

As we describe below, the emergence of new professional standards for teaching has been an important element of the policy context for teacher education and teacher learning over the past twenty years, and may offer new possibilities for ways to improve professional learning and practice in the years ahead.

The emergence of standards for teaching

The past two decades have marked the emergence of professional standards for teaching, stimulated in large part by the view that heightened expectations for student learning can be accomplished only by greater expectations for teaching quality. As part of the standards-based reform movement initiative launched in the United States in the late 1980s, new standards for teacher education accreditation and for teacher licensing, certification, and ongoing evaluation have become a prominent lever for promoting system-wide change in teaching. For example, the NCTAF argued that:

> Standards for teaching are the linchpin for transforming current systems of preparation, licensing, certification, and ongoing development so that they better support student learning. [Such standards] can bring clarity and focus to a set of activities that are currently poorly connected and often badly organized . . . clearly, if students are to achieve high standards, we can expect no less from their teachers and from other educators. Of greatest priority is reaching agreement on what teachers should know and be able to do to teach to high standards.
>
> (1996, p. 67)

Professions generally set and enforce standards in three ways: (1) through professional accreditation of preparation programs; (2) through state licensing, which grants permission to practice; and (3) through advanced certification, which is a professional recognition of high levels of competence.[2] In virtually all professions other than teaching, candidates must graduate from an accredited professional school in order to sit for state licensing examinations that test their knowledge and skill. The accreditation process is meant to ensure that all preparation programs provide a reasonably common body of knowledge and structured training experiences that are comprehensive and up-to-date. Licensing examinations are meant to ensure that candidates have acquired the knowledge they need to practice responsibly. The tests generally include both surveys of specialized information and performance components that examine aspects of applied practice in the field: Lawyers must analyze cases and, in some states, develop briefs or memoranda of law to address specific issues; doctors must diagnose patients via case histories and describe the treatments they would prescribe; engineers must demonstrate that they can apply certain principles to particular design situations. These examinations are developed by members of the profession through state professional standards boards.

In addition, many professions offer additional examinations that provide recognition for advanced levels of skill, such as certification for public accountants, board certification for doctors, and registration for architects. This recognition generally takes extra years of study and practice, often in a supervised internship and/or residency, and is based on performance tests that measure greater levels of specialized knowledge and skill. Those who have met these standards are then allowed to do certain kinds of work that other practitioners cannot. The certification standards inform the other sets of standards governing accreditation, licensing, and re-licensing: They are used to ensure that professional schools incorporate new knowledge into their courses and to guide professional development and evaluation throughout the career. Thus, these advanced standards may be viewed as an engine that pulls along the knowledge base of the profession. Together, standards for accreditation, licensing, and certification comprise a "three-legged stool" (NCTAF, 1996) that supports quality assurance in the mature professions.

This three-legged stool, however, has historically been quite wobbly in teaching, where each of the quality assurance functions has been much less developed than in other professions. Until recently, there was no national body to establish a system of professional certification. Meanwhile, states have managed licensing and the approval of teacher education programs using widely varying standards and generally weak enforcement tools. Furthermore, the utility of each of these functions has been hotly contended within and outside the profession on a variety of ideological and political grounds. In recent years, these debates have led to an array of empirical studies seeking to establish whether and how licensing, accreditation, and certification make a difference for teacher quality, as well as teacher learning and the distribution of teachers. This phenomenon is largely unique to education, as the mature professions have adopted such quality controls without questioning their outcomes.

The National Board for Professional Teaching Standards

A set of efforts to set standards for teaching has been led by the NBPTS (the National Board), an independent organization established in 1987 as the first professional body—comprised of a majority of classroom teachers—to set standards for the advanced certification of highly accomplished teachers. The Board's mission is:

> [to] establish high and rigorous standards for what accomplished teachers should know and be able to do, to develop and operate a voluntary national system to assess and certify teachers who meet those standards, and to advance related education reforms—all with the purpose of improving student learning.
>
> (Baratz-Snowden, 1990, p. 19)

The standards developed by the National Board incorporate knowledge about teaching and learning that supports a view of teaching as complex, contingent on students' needs and instructional goals, and reciprocal, that is, continually shaped and reshaped by students' responses to learning events. The new standards and assessments take into explicit account the teaching challenges posed by a student body that is multicultural and multilingual and that includes diverse approaches to learning. By reflecting new subject matter standards for students which were articulated by the national professional associations in the 1990s, the demands of learner diversity, and the expectation that teachers must collaborate with colleagues and parents in order to succeed, the standards define teaching as a collegial, professional activity that responds to considerations of subjects and students. By examining teaching in the light of learning, they put considerations of effectiveness at the center of practice. This view contrasts with that of the previous "technicist" era of teacher training and evaluation, in which teaching was seen as the implementation of set routines and formulas for behavior, unresponsive to the distinctive attributes of either clients or curriculum goals.

Another important attribute of the new standards is that they are *performance-based*, that is, they describe what teachers should know, be like, and be able to do rather than listing courses that teachers should take in order to be awarded a license. This shift toward performance-based standard-setting is in line with the approach to licensing taken in other professions and with the changes already occurring in a number of states. This approach aims to clarify what the criteria are for determining competence, placing more emphasis on the abilities teachers develop than the hours they spend taking classes.

To achieve National Board Certification, candidates must complete a rigorous two-part assessment. The assessment includes a portfolio completed by the teacher at the school site, which incorporates student work samples, videotapes of classroom practice, and extensive written analyses and reflections based upon these artifacts. The portfolio is meant to allow teachers to present a picture of their practice as it is shaped by the particular needs of the students with whom the teachers work and the particular context of the teacher's school. The assessment also includes a set of exercises completed at a local assessment center during which candidates demonstrate both content knowledge and pedagogical content knowledge through tasks such as analyzing teaching situations, responding to content matter prompts, evaluating curriculum materials, or constructing lesson plans.

Influences of the Board

By 2009, the National Board had offered advanced certification to more than 82,000 accomplished teachers, about 2% of the U.S. teaching force. This represents about 40% of those who apply for certification. However, the Board has had much greater impact than the initial numbers of certified teachers suggested. As many states and districts have provided salary supplements to teachers who earn Board Certification, the notion that teachers might be compensated based on their demonstrated skill has been established.

Perhaps most important, as the first professional effort to define accomplished teaching, the National Board has also had an enormous influence on standard-setting for beginning teacher licensing, teacher education programs, teacher assessment, on-the-job evaluation, and professional development for teachers throughout the United States. A number of districts have incorporated National Board certification into teacher evaluation processes, compensation systems, and career ladders that identify teachers for new roles and responsibilities, such as master or mentor teacher positions.

The standard-setting work completed by the National Board influenced the setting of national standards for the licensing of beginning teachers through the work of the Interstate New Teacher Assessment. These standards have been adopted or adapted by most states as part of their licensing standards and incorporated into the standards of the National Council for Accreditation of Teacher Education (NCATE). NCATE then began working with universities to help them design advanced Master's degree programs focused on the development of teaching practice and organized around the standards of the National Board.

As a result of these combined initiatives, systems of licensing and accreditation that seek to assess what teachers know and can do are gradually replacing the traditional methods of tallying specific courses as the basis for granting program approval or a license. Furthermore, because these three sets of standards are substantively connected and form a continuum of development along the career path of the teacher, they conceptualize the main dimensions along which teachers can work to improve their practice. By providing vivid descriptions of high quality teaching in specific teaching areas, some analysts argue, "[the standards] clarify what the profession expects its members to get better at . . . profession-defined standards provide the basis on which the profession can lay down its agenda and expectations for professional development and accountability" (Ingvarson, 1997, p. 1).

These standards and the Board's assessment process have stimulated initiatives in teacher education to focus coursework on standards of practice and to use portfolios to evaluate teaching. Documenting the spread of portfolio assessments throughout teacher education, and into teacher evaluation and teacher development enterprises as well, Nona Lyons directly attributes to the National Board the widespread move to performance assessments focused on documentation of practice. In addition, Lyons argues that portfolios hold the seed of a "new professionalism" that supports teaching quality in a number of ways:

> Portfolio assessment systems hold out standards of rigor and excellence; require evidence of effective learning; foster one's own readiness to teach, to author one's own learning; make collaboration a new norm for teaching, creating collaborative, interpretive communities of teacher learners who can interrogate critically their practice; and uncover and make public what counts as effective teaching in today's complex world of schools and learners.
>
> (1998, p. 21)

The effectiveness of Board certified teachers

As the Board certification process has spread, policymakers and researchers have begun to look for evidence about its effects on teacher learning as well as its validity as a measure of teacher effectiveness. A number of studies have found that the National Board Certification assessment process identifies teachers who are more effective in raising student achievement than others who failed to achieve certification (Bond, Smith, Baker, & Hattie, 2000; Cavaluzzo, 2004; Goldhaber & Anthony, 2005; Smith, Gordon, Colby, & Wang, 2005; Vandevoort, Amrein-Beardsley, & Berliner, 2004).

Equally important, many studies have found that teachers' participation in the National Board process supports their professional learning and stimulates changes in their practice. Teachers note that the process of analyzing their own and their students' work in light of standards enhances their abilities to assess student learning and to evaluate the effects of their own actions, while causing them to adopt new practices that are called for in the standards and assessments (Athaneses, 1994; NBPTS, 2001a; Sato, 2000; Tracz, Sienty, & Mata, 1994; Tracz *et al.*, 1995). Teachers report significant improvements in their knowledge and performance in each area assessed — planning, designing, and delivering instruction, managing the classroom, diagnosing and evaluating student learning, using subject matter knowledge, and participating in a learning community

— and observational studies have documented that these changes do indeed occur (Lustick & Sykes, 2006; Sato, Chung Wei, & Darling-Hammond, 2008). David Haynes' statement is typical of many:

> Completing the portfolio for the Early Adolescence/Generalist Certification was, quite simply, the single most powerful professional development experience of my career. Never before have I thought so deeply about what I do with children, and why I do it. I looked critically at my practice, judging it against a set of high and rigorous standards. Often in daily work, I found myself rethinking my goals, correcting my course, moving in new directions. I am not the same teacher as I was before the assessment, and my experience seems to be typical.
>
> (1995, p. 60)

A survey which reported similar results regarding self-reported improvements in practice found that most (80%) teachers who had gone through the certification process felt it was more productive than other professional development experiences they had had. Nearly 80% of teachers involved as assessors similarly felt that serving as an assessor was a useful professional development activity. Large majorities of both the Board certified teachers and assessors felt their experiences had a strong effect on their teaching (NBPTS, 2001b). Teachers comment that videotaping their teaching and analyzing student work makes them more aware of how to organize teaching and learning tasks, how to analyze student learning, and how to intervene and change course when necessary.

Performance assessments of beginning teaching

Recently, similar performance assessments have been developed for evaluating the effectiveness of beginning teachers, including pre-service teachers and the programs that prepare them. Although most states require a battery of paper and pencil tests to enter teacher education or for an initial license (usually tests of basic skills, subject matter knowledge, and/or pedagogical knowledge), these have generally proved to be rather poor predictors of teachers' eventual success in the classroom (Ayers, 1988; Haney, Madaus, & Kreitzer, 1987; Haertel, 1991; Mitchell, Robinson, Plake, & Knowles, 2001). To correct these shortcomings, teaching performance assessments, modeled after the National Board assessments, have been developed for use either in teacher education, as a basis for the initial licensing recommendation (California, Colorado, Kentucky, Oregon), or in the teacher induction period, as a basis for moving from a probationary to a professional license (Connecticut).

The assessments require teachers to document their plans and teaching for a unit of instruction, videotape and analyze lessons, and collect and evaluate evidence of student learning. Like the National Board assessments, beginning teachers' ratings on the Connecticut BEST assessment have been found to significantly predict their students' value-added achievement on the state reading tests (Wilson, Hallam, Moss, & Pecheone, 2007).

Meanwhile, in California, the state legislature requires all traditional and alternative preparation programs to evaluate candidates using a teacher performance assessment, which is used both to determine licensing and—when scores are aggregated—to evaluate programs for accreditation purposes. The Performance Assessment for California Teachers (PACT), used by 33 teacher education programs in the state, has been shown to be reliable, valid, and a strong lever for improving both teacher competence and program quality (Pecheone & Chung, 2006). Like the Connecticut BEST assessment, a preliminary validity study of PACT also found that teachers' scores on the assessment are positively associated with their value-added effectiveness when they later become full-time teachers (Newton, 2010). These performance assessments also help beginning teachers improve their practice in ways that continue after the assessment experience has ended (Chung, 2008; Pecheone & Chung, 2006).

Faculty and supervisors score these portfolios using standardized rubrics in moderated sessions following training, with an audit procedure to calibrate standards. Faculties use the PACT results to revise their curriculum. Like the National Board assessments, these promise to have learning effects that may affect the system more broadly, through the learning that occurs for assessors as well as for candidates (Darling-Hammond, 2006). For example, participants report:

> For me the most valuable thing was the sequencing of the lessons, teaching the lesson, and evaluating what the kids were getting, what the kids weren't getting, and having that be reflected in my next lesson ... the "teach-assess-teach-assess-teach-assess" process. And so you're constantly changing—you may have a plan or a framework that you have together, but knowing that that's flexible and that it has to be flexible, based on what the children learn that day.
>
> (Prospective teacher)

> This [scoring] experience ... has forced me to revisit the question of what really *matters* in the assessment of teachers, which—in turn—means revisiting the question of what really *matters* in the *preparation* of teachers.
>
> (Teacher education faculty member)

> [The scoring process] forces you to be clear about "good teaching;" what it looks like, sounds like. It enables you to look at your own practice critically, with new eyes.
>
> (Cooperating teacher)

> As an induction program coordinator, I have a much clearer picture of what credential holders will bring to us and of what they'll be required to do. We can build on this.
>
> (Induction program coordinator)

Based on this work, twenty states have recently come together as a Teacher Performance Assessment Consortium under the auspices of the American Association of Colleges of Teacher Education and the Council of Chief State School Officers to create a common initial licensing assessment that can be used nationwide to make preparation and licensing performance-based, as well as predictive of teacher effectiveness. It is hoped that this measure will resolve the questions about which pathways into teaching are preferable by establishing a common standard for entry into the profession that also provides information about the efficacy of different approaches to preparation.

Standards for accrediting teacher education

A final element of the professional standards picture is the increasing use of such standards and performance assessments for evaluating schools of education. Until recently, the program approval process for schools of education, generally coordinated by the state's department of education, has typically assessed "the types of learning situations to which an individual is exposed and . . . the time spent in these situations, rather than . . . what the individual actually learned" (Goertz, Ekstorm, & Coley, 1984, p. 4). The 20th-Century custom of admitting individuals into practice based on their graduation from a state-approved program was a wholesale approach to licensing. It assumed that program quality could be well defined and monitored by states; that programs would be equally effective with all of their students; and that completion of the courses or experiences mandated by the state would be sufficient to produce competent practitioners. The state approval system also assumed that markets for teachers were local: that virtually all teachers for the schools in a given state would be produced by colleges within that state, a presumption that has become increasingly untrue over time.

Most states, meanwhile, have routinely approved virtually all of their teacher education programs, despite the fact that these programs offer dramatically different kinds and qualities of preparation (Goodlad, Soder, & Sirotnik, 1990; NCTAF, 1996; Tom, 1997). Many state education agencies have inadequate budgetary resources and person power to conduct the intensive program reviews that would support enforcement of high standards (David, 1994; Lusi, 1997). And even when state agencies find weak programs, political forces make it difficult to close them down. Teacher education programs bring substantial revenue to universities and local communities, and the availability of large numbers of teaching candidates, no matter how poorly prepared, keeps salaries relatively low. As Dennison notes, "The generally minimal state-prescribed criteria remain subject to local and state political influences, economic conditions within the state, and historical conditions which make change difficult" (1992, p. A40).

Since the 1990s, however, states have been moving toward a common set of accreditation and teacher preparation standards linked to the National Board's professional standards for accomplished teachers and INTASC's standards for beginning teachers. This movement has been facilitated by a growing interest in national accreditation. In 1989, NCATE launched a new state partnership program in which its professional review of colleges of education is integrated with states' own reviews. The number of partnerships increased from 19 in 1990 to 48 in 2000.

One important result of these state partnerships is the alignment of state and professional standards. Another is increasing emphasis on teacher education outcomes, as the move to performance-based accreditation requires that programs provide evidence of competent teacher candidate performance rather than merely showing that candidates have been exposed to curriculum. Some studies indicate that the NCATE review process has led to substantial changes in weak education programs (e.g., Altenbaugh & Underwood, 1990; Williams, 2000), highlighting the fact that professional accreditation can spur program reform efforts. However, much is yet to be learned about how the use of standards and evidence can support teacher education improvements on a wide scale.

Conclusion

Debates about teacher education policy have arisen from both technical and political disagreements about which qualifications and preparation predict effectiveness and which principles should guide teacher selection and learning opportunities. At the root of some of these debates is the question of whether all students are equally entitled to teachers of comparable quality, as well as questions of what kinds of qualifications and training matter most.

Current research suggests that there are many teacher characteristics and abilities which, in combination, predict teaching effectiveness. The fact that teachers' effectiveness is greatly enhanced when they have had many opportunities to learn—including high-quality general education, deepening of both content and pedagogical knowledge, teaching experience, and opportunities to develop specific practices through professional development and assessment—suggests a multi-faceted approach to policy development on behalf of stronger teaching. Evidence suggests that if policies were to support the recruitment of well-educated candidates into high-quality preparation programs that ensure substantial opportunities to learn subject matter and pedagogy, and support their ongoing learning focused on effective practices, the overall quality of teaching could be expected to be significantly higher.

Such policies would need to include effective incentives for recruiting, retaining, and distributing teachers to the places where they are needed (for examples, see Darling-Hammond & Sykes, 2003) as well as professional policies governing accreditation, licensure, and advanced certification that encourage schools of education to adopt the kinds of connected coursework and clinical experiences that enhance teachers' capacities and effectiveness.

Promising among these policy possibilities are supports for teacher assessment strategies—such as standards-based teacher evaluations and assessments like those of the NBPTS and PACT—that have been found not only to measure features of teaching associated with effectiveness, but actually to help develop effectiveness at the same time. Particularly useful are those approaches that develop both greater teaching skill and understanding for the participants and for those involved in mentoring and assessing these performances. These approaches may be particularly valuable targets for policy investments, as they may provide an engine for developing teaching quality across the profession—through their contributions to program improvement and to measures of how teachers contribute to student learning.

Chapter 9

Teacher education around the world

What can we learn from international practice?

Linda Darling-Hammond and Ann Lieberman

There may be agreement internationally that the quality of the teaching is a critical element in 21st-Century learning, but there is a wide range of views about how to develop it. This collection of chapters includes countries large and small, from Asia, the Americas, and Europe, with distinctive cultures, and, more importantly, with some major differences in the commitments they are willing to make to support high-quality preparation for teachers.

We highlight, first, the way these countries think about teacher education policy and practice. We then describe their practices in the areas of recruitment, preparation, induction, ongoing professional development, and collective improvement of practice. Last, we describe the challenges and obstacles that inevitably develop as policies and practices for changing institutions are put in place.

Defining teacher quality: competing perspectives around the globe

Of the nations represented in this volume, the highest achieving on international assessments such as the Program in International Student Assessment (PISA) are Finland, Singapore, and Canada, followed by the Netherlands and Australia, with Britain further behind, and the United States generally at the rear. To a noticeable extent, these rankings reflect the extent to which teaching has been organized and supported as a strong profession within these nations, with extensive investments in knowledge and skill.

Hong Kong is an anomaly in this group. As a recent addition to China, not highly representative of the rest of the country, Hong Kong has had a unique history in the past two decades, with an out migration of teachers as one side-effect of the anxiety that ensued when agreements were forged for it to become part of China. In the years since, aspirations for professionalizing teaching have competed with concerns for teacher shortages that emerged during that period. As we discuss later, the context in Hong Kong is extraordinarily complex.

Whilst Finland, Singapore, and Canada have forged a clear purpose and direction for a universally strong teacher preparation enterprise, all of the other countries described here have experienced, to greater or lesser extents, competing influences regarding both teacher education and the profession of teaching. On the one hand, there is much rhetoric about professionalizing teaching and upgrading the quality of teachers—and there are some programs and initiatives that indeed offer strong preparation for teaching in each of these jurisdictions. On the other hand, there are also recurring initiatives, such as alternative pathways into teaching, which effectively reduce standards and preparation for the profession. In nations like Great Britain and the United States, concerns about the quality of teachers seem to be as frequently met by efforts to reduce standards as by efforts to strengthen them.

Where teaching is viewed as a profession, there is also clarity about a strong mission for a knowledge-based system of education that strives to offer equitable opportunity. For example, Finland's strong press for an equitable high-quality education system has changed the country's culture in the past thirty years. In a single generation, Finland has leapt from a relatively poorly educated nation to a 21st-Century powerhouse with a current literacy rate of 96%, high graduation and college-going rates, and top scores in all areas on the PISA assessments.

In the process of greatly expanding educational opportunity, the Finns have created a sophisticated profession of teaching, with all teachers holding a Master's degree that encompasses both strong subject matter and pedagogical preparation, and that integrates research and practice. Teaching has become the most sought-after profession after medicine. Teachers are highly respected and supported. One hundred percent of the teachers are in a union which works collaboratively with the government to support teacher learning and school improvement.

Many teachers in Finland pursue a PhD and then remain in teaching. Clearly the Finnish view is that teaching should be a long-term profession where people can grow into leadership positions and develop expertise over time.

Similarly, Singapore has shifted from just *getting* teachers to *providing* teachers of quality. In 1997, the *Thinking Schools, Learning Nation* reform explicitly redefined the role of teachers. As Prime Minister Gok proclaimed:

> Every school must be a model learning organization. Teachers and principals will constantly look out for new ideas and practices, and continuously refresh their own knowledge. Teaching will itself be a learning profession, like any other knowledge-based profession of the future.

This reform has fueled changes in recruitment, preparation, compensation, status and the professional development of teachers. As in Finland, standards for admission to teacher preparation are stringent, and they include strong demonstrated academic ability and a passion to teach. Also as in Finland, candidates' preparation is fully paid by the government, with a salary while they train. Preparation is well designed and followed by strong induction and professional development. Compensation is high, relative to other occupations. Not a single teacher has entered without this strong preparation and there are none who fail to receive these kinds of support. Singapore has created a career ladder to provide for a variety of different kinds of leadership positions over the course of what is generally a lifelong career.

While somewhat less generous than these world leaders, provincial governments in Canada also generally support teachers financially during their training (usually at the graduate level), and compensate them reasonably well. Despite occasional debates, teachers have typically been considered well prepared and, at least in Ontario (the province we discuss in this volume), they have plentiful opportunities for learning throughout the career. Although there have been some vocal debates about teaching in Australia in recent years, teacher preparation has also been generally well supported there, and the vast majority of teachers enter the profession with full preparation and receive ongoing support. And, despite countervailing policies in Great Britain, the governments of Wales and Scotland have maintained and strengthened university-based preparation for teachers at the graduate level over recent years and have worked to develop a strong profession.

By contrast, England, the United States, the Netherlands, and Hong Kong have, to varying extents, developed a range of "market-driven" pathways into teaching. In these countries, candidates can choose from an array of alternatives that lead to becoming a teacher. They can participate in a range of different pre-service preparation models or undertake a pathway that provides "on-the-job training," generally through a graduate program. Some teachers can receive a permit to teach before receiving any training. Standards that have evolved on paper are not universally enforced. It is unclear what these governments think a *qualified* teacher looks like or should be.

It is also noteworthy that governments in most of these jurisdictions do not provide strong financial support for individuals preparing to enter teaching. Although Dutch students are generally supported with forgivable loans, there are no special arrangements to induce candidates into teaching. British students are also on their own to support themselves in teacher preparation. Perversely, in Hong Kong and most parts of the United States, there are currently greater subsidies for candidates entering teaching through alternative routes where they train on the job than there are for candidates who choose to enter pre-service programs that would prepare them before they enter. Because of inequalities in U.S. school funding, teacher salaries, and ongoing supports, prepared and qualified teachers are also unequally allocated to students of different socioeconomic backgrounds, and those who teach in poorer districts are less likely to receive ongoing professional development. This exacerbates inequality in students' access to quality teaching.

The nature of the debates about teaching

While analysts describe a wave of teacher bashing in the United States, and a "war on teachers" in England, nations that have a strong professional ideal for teaching deliberately celebrate teachers, teaching, and education. The contrasts are stark. For example, in England and the US, conservative governments over the past thirty years have challenged the idea that there is a knowledge base for teaching, have questioned the role of universities in the preparation of teachers, and have characterized the individuals entering teaching as less intelligent and capable than individuals who have entered other occupations (often in the face of contradic- tory evidence).

These governments have promoted pathways into teaching that avoid the "barriers" of preparation and have supported the lowering of standards for teachers entering communities that offer fewer incentives to teach—those with needier students, lower salaries, and poorer working conditions. Initiatives like Teach for America in the United States and Teach First in England glorify candidates who enter teaching in high-needs schools with little training and a commitment of only two years to an occupation that is a way station on the way to a real job. These governments have invested more money in such programs than they have in pre-service preparation for candidates who intend to make teaching a career.

In part influenced by these Anglophone colleagues, debates have emerged in Australia in more recent years. Although Australia has a voiced commitment to improving teaching and has a substantial body of work underway, the federal government's new proposals are a confusing blend of professionalizing and de-professionalizing initiatives. The *Teacher Quality National Partnership* (*TQNP*) program was designed to attract, prepare, place, develop, and retain quality teachers and school leaders, and to improve the quality of teaching. On the one hand, reforms include new national standards for teacher registration and improvements in teacher education, to be implemented through the Australian Institute for Teaching and School Leadership. On the other hand, the package included efforts to attract new candidates to teaching through alternative pathways that reduce training, as well as programs like Teach for Australia that suggest teaching is a short-term junket—especially for teachers of the urban and rural poor.

Although teacher quality is an important idea that is spoken about in policy circles, it has taken on a variety of meanings. The political battles pit deregulation and marketization of university-based professional training, often in tandem with calls for increasingly centralized control of curriculum and pedagogy, against a defense of professionalism grounded in the academy. Those promoting deregula- tion argue there is little valid evidence to support the contributions of teacher education as it is currently practiced, and argue instead for regulatory standards and performance indicators in lieu of traditional teacher education pathways.

A similar debate has emerged in the Netherlands, as recommendations for the preparation of teachers have taken shape while a teacher shortage is looming. On the heels of a decline in public confidence in teacher quality, beginning in about 2007, calls for higher standards have been accompanied by a call for the establish- ment of alternative routes to allow people from other occupations to work as teachers while training at the same time. Such routes were established through an

Intern Teacher Act in 2000, and have grown at a fast rate, preparing more than 3000 teachers for primary and secondary schools. However, research suggests that these entrants have not stayed in teaching at high rates.

Hong Kong has increased its rhetorical calls for a strong professional teaching force in recent years, and has not engaged in debilitating debates about teacher quality. In spite of the stated preference for teachers being professionally qualified, however, the predominance of the in-service initial teacher education route means that students in schools are regularly taught by those who have not been trained to teach. This clearly raises questions about the extent to which teaching is regarded in Hong Kong as a profession, with its own specialist body of knowledge and skills beyond subject knowledge, despite many government statements to the contrary.

By contrast, nations like Finland and Singapore have made teaching an attractive lifelong career and have increased incentives rather than lowering standards to ensure an adequate supply of candidates for the profession. In Singapore, for example, prime ministers and other leading officials frequently emphasize the importance of teachers to the national welfare through speeches, public ceremonies, the media, national competitions and scholarship programs, traditions and rituals such as the teachers' investiture ceremony, and use of the internet to highlight teachers' work and accomplishments. These inducements are on top of generous resource allocations for salaries, training, and professional learning support throughout the career. The Finns quietly provide the same kinds of support and reinforce their respect for teachers through the actions they take. Both of these nations have transformed what was once an unsupportive context for professional teaching as part of their nationwide education reforms several decades ago.

Ontario, Canada, turned around a teacher-bashing context more recently, when a new government explicitly set out to rebuild the profession and the public's respect for teachers. A new Premier and Minister of Education elected in 2003 came into office with a strong commitment to strengthening public education and the profession of teaching as a key element in improving student outcomes. They set out to spread evidence-based practices throughout classrooms and schools by increasing teachers' and leaders' access to knowledge. Their approach, focused on improvement and capacity building, quickly turned around outcomes. By 2007, all measures of student achievement, including graduation rates, had increased substantially, and teacher attrition had dropped dramatically. That trajectory has continued since, demonstrating the possibilities for sustained improvement built on a strong foundation.

Standards for teaching as a strategy for profession-building

In the midst of the debates about how to improve teaching quality, an emerging strategy across a number of nations has been the articulation of standards for what teachers should learn and be able to do. The theory of action is that such standards—used to guide licensing or certification of candidates and/or accreditation of programs—can guide teacher learning and influence entry, continuation, or recognition in the field.

The United States has been the leader in this regard, with the creation of the National Board for Professional Teaching Standards in 1987, which not only articulated standards and developed assessments for evaluating accomplished teaching, but also led to revisions of standards for beginning teacher licensing and preparation through the Interstate New Teacher Assessment and Support Consortium (INTASC). Research has found that veteran teachers who meet the National Board's standards are more effective than those who do not and that the process of becoming Board-certified helps teachers improve their practice. In recent years, the creation of a performance assessment for evaluating new teachers has also taken hold, with more than twenty states currently collaborating to create a national version of an assessment that can inform initial licensure and provide leverage on improving teacher preparation. If such a high-quality performance assessment can be developed and demonstrated to validly predict teachers' effectiveness, it could create an entry standard that puts to rest the futile arguments about the quality of various traditional and alternative routes and set a meaningful benchmark for all programs and candidates to meet.

The strategy of setting standards for teaching has had some recent currency around the world. In keeping with Singapore's commitment to "evidence-based curricula informed by research," educators study other countries' efforts to keep pace with educational innovations. Thus, it is not surprising that Singapore has adapted the concept of INTASC's standards—which are expressed as knowledge, skills and dispositions—in its Values, Skills, and Knowledge (VSK) criteria that followed the 2005 re-design of initial teacher preparation programs. In line with the focus of *Thinking Schools, Learning Nation*, the VSK model emphasizes "Innovation, Independent Learning, Critical Thinking, Commitment and Service." Similarly, in 2004, the Dutch parliament passed legislation requiring teachers at all levels (primary and secondary) to be "not only qualified, but competent" and subsequently identified six key competencies that all teachers would be expected to meet.

In Hong Kong, a competency framework was developed by the Advisory Committee on Teacher Education and Qualifications (ACTEQ) in 2003. Outlining professional competencies and core values, the framework articulates three levels of competent performance for beginning teachers across four domains of professional practice: teaching and learning, student development, school development and professional relationships. These are underpinned by six core values: belief that students can learn; love and care for students; respect for diversity; commitment and dedication to the profession; collaboration and team spirit; and passion for continuous learning and excellence. For each domain and for each level, descriptors of practice have been elaborated which acknowledge and highlight the complexity of the teaching role in a context which aims to enable children and young people to develop as whole rounded people, in line with the reforms. The competency framework is beginning to be used to frame school placement and its assessment and may, thus, begin to bring more common expectations to preparation and teaching.

Most recently, in Australia, the Australasian Teacher Regulatory Authorities (the association established by the teacher registration and accreditation authorities across Australia and New Zealand) have been developing a new national professional standards framework for teachers, which is being seen as the cornerstone of the TQNP program. It outlines what teachers, at all levels of responsibility, know and do across the domains of professional knowledge, professional practice and professional engagement. Much like the framework of the National Board for Professional Teaching Standards in the US, this in turn defines an architecture within which generic, specialist and subject-area standards are to be developed.

The critical question for the teacher standards movement, where it is emerging, is how the standards will be used, how universally they will be applied, and how they may leverage stronger learning opportunities and a more common set of knowledge, skills, and commitments across the profession. Robust standards weakly applied can be expected to have much less effect than those that are used, as in other professions, as an inviolable expectation for candidates and institutions to meet.

Entry into the profession

Recruitment

Countries that are focused on building a strong profession understand the interdependence among standards, preparation, and supports. Several of these countries provide significant financial support to offset the costs of teachers' training, which, in turn, allows them to be highly selective in choosing candidates and to insist that all candidates complete a comprehensive, rigorous program of preparation. Thus, in Finland, preparation is fully funded by the government, and candidates earn a living stipend or a salary while they are in training. All candidates receive uniformly high-quality preparation. Among young Finns, teaching is a most desired profession, and competition for slots is severe, with only 1 in 4 applicants to teacher training accepted overall, including only 1 in 10 for primary school teacher preparation.

Similarly, in Singapore, generous support for teaching candidates (the equivalent of $30,000–$50,000 per year in salary, plus tuition, books, and laptop computers) is part of a bond with the government to teach for 3–5 years, depending on the kind of program completed. If the service requirement is not fulfilled, this funding must be repaid. This structure, along with the supportive induction program, enhances retention as well as recruitment. Salaries are commensurate with other fields like engineering, law, and business.

In Australia and Canada, a major portion of candidates' cost of teacher preparation is underwritten by the government. Interestingly, the Canadian reforms aimed at more explicitly supporting teachers have both dramatically reduced attrition from teaching and made recruitment less necessary. Prior to 2004, due to high teacher turnover, Ontario added additional spaces to university teacher education, but since 2008 the province has had a significant surplus of teachers (even though many new positions have been created) and these additional spaces have not been necessary.

The Netherlands has a national stipend system for all students in higher education. Students who enter college are provided with a loan to pay for their expenses, which will be converted into a gift if they finish their exams in time. If they take more time to complete their program than is expected, or fail their exams, the loan will not be converted into a gift. While this may serve as a strong incentive to enter higher education in general, whether teaching itself is a career choice depends on other factors.

Concern about shortages has led to new routes for mid-career changers, on the one hand, and a half-year course of study for undergraduates at some research universities, which earns them a special teaching certificate allowing them to teach their major subject in the lower secondary grades. These options, however, reduce the expectations for pre-service training, rather than the opposite.

In Hong Kong and the US, teachers are more likely to fund their own education, unless they pursue a subsidized alternative route. In Hong Kong, professional training costs are partly covered by the government which sets quotas for paid places for all entry routes. Students who study full-time pay fees in line with undergraduate and postgraduate fee structures; there is no subsidy and no stipend. Those who study part-time in the evening and work as teachers or teaching assistants during the day, pay a pro-rata fee and fund their studies from their work. In the United States, the federal service scholarships and forgivable loans that were once a major tool for recruiting teachers in the 1960s and 1970s were dramatically reduced or ended during the 1980s, and current federal support covers only a small portion of costs for only a small subset of teachers in specific shortage fields.

One might think that greater recruitment supports would be offered in countries where teachers' salaries are relatively less competitive with other occupations, in order to offset the wage disincentives. However, the nations that pay higher teacher salaries also offer more support for training, as illustrated in a recent OECD report comparing teacher salaries to those of other college graduates. The report included four of the nations we studied. At the top of the salary rankings were Australia and Finland, where teacher salaries are, on average, nearly equivalent to those of other college-educated workers, followed by the Netherlands, with teachers' salaries pegged at about 80% of those of other college-educated workers, followed at some distance by the United States, with a ratio of only 60%, one of the lowest rates in the survey (OECD, 2011, p. 13).

Initial preparation

While common and uniformly high-quality preparation for teachers is a very explicit goal in Finland—where teachers all complete a two- or three-year Master's degree before they enter teaching, there is more variability in pathways in the other countries we studied, and a broader range of quality in many of them. All of the others offer some combination of undergraduate and graduate-level programs for candidates who enter at different junctures in their studies. As we noted above, a number of countries also offer pathways that allow candidates to assume teaching responsibilities while they are still in training. These pathways are an option for relatively few candidates in Australia and for many more in England, the Netherlands, the US, and Hong Kong.

In Canada, Australia, and the United States, standards governing certification or registration for teachers, as well as accreditation for programs, create some regularities across university-based pre-service programs, even when other pathways offer substantially different levels and kinds of preparation.

Although variability in the kind and quality of preparation is much greater in some countries than others, all of the places we studied have some excellent programs that offer high-quality preparation and are innovating in interesting ways. In this section, we highlight some of these program features across various countries. Recurring themes for improvement in nearly all of these countries include strengthening connections between theory and practice and developing teachers' capacities to teach diverse learners, as nations deal with growing immigration and growing expectations of teachers.

In Finland, teacher education aims at balanced development of the teacher's personal and professional competences. Particular attention is focused on building pedagogical thinking skills that enable teachers to manage the teaching process in a diagnostic manner, using research as a base, and conducting action research as a guide. In addition to studying child development, learning, and pedagogy in the content areas, each student completes a Master's thesis in which he or she takes up a problem of practice and studies it in a rigorous way. There is a strong emphasis on learning to teach students who struggle to learn, on the theory that if teachers can understand and respond to these students' unique needs, they will be able to teach all children successfully.

Clinical learning takes place in special Teacher Training Schools, governed by the universities, which have similar curricula and practices as normal public schools, but which are committed to training beginning teachers and staffed by teachers who are especially selected for their teaching skills. These teachers are well prepared in supervision and teacher professional development and assessment strategies. Teacher Training Schools are also expected to pursue research and development roles in collaboration with the Department of Teacher Education and, sometimes, with the academic faculties who participate in teacher education. These schools can, therefore, introduce alternative curricular designs to student teachers. Some regular public schools (called Municipal Field Schools) serve the same purpose. These schools also have higher professional staff requirements, and supervising teachers have to prove that they are competent to work with student teachers.

Singapore has also made a strong commitment to high-quality, equal education for prospective teachers, although this preparation can be delivered through both undergraduate and graduate pathways at the National Institute of Education, the nation's only teacher training institution. Standards for entry and continuation in preparation are equivalent and rigorous in both pathways, as are coursework and clinical work. There is a strong emphasis on mastering both content and content pedagogy—with academic subjects and curriculum studies courses not only aligned, but taken concurrently and designed to be mutually reinforcing. In a reflection of the national quest to deliver a 21st-Century curriculum that infuses technology and favors project-based learning and collaboration, all student teachers must take a course in "Interactive computer technology for meaningful learning" and, in another course, must work collaboratively with peers to complete the Group Endeavors in Service Learning (GELS) Project, which demands 20 hours of direct service in the community, beyond project design, planning and presentation.

Partner schools are increasingly developed as sites for clinical practice. School–university collaboration also takes place through shared decision-making about student teachers, and opportunities for teachers to serve at the National Institute of Education (NIE) and for faculty to serve in schools through a "school attachment" opportunity.

Teacher education in the Netherlands reflects a tiered system. The four-year teacher education programs provided by the universities for applied sciences prepare students to teach in primary and secondary education, and vocational education, but not the higher classes of higher general secondary education and pre-university education (VWO). These higher classes are reserved for graduates of the research universities, who receive a year-long teacher education program after they have already acquired a Master's in the discipline related to the school subject. The graduates of these programs receive a *first level teaching qualification*, which allows them to teach in all classes of secondary and vocational education, while the graduates of teachers' colleges receive a *second level teaching qualification*.

Teacher education initiatives in both kinds of institutions reflect a strong emphasis upon combining clinical work and coursework in ways that better prepare teachers for the realities of classroom teaching. As in Finland, some universities place student teachers in "opleidingsscholen" (training schools) that have additional resources for coaching student teachers on the job. These schools have a school-based teacher educator who supervises the student teachers, along with the university-based supervisor. Opleidingsscholen can apply to the Ministry of Education for subsidies for their teacher education activities, and the schools can also take advantage of professional development opportunities offered to their school faculty by the university-based teacher education institute. Recently, efforts have evolved to create standards and a registration process for these school-based teacher educators.

One-year Master's degree programs at places like Leiden University are similar in form and content to post-baccalaureate programs at U.S. universities like Stanford and Columbia, Teachers College. In these models, prospective teachers begin working in schools in the classrooms of cooperating teachers from the first weeks of the program and do so until the end of the school year, while they are taking tightly linked coursework at the same time.

One of Leiden's more interesting innovations has replaced traditional courses, such as Foundations and Methods, with a set of modules designed to help new teachers develop six critical teaching roles. The roles map onto the key competencies outlined in the Dutch teaching standards: subject teacher, classroom manager, expert in adolescent psychology, member of the school organization, colleague, and professional.

Prospective teachers focus their studies and clinical work on each of these roles in turn as they move through the modules. From the beginning of the program, students are provided with rubrics that articulate competence in each role, so that they can track and evaluate their own progress, thus developing the capacity to become reflective professionals who are active learners. Modules typically are launched with an introduction of the relevant theory in a lecture by a specialist in this field. This lecture, often illustrated with extensive use of teaching videos as a basis for analysis, provides a frame of reference, or "language," for students to think and talk about their experiences in their own classrooms. Research findings are presented about the links between specific teaching approaches and student learning, motivation, and other outcomes.

Aside from their efforts to apply what they are learning in their classroom placements, candidates may engage in role-playing exercises to rehearse and test out strategies and responses to classroom situations. As students develop each role, they complete relevant assignments that are eventually collected in a final, culminating portfolio demonstrating their development as teachers. These assignments help them apply what they are learning in the classroom, collecting data and evidence about their own practice and its outcomes—using, among other things, videotapes of their teaching, evidence of student work and learning, and student surveys—and analyzing this evidence in relation to research on best practices.

At Utrecht University, teacher educators have developed what is called a *realistic approach to teacher education*, seeking to bring into the program aspects of what many teachers experience as "reality shock" when they first start teaching, so that teachers can bring relevant theory to bear upon the concerns that may otherwise feel overwhelming and difficult to understand. They are supported by both teacher educators and supervising teachers at the schools as they experience key parts of the process of beginning to teach independently.

In undergraduate programs, such as that at the Amsterdam School of Education, an emphasis on "authentic learning" drives a very deliberate process for assuming a professional role and activities over the four years of preparation, with growing practical engagement each year and ongoing support for reflection and metacognition. During their final year, students have a special Teacher-in-Training contract and serve as an independent teacher with full responsibilities, sometimes receiving a salary from the school, with their mentor giving support at a distance.

Part of the preparation process at the Amsterdam School of Education directly addresses the need for teachers to become culturally competent, as concerns for multicultural education have grown while the Netherlands' population has a 20% racial/ethnic minority. Students undertake a project focused upon understanding diverse cultures and language in the classroom. During the project, faculty members provide lectures that are intended to help student teachers develop background knowledge on different cultures, the role of language in classrooms, and intercultural communication. These lectures then serve as the basis for the student teachers to design lessons with a specific focus on language use and inclusive approaches in teaching and to write small case-studies focusing on dilemmas in multicultural schools. The project ends with an event where students present the multicultural landscape of schools in Amsterdam, sharing the outcomes of their case studies.

As these examples suggest, in many parts of the world, student teachers now spend far more time in schools during their initial teacher preparation programs than they did a decade or two ago. This additional time has usually been accompanied by greater attention to the quality of that in-school experience—the quality of the cooperating teachers selected, their training for the role, and the creation of something beginning to resemble a clinical curriculum—an intentional set of experiences and learning during the clinical part of the program.

In the United States, more attention is being paid to the development and assessment of clinical practice, with the development of structured performance assessments for novice teachers, tied to professional standards, being used as a means for leveraging both individual learning and institutional learning for teacher education programs. Interest in such strategies has also grown in Australia, where portfolios and performance assessments for evaluating beginners' capacity to teach are receiving more emphasis.

Most would agree that the greater attention to clinical preparation has been a net benefit to teacher preparation. This has been a major thrust of teacher education reforms in England, as school-based preparation has become a much more prominent element of the process and teachers-in-training spend much more time in classrooms. However, there is some danger, as MacBeath notes in Chapter 4 in this volume, that the school-based emphasis has come at the expense of the other components of preparation. He notes that the steep fees that higher education institutions have to pay schools for their clinical contributions have destabilized the staffing structure of many university schools of education. Finding the right balance between theory and practice, creating truly integrated forms of preparation, and ensuring adequate resources for the task will continue to be a challenge in many programs for some time to come.

Continuing in the profession

Of course, teacher learning is not complete when teachers leave pre-service preparation. In many ways, the most powerful learning is just beginning as teachers enter their first classroom assignments. And many societies have begun to provide much more organized support for teachers as they enter and continue in the career.

Induction

Perhaps the most comprehensive supports for new teachers are offered in Singapore, where mentor teachers, who are recognized and compensated through the nation's career ladder, have an explicit mission to support new teachers. Novices receive a package of supports, including mentoring, in-service courses, and a buddy system. The structured induction program in place in all schools typically involves four core in-service courses that new teachers attend within their first two years of service. These cover classroom management, basic counseling, working with parents, and reflective practice. In addition to their experienced mentor teacher, new teachers are assigned a buddy—a peer teaching the same subject, plus a supervisor (usually the department head) to help them learn and acclimatize.

In Ontario, the reforms launched in 2003 focused more on in-service rather than pre-service supports for teachers, because teacher education was viewed as strong, offering a sufficient supply of new teachers who are viewed as capable and well educated. However, supports after entry were not highly developed, and the newly elected government introduced a high-quality induction program for all new teachers, providing first year teachers with extra release time, targeted professional development, and mentoring. This has contributed to major improvements in teacher retention.

In Australia, most states initially offer teachers a provisional registration upon graduation from an approved teacher education program and then full registration after a period of 12–18 months, during which time the beginning teacher must provide evidence that they have achieved the standards of professional practice required for full registration. This time usually involves an induction program including school-based mentoring and workshops and other professional learning opportunities. Induction programs are usually state- or employer-run and mentors are sometimes given classroom release time to carry out their mentoring role.

A similar structure of two-stage certification is now common in the United States, and most states now require some form of induction, including mentoring, for beginning teachers in their first year or two of teaching. Nearly 75% of beginning teachers now receive induction support, although only 5% receive the combination of supports—regular coaching and mentoring, shared planning time, and a reduced teaching load—that are common in some other nations (Wei, Darling-Hammond, & Adamson, 2010).

In Hong Kong, an induction scheme launched in 2008 draws on the ACTEQ competency framework mentioned earlier, which also guides ongoing professional development. Based on the identified needs and concerns of beginning teachers, the government developed a "tool kit" to help schools develop support systems for new teachers, including mentoring.It also offers staff development support, a network for sharing, and the dissemination of research and good practice.

Around the world, many teachers are getting a better launch to their careers than was true a decade or more ago.

Ongoing professional development

Enabling teachers to continue to grow, learn, and be excited about their work depends on both ongoing high-quality learning opportunities and career opportunities that enable them to share their expertise in a variety of ways. Around the world, job-embedded forms of professional learning are taking greater root, often organized around teachers' work with curriculum development through collaborative planning, lesson study, and action research of various kinds. Also increasing are opportunities for teachers to share their expertise with one another.

Embedding learning in teachers' work and roles

In Finland, teachers take responsibility for curriculum and assessment development, as a major part of their professional role. Since the national curriculum offers very lean guidance and there is no external standardized testing, teachers are expected to work collectively to develop the work that occurs at the school level. This is one source of ongoing learning. In addition, teachers are encouraged and supported to continue to study, and most engage in both school-based and university-based learning opportunities. Many Finnish teachers earn a PhD in educational studies and continue to practice in the classroom.

Singapore offers extensive job-embedded time for teachers to plan and work collaboratively, and the NIE supports teachers in learning and practicing action research. Along with lesson study and other tools for productive collaboration on curriculum, action research is generally implemented in grade-level and department teams. The government also supports about 100 hours of professional development time (more than 12 days) each year.

In addition, Singapore has perhaps the best-defined career ladder, providing leadership opportunities for teachers within as well as outside the classroom. Through a well-developed evaluation process that provides extensive feedback to teachers—and that attends to collaboration and leadership skills as well as teaching skills—teachers are encouraged to develop their interests and talents. With government support for additional training and compensation, they can pursue a pathway as a master teacher who will take on roles as a mentor and coach to others, a specialist who will engage in curriculum and assessment development work, or a school leader who will move into administrative roles at the school level or, eventually, the regional level or ministry.

The notion of a career ladder also motivates ongoing professional development in the UK. Beyond school-level collaboration time, the government has provided five professional development days for teachers. In England, university-based professional learning opportunities for teachers tend to take the form of a ladder of qualifications—from the Certificate of Professional Studies (CfPS), to the Post-graduate Diploma of Educational Studies, in turn leading to a Master of Education degree (MEd).

The ladder is also a common feature of continuing professional development in Wales and in Scotland, but in both places with the addition of the Chartered Teacher route. This was created to reward and retain excellent teachers in the classroom rather than expecting them to follow a promotion pathway into administration. In Scotland's *Standards for Chartered Teacher* guidelines, the role is described as "reviewing practice, searching for improvements, turning to reading and research for fresh insights, and relating these to the classroom and the school." The chartered teacher is expected to bring to his or her work "more sophisticated forms of critical scrutiny, demonstrate a heightened capacity for self-evaluation, and a marked disposition to be innovative and to improvise."

The Chartered Teacher programme is made up of 12 modules, each involving around 150 hours of study. The modules are provided through universities and result in the award of a Master's degree. Moving up the qualifications ladder by undertaking further post-graduate study is a growing trend in the UK, and in 2008 the Labour Government issued a White Paper that floated the idea that a required, government-sponsored Master's degree in teaching and learning for all teachers would be an expectation of a new license to teach, renewable every five years. This was seen by many commentators as marking a watershed in government thinking and policy: "After 30 years of policy that has been driven by a mistrust of teachers, this could signal a new age for education policy', suggested a BBC report in July 2009.

As part of another effort to re-establish trust with teachers, in Canada, Ontario's new government in 2003 reached out to teachers' unions as part of its agenda to professionalize teaching. The unions have received substantial government funding to offer professional development sessions to teachers as a way of recognizing and strengthening the role of unions in promoting good professional practice. As one example, the federations developed the "teacher leader learning program," which encouraged teacher leaders in and across schools to engage with leading experts and each other to strengthen teaching practices.

The province's extensive professional development efforts also focused on schools and districts, seeking to avoid one-shot workshops in favor of job-embedded learning through coaching, mentoring and other strategies. The province added two professional development days to the school calendar and required that districts, in consultation with the Ministry, decide how best to use those days to support their own goals and strategies. Every school and every district created a leadership team for literacy and numeracy in elementary schools and a leadership team for student success in secondary schools. These teams create and support the local strategy for improvement, in collaboration with the principal.

The conceptualization of ongoing professional learning as being part of a collective effort, rather than only an individual undertaking, is the next emerging horizon for teacher learning—and, for that matter, the learning of school leaders as well. As we describe in the next section, some governments are developing new conceptions of school improvement that are rooted in professional learning that is designed to be profession-wide.

A profession-wide approach to the collective improvement of practice

In a number of countries, including Finland and Singapore, teachers and leaders are encouraged to visit other schools to look at and share practices. In the UK and Australia, as part of literacy and numeracy initiatives, networks of schools have been formed to support cross-school learning. Perhaps the most extensive investment in this approach has taken place in Ontario, Canada, which has taken the idea of professionalism to a system-wide level, by investing in the spread of knowledge across classrooms, schools, and the system as a whole. As Levin explains in this volume:

> We were confident that almost everything that needed to be done in our schools was being done somewhere among Ontario's nearly 5000 schools. If we could find and share good practices, we could have an organic process of improvement led by educators, which is necessary for sustainability.

The improvement of collective practice took many forms. In addition to teacher and principal professional development, these strategies included: helping districts and schools set reasonable and ambitious goals and work towards them; setting up and supporting learning networks across the province to share practices and outcomes; providing intellectual resources, from curriculum support documents to webcasts to DVDs of good practice, so that schools could readily access knowledge. Successful "Lighthouse Schools" are publicized and given additional funds to share their good practices with other schools. The Ontario Focused Intervention Program provides additional support and advice to struggling or coasting schools, which are then networked for mutual learning with similar schools that have had greater success. The government funds Student Success Leaders in every district to lead the effort to improve high school graduation rates. These leaders meet regularly to share their learning.

So as not to support a never-ending set of pilot projects that produce results and then fade away, Ontario has funded learning projects in a wide range of schools to support experimentation with various approaches to improvement. Then, the number of new projects was steadily reduced in favor of wider implementation of those found to be most effective. As Levin notes, "The goal of experimentation is to learn, and to use what we learn across the system, an approach that has been sadly lacking in education in many places."

The work exemplifies what some US leaders have called "top down support for bottom-up reform." Responding to district initiatives, the Ontario Ministry of Education supported a network of 20 districts that wanted to work together to improve outcomes for Aboriginal students. Ontario's directors of education (its local superintendents) also led a major effort, financed by the Ministry, to strengthen the capacity of teachers to work with more diverse students, thereby reducing rates of referral to special education.

One element in the government's strategy was to increase the use of research across Ontario schools. The Ministry embedded research elements in all major strategies, giving public profile to high quality research, and implementing an education research strategy to increase capacity and strengthen partnerships among researchers, school districts and schools. As one example, the annual Ontario Education Research Symposium, which brings together all these partners, started in 2005; it is now one of the most oversubscribed events in the annual education calendar, always having to turn away participants to maintain a reasonable size. It has now been replicated by several universities at a regional level, a further sign of success and impact. That educators and researchers could work together to advance learning and improve practice is, ultimately, the goal of a well-functioning profession.

Leading practices and challenges

Looking across these many examples, there are some practices that stand out as promising for the improvement of teacher learning and teaching, including:

- Recruitment of highly able candidates into high-quality programs by ensuring competitive salaries, financial subsidies for training, and greater commonality in the design and quality of preparation, as Finland and Singapore have done.
- Connecting theory and practice through both the design of thoughtful coursework and the integration of high-quality clinical work in settings where good practice is supported. Programs in Finland and the Netherlands, as well as some institutions in the United States, have created new models for student teaching, often in "training schools."
- Using professional teaching standards to focus attention on the learning and evaluation of critical knowledge, skills, and dispositions as illustrated in the United States, Australia, Hong Kong, the Netherlands, and Singapore.
- Creation of teacher performance assessments, based on professional standards, that connect student learning to classroom teaching. As developed in the US and under construction in Australia, these assessments leverage improvements in both candidate competence and program improvement.
- Establishing induction models that support beginning teachers through skillful mentoring, collaborative planning, and reduced teaching loads that allow

time for in-service seminars and careful building of a repertoire of practice, as organized in Singapore, Australia, Canada, Hong Kong, and some parts of the United States.

- Supporting thoughtful professional development that routinely enables teachers to learn with and from one another, both within and across schools and universities, as Singapore, Australia, and Canada have done.
- Career ladders, like those in Singapore and the UK, that allow teachers to develop and share expertise in teaching, mentoring, curriculum development, and leadership.
- Profession-wide capacity building, like that underway in Ontario, which creates strategies for wide sharing of research and good practice, recognizes successful classroom and school practices, and enables expert teachers and principals to provide leadership to the system as whole.

Challenges to building a teaching profession

Teacher education has been differently positioned in different countries and at different times in history. Marilyn Cochran-Smith notes that, in nations like the US, the UK, Australia, and Canada, it was first positioned as a "training problem," then as a "learning problem," and more recently as a "policy problem"(Cochran-Smith & Fries, 2005).

In the first of these stages, teacher education was self-governed by teacher preparation institutions. In the second stage, teacher education governance increasingly focused on outcomes. This led both to a greater diversity of providers, on the grounds that traditional university programs might not focus adequately on preparing teachers to succeed in practice, and, in some nations, to teacher certification tests, meant to confirm whether teachers had actually gained certain kinds of knowledge. The concern for outcomes also raised questions about whether teacher education contributes to student learning. Most recently, in the era of teacher education as a policy problem, some have argued that the most appropriate policies for teacher education—including whether, where, and how it should take place—should be decided according to empirical evidence about its contribution to student achievement.

In this contested context, politicians, bureaucrats, the business community, public and community representatives, and even members of the teaching profession, are increasingly asking questions about the professional preparation of teachers, including: What is the value of teacher education? What should beginning and veteran teachers know and be able to do? How can judgments be made about the quality of teaching practice? We have seen that there are contending values about what it means to be a well-prepared teacher and about the strategies that might be used to achieve this goal.

Some would deregulate entry to teaching and create a marketplace of unregulated options for training. This notion is often accompanied by proposals to judge practice based on the standardized test scores of students—leading to greater centralization and narrowing of curriculum, instruction, and testing. The bargain calls for less regulation of teacher education and entry to teaching, but more regulation of the act of teaching itself. Others call for increased professionalization achieved through more comprehensive and rigorous preparation, allowing more autonomy and professional self-regulation for educators in practice. Perhaps the central challenge for educators is whether they can create means for self-regulation that are sufficiently robust that they will inspire public confidence in the process.

No changes of a systemic nature can avoid or ignore the challenges that have been described in the countries featured in this collection. In places where salaries and supports for teaching are inadequate, teacher shortages are often addressed by lowering standards to get people into classrooms. This not only de-professionalizes teaching, it also ensures that the system will be inequitable, with the effects falling most heavily on the least advantaged students. Furthermore, inadequate investments in professional knowledge will undermine the capacity of educators and societies to meet the needs of students who are immigrating from a variety of countries with a range of educational, cultural, and language needs.

The changes that are needed to build a strong profession of teaching that can meet these challenges around the globe will require us to learn from each other about what matters and what works in different contexts. We will need a deep understanding of the possible strategies for making major improvements in teachers' learning opportunities and a clear theory of change for how to bring these strategies about. As we consider these possibilities, we should keep in mind that while there are many different roads to the same ends, it is important that we keep a sharp focus on approaches that will, ultimately, build powerful and equitable learning systems for students and teachers alike.

Notes

2 Quality teachers, Singapore style

1 I acknowledge here that the notion of "developed" and "developing" worlds constitutes a constructed binary that privileges colonizers and allows them to maintain their position of power.
2 "Pre-university" is the equivalent of 11th and 12th grades in the US.
3 In this chapter, all Chinese names are written according to Chinese cultural norms whereby family or surnames precede birth or given names. Thus, Prime Minister Goh Chok Tong's family name—Goh—comes before his given name "Chok Tong."
4 Every working Singapore citizen or permanent resident is eligible for and required to contribute to the CPF (Central Provident Fund) which is minimally analogous to social security in the US. However, there are two key differences: (1) employers are required to match employee contributions (for teachers, this equals 13% of monthly salaries); and (2) while Singaporeans typically cannot withdraw from CPF until retirement, they actually own a physical account that accumulates interest and provides regular statements.
5 Quotes without attribution are either taken from interviews or conversation with Singaporean educators/university faculty, or from various PowerPoint presentations conducted by NIE faculty.
6 Of the 3000 student teachers admitted in 2009, "some are first posted to schools as contract teachers to help ease the bubble intake problem [by] staggering their entry into NIE."
7 "Glocal" is a term coined in Singapore to express the necessary and natural symbiosis of the global and the local.
8 The Bachelor of Education was introduced as a part-time program to accommodate the needs of practicing teachers who already hold diplomas in education and can now continue their professional education and upgrade their credentials.

3 Teacher preparation in the Netherlands: Shared visions and common features

1 These three reforms represented large-scale systematic change for Dutch secondary education. The total cost of these reforms was approximately 2.2 billion Euros (Commissie Parlementair Onderzoek Onderwijsvernieuwing, 2008).
2 The challenges facing these reform efforts are consistent with research on the implementation of school reforms that suggests that large-scale reforms will be unsuccessful without building the capacity of all educators involved (especially, in this instance, classroom teachers) who need to be well supported and provided with professional development in order to carry them out (Hatch, 2009).

3 While a growing body of research has developed that attends to these issues in the U.S. (Ladson-Billings, 1995, 2001; Villegas, 2008) this is still an issue that is underexamined in Dutch teacher preparation programs.

4 The Committee also called for the establishment of alternative routes into teaching, and established the Intern Teacher Act in 2000, allowing people from other occupations to work as teachers while training at the same time. While these alternative routes have been growing at a fast rate, those who are prepared do not appear to have a high retention rate. Brouwer (2007) reports that between 2000 and 2005, alternative routes had prepared approximately 3,550 teachers for primary and secondary schools but that a substantial number of those teachers seem to have left teaching within five years. Indeed, recent reports by the Ministry of Education, Science and Culture on the intake of teachers into teacher preparation did not mention these routes or provide information on figures related to those programs (2008). Brouwer argues that the lack of mentoring and loose coordination between placement schools and preparation programs could be contributing to the attrition and asks for more research on the features of these programs that may strengthen alternative preparation.

5 Universities for applied sciences are referred to as "Hogescholen" in Dutch.

6 For students who hold a master's in one of the languages or in history from one of the research universities such as Leiden University, becoming a teacher is a clear and obvious option. For example, students who study classical languages (Latin and Ancient Greek) may select teaching because there is both a serious shortage of teachers in those areas and there are also fewer options beyond teaching. While there are many other career options for those graduating in biology, job opportunities for these graduates outside education are less positive compared with other sciences, and so many of those graduates opt for teaching. For mathematicians, it is very easy to find a job as a teacher because of the large teacher shortages. Students who hold a master's degree in one of the social sciences and economics can also teach this subject in secondary education, but the number of teaching positions for these subjects is limited, and the number of students who hold a master's degree in economics and the social sciences is large. Therefore for these groups becoming a teacher is not an obvious option. For students who prepared for teaching in primary education, the overall prospects for finding a job are excellent, especially in the major cities, because of the teacher shortages.

7 Indeed, recent studies of 26 teacher preparation programs in New York city suggest that few programs stood out as having unique features, due, in part to institutional pressure and heightened regulatory contexts (Boyd *et al.*, 2008).

8 The organization of the coursework in this way is one of the many changes that took place in the 2004 reform of the Leiden University program. Up to 2003, the program had been organized into separate classes that were designed to teach key ideas about teaching and learning—and in each course, students were assessed separately at the end of the class. However, an assessment of students' perceptions in 2004 revealed that they felt ill-prepared for teaching and, subsequently, a number of key curricular changes were made, including, in addition, organizing the curriculum around roles.

9 The Dutch word for this particular role, which includes knowledge about youth culture and child development (including moral and ethical development), is "pedagog."

10 The survey used in the program is entitled "The Questionnaire on Teacher Interaction." The survey, and the theory behind it, are described in more detail by Wubbels and his colleagues (2006).

4 Teacher training, education or learning by doing in the UK

1 A Google search on war on teachers ironically provides only a reference to Obama's speech on 5 November 2009 in which it is said he declared war on teachers.

7 Rethinking teacher education in Australia: The teacher quality reforms

1 Also known as the Australian Government or the Federal Government. Australia has three levels of government: Commonwealth, state or territory, and local. In relation to education, the Commonwealth manages the university or higher education sector while the states and territories manage school education, early childhood education, and Vocational Education and Training (VET) or Technical and Further Education (TAFE) providers which offer courses that focus on work skills. However, taxes are collected federally and then budgets are allocated to the states and territories.
2 The areas for reform also include the following, but these areas are not the focus of this chapter:

   • knowledge of teachers and school leaders through their careers; and
   • improving the quality and availability of teacher workforce data.

3 The Ministerial Council on Education, Employment, Training and Youth Affairs (MCEETYA) was formed in June 1993, when the Council of Australian Governments (COAG) amalgamated with a number of ministerial councils to coordinate policy-making nationally.

8 Teacher preparation and development in the United States: A changing policy landscape

1 The seven institutions were Alverno College in Milwaukee, WI; Bank Street College in New York City; Trinity College in San Antonio, TX; University of California at Berkeley; University of Virginia in Charlottesville; University of Southern Maine; and Wheelock College in Boston, MA.
2 In U.S. education, the term "certification" has historically been used to describe states' decisions regarding admission to practice, commonly termed licensing in other professions. Now, advanced certification for accomplished veteran teachers is granted by a National Board for Professional Teaching Standards. To avoid confusion between the actions of this professional board and those of states, we use the terms licensing and certification here as they are commonly used by professions: "licensing" is the term used to describe state decisions about initial admission to practice and "certification" is the term used to describe the actions of the National Board in certifying accomplished practice.

References

Chapter 1: The most wanted: Teachers and teacher education in Finland

Aho, E., Pitkänen, K., & Sahlberg, P. (2006). *Policy development and reform principles of basic and secondary education in Finland since 1968.* Washington, DC: World Bank.

Darling-Hammond, L. (2006). *Powerful teacher education: Lessons from exemplary programs.* San Francisco: Jossey-Bass.

European Commission (2004).*Common European principles for teacher competences and qualifications.* Brussels: Directorate-General for Education and Culture. Available at: http://www.see-educoop.net/education_in/pdf/01-en_principles_en.pdf.

Häivälä, K. (2009). Voice of upper secondary school teachers: Subject teachers' perceptions of changes and visions in upper secondary schools. *Annales Universitatis Turkuensis* C 283 (in Finnish). Turku: University of Turku.

Helsingin Sanomat (2004). Ykkössuosikki: Opettajan ammatti [Top favorite: teaching profession]. February 11.

Helsingin Sanomat (2008). Millä ammatilla pääsee naimisiin? [Which profession to marry?] Koulutusliite, February 27, pp. 4–6.

Jakku-Sihvonen, R., & Niemi, H. (Eds.) (2006). *Research-based teacher education in Finland: Reflections by Finnish teacher educators.* Turku: Finnish Educational Research Association.

Jokinen, H., & Välijärvi J. (2006). Making mentoring a tool for supporting teachers' professional development. In R. Jakku-Sihvonen, & H. Niemi (Eds.), *Research-based Teacher education in Finland: Reflections by Finnish teacher educators* (pp. 89–101). Turku: Finnish Educational Research Association.

Jussila, J., & Saari, S. (Eds.) (2000). *Teacher education as a future-molding factor: International evaluation of teacher education in Finnish universities.* Helsinki: Higher Education Evaluation Council. Available at: http://www.kka.fi/?l=en&s=4.

Kim, M., Lavonen, J., & Ogawa, M. (2011). Experts' opinion on the high achievement of scientific literacy in PISA 2003: A comparative study in Finland and Korea. *Eurasia Journal of Mathematics, Science & Technology Education, 5*(4), 379–393.

Kivi, A. (2005). *Seven brothers.* [Seitsemän veljestä, first published in 1870, trans. R. Impola]. Beaverton: Aspasia Books, Inc.

Kumpulainen, T. (Ed.) (2008). *Opettajat Suomessa 2008* [Teachers in Finland 2008]. Helsinki: Opetushallitus.

Lavonen, J., Krzywacki-Vainio, H., Aksela, M., Krokfors, L., Oikkonen, J., & Saarikko, H. (2007). Pre-service teacher education in chemistry, mathematics and physics. In E. Pehkonen, M. Ahtee, & J. Lavonen (Eds.), *How Finns learn mathematics and science.* (pp. 49–68). Rotterdam: Sense Publishers.

Ministry of Education (2007). *Opettajankoulutus 2020* [Teacher education 2020]. Committee Report 2007: 44. Helsinki: Ministry of Education.

Ministry of Education (2009). *Ensuring professional competence and improving opportunities for continuing education in education.* Committee Report 2009: 16. Helsinki: Ministry of Education.

Niemi, H. (2002). Active learning: A cultural change needed in teacher education and in schools. *Teaching and Teacher Education, 18*(7), 763–780.

OECD (2005). *Teachers matter: Attracting, developing and retaining effective teachers.* Paris: OECD.

OECD (2008). *Education at a glance: Education indicators.* Paris: OECD.

OECD (2011). *Education at a glance: Education indicators.* Paris: OECD.

Pechar, H. (2007). "The Bologna Process": A European response to global competition in higher education. *Canadian Journal of Higher Education, 37*(3), 109–125.

Piesanen, E., Kiviniemi, U., & Valkonen, S. (2007). *Opettajankoulutuksen kehittämisohjelman seuranta ja arviointi. Opettajien täydennyskoulutus 2005 ja seuranta 1998–2005 oppiaineittain ja oppialoittain eri oppilaitosmuodoissa* [Follow-up and evaluation of the teacher education development program: Continuing teacher education in 2005 and its follow-up 1998–2005 by fields and teaching subjects in different types of educational institutions]. Jyväskylä: University of Jyväskylä, Institute for Educational Research.

Saari, S., & Frimodig, M. (Eds.) (2009). Leadership and management of education. evaluation of education at the University of Helsinki 2007–2008. *Administrative Publications 58.* Helsinki: University of Helsinki.

Sahlberg, P. (2007). Education policies for raising student learning: The Finnish approach. *Journal of Education Policy, 22*(2), 147–171.

Sahlberg, P. (2011). *Finnish lessons: what can the world learn from educational change in Finland?* New York: Teachers College Press.

Statistics Finland (2009). Education. Retrieved May 8, 2009 from http://www.stat.fi/til/kou_en.html.

Välijärvi, J., & Sahlberg, P. (2008). Should a "failing" student repeat a grade? Retrospective response from Finland. *Journal of Educational Change, 9*(4), 385–389.

Westbury, I., Hansen, S-E., Kansanen, P., & Björkvist, O. (2005). Teacher education for research-based practice in expanded roles: Finland's experience. *Scandinavian Journal of Educational Research, 49*(5), 475–485.

Zgaga, P. (2007). *Looking out: The Bologna Process in a global setting. on the "external dimension" of the Bologna Process.* Oslo: Norwegian Ministry of Education and Research.

Chapter 2: Quality teachers, Singapore style

Akiba, M., LeTendre, G. K., & Scribner, J. P. (2007). Teacher quality, opportunity gap, and national achievement in 46 countries. *Educational Research, 36*(7), 369–387.

Buchberger, F., Campos, B. P., Kallos, D., & Stephenson, J. (2000). *Green paper on teacher education in Europe*. Umea, Sweden: Thematic Network of Teacher Education in Europe.

Cochran-Smith, M., & Zeichner, K. (2005). *Studying teacher education: The report of the AERA panel on research and teacher education*. Mahwah, NJ: Erlbaum.

Darling-Hammond, L. (2001). *The research and rhetoric on teacher certification: A response to "Teacher certification reconsidered."* Retrieved June 15, 2006 from: http://www.nctaf.org/documents/nctaf/abell_response.pdf.

Darling-Hammond, L., & Bransford, J. (Eds.) (2005). *Preparing teachers for a changing world*. San Francisco: Jossey-Bass.

Darling-Hammond, L., & Youngs, P. (2002). Defining "highly qualified teachers": What does "scientifically-based research" actually tell us? *Educational Researcher*, *31*(9), 13–25.

Duncan, A. (2009). Teacher preparation: Reforming the uncertain profession. Speech delivered at Teachers College, Columbia University, New York, October 22.

Goh, C. B., & Gopinathan, S. (2008). The development of education in Singapore since 1965. In S. K. Lee, C. B. Goh, B. Fredriksen, & J. P. Tan (Eds.), *Toward a better future; Education and training for economic development in Singapore since 1965* (pp. 12–38). Washington, DC: The World Bank.

Goh, C. B., & Lee, S. K. (2008). Making teacher education responsive and relevant. In S. K. Lee, C. B. Goh, B. Fredriksen, & J. P. Tan (Eds.), *Toward a better future; Education and training for economic development in Singapore since 1965* (pp. 96–113). Washington, DC: The World Bank.

Goh, C. T. (1997). Shaping our future: Thinking schools, learning nation. Speech delivered at the 7th International Conference on Thinking, Singapore. June 2. Retrieved October 20, 2009 from http://www.moe.gov.sg/media/speeches/1997/020697.htm.

Goodwin, A. L., Genishi, C., Asher, N., & Woo, K. (1997). Voices from the margins: Asian American teachers' experiences in the profession. In D. M. Byrd, & D. J. McIntyre (Eds.), *Research on the education of our nation's teachers: Teacher education yearbook V* (pp. 219–241). Thousand Oaks, CA: Corwin Press.

Goodwin, A. L., & Oyler, C. (2008) Teacher educators as gatekeepers: Deciding who is ready to teach. In M. Cochran-Smith, S. Feiman-Nemser, & J. McIntyre (Eds.), *Handbook of research on teacher education: Enduring questions in changing contexts* (3rd ed., pp. 468–490). New York: Routledge.

Gopinathan, S. (2007). Globalisation, the Singapore developmental state and education policy: A thesis revisited. *Globalisation, Societies and Education*, *5*(1), 53–70.

Hogan, D., & Gopinathan, S. (2008). Knowledge management, sustainable innovation, and pre-service teacher education in Singapore. *Teachers & Teaching*, *14*(4), 369–384.

INTASC (Interstate New Teacher Assessment Standards). (2007). Retrieved September 17, 2009 from: http://www.ccsso.org/Projects/interstate_new_teacher_assessment_and_support_consortium/.

International Alliance of Leading Education Institutes. (2008). *Transforming teacher education: Redefined professionals for 21st century schools*. Singapore: NIE.

International Reading Association. (2008). *Status of teacher education in the Asia-Pacific region*. New York: UNESCO.

Luke, A., Freebody, P., Shun, L., & Gopinathan, S. (2005). Towards research-based innovation and reform: Singapore schooling in transition. *Asia Pacific Journal of Education, 25*(1), 5–28.

Ministry of Education (MOE). (2007). *Mission and vision statement.* June 29. Retrieved October 12, 2009 from http://www3.moe.edu.sg/corporate/mission_statement. htm#vision.

Ministry of Education (MOE). (2008). *Education in Singapore.* Singapore: MOE.

Ministry of Education (MOE). (2009a). *Education statistics digest.* Singapore: MOE.

Ministry of Education (MOE). (2009b). *Teaching as a career.* Retrieved October 12, 2009 from http://www.moe.gov.sg/careers/teach/.

Ministry of Education (MOE). (n.d.a). *Teachers network.* Retrieved November 30, 2009 from http://sam11.moe.gov.sg/tn/index.htm.

Ministry of Education (MOE). (n.d.b). *The teachers' pledge.* Retrieved October 12, 2009 from http://www3.moe.edu.sg/purposeofteaching/teacherPledge.html.

National Center for Education Statistics (NCES). (n.d.). *Trends in International Mathematics and Science Study (TIMSS).* Retrieved October 10, 2009 from http:// nces.ed.gov/timss/results07.asp.

National Institute of Education (NIE). (2009). *TE21: A teacher education model for the 21st Century.* Singapore: NIE.

National Institute of Education (NIE). (n.d.a). *Foundation programmes.* Retrieved October 15, 2009 http://www.nie.edu.sg/nieweb/programmes/load.do?id=Foundation.

National Institute of Education (NIE). (n.d.b). *Office of Education Research.* Retrieved October 15, 2009 from http://www.nie.edu.sg/nieweb/research/load.do?id=Office of Education Research.

National Institute of Education (NIE). (n.d.c). *Practicum office.* Retrieved November 15, 2009 from http://eduweb.nie.edu.sg/practicum/.

Peng, H. (2009). Singapore education system at an inflexion point. Speech delivered at the 2009 Teachers' Mass Lecture, Singapore. August 26. Retrieved December 10, 2009 from http://sam11.moe.gov.sg/tn/TeachersVision/messages.htm.

Shulman, L. S. (1986). Those who understand: Knowledge growth in teaching. *Educational Researcher, 15*(2), 4–14.

Singapore Department of Statistics. (2009). *Population trends 2009.* Singapore: Singapore Department of Statistics.

Singapore Education Milestones, 2004–2005. Retrieved October 25, 2009 from http:// www.moe.gov.sg/about/yearbooks/2005/teach.html.

Statistics Singapore. (2009). Retrieved December 5, 2009 from http://www.singstat.gov. sg/stats/keyind.html.

Tan, C. (2005). Driven by pragmatism: Issues and challenges in an ability-driven education. In J. Tan, & P. T. Ng (Eds.), *Shaping Singapore's future: Thinking schools, learning nation,* (pp. 5–21). Singapore: Prentice-Hall/Pearson.

Walsh, K. (2001). *Teacher certification reconsidered: Stumbling for quality.* Baltimore, MD: Abell Foundation.

World Bank. (2008). *2005 International comparison program: Tables of final results.* Washington, DC: World Bank. Retrieved October 20, 2009 from http://www.finfacts. ie/biz10/globalworldincomepercapita.htm#.

Yip, J. S. K., Eng, S. P., & Yap, J. Y. C. (1997). 25 years of education reform. In J. Tan, S. Gopinathan, & W. K. Ho (Eds.), *Education in Singapore: A book of readings* (pp. 3–32). Singapore: Prentice-Hall.

Chapter 3: Teacher preparation in the Netherlands: Shared visions and common features

Boyd, D., Grossman, P., Hammerness, K., Lankford, H., Loeb, S., McDonald, M., Reininger, M., Ronfedlt, M., & Wyckoff, J. (2008). Surveying the landscape of teacher preparation in New York City: Constrained variation and the challenge of innovation. *Educational Evaluation and Policy Analysis, 30*(4), 319–342.

Boyd, D., Grossman, P., Lankford, H., Loeb, S., & Wyckoff, J. (2006). Complex by design: Investigating pathways into teaching in New York City Schools. *Journal of Teacher Education, 57*(2), 155–166.

Bransford, J., Brown, A. L., & Cocking, R. R. (Eds.). (2000). *How people learn: Brain, mind, experience, and school (Expanded ed.).* Washington, DC: National Academy Press.

Britzman, D. (1986). Cultural myths in the making of a teacher: Biography and social structure in teacher education. *Harvard Educational Review, 56*(4), 442–456.

Brouwer, N. (2007). Alternative teacher education in the Netherlands 2000–2005: A standards-based synthesis. *European Journal of Teacher Education, 30*(1), 21–40.

Brouwer, N., & Korthagen, F. A. (2005). Can teacher education make a difference? *American Educational Research Journal, 42*(1), 153–224.

Centraal Bureau voor de Statistiek (2009). Participation rate Dutch youth in education above European average Retrieved December 15, 2009, from http://www.cbs.nl/en-GB/menu/themas/onderwijs/publicaties/artikelen/archief/2009/2009-2907-wm.htm.

Central Bureau for the Statistics (CBS). (2011). *Statline.* Retrieved October 25, 2011, from: http://statline.cbs.nl.

Comiteau, L. (2007). Why Dutch kids are happier than yours. *Time Magazine,* July 11.

Commissie Parlementair Onderzoek Onderwijsvernieuwing (2008). [*Parliamentary investigation on educational innovation*] Parlementair Onderzoek Onderwijsvernieuwingen. Amsterdam: SDU.

Commissie Toekomst Leraarschap (CTL) (1993) *Een beroep met perspectief: de toekomst van het leraarschap* [A profession with perspective: the future of teaching]. Zoetermeer, Ministerie van OC&W.

Darling-Hammond, L. (Ed.) (2000). *Studies of excellence in teacher education* (3 vols). Washington, DC: American Association of Colleges for Teacher Education.

Darling-Hammond, L. (2006). *Powerful teacher education: Lessons from exemplary programs.* San Francisco: Jossey-Bass.

ECHO (2009). Welcome to ECHO. Available at: http://www.echo-net.nl/. (accessed December 11, 2009).

Ericsson, K. A. (2006). The influence of experience and deliberate practice on the development of expert performance. In K. A. Ericsson, N. Charness, P. J. Feltovich, & R. R. Hoffman (Eds.), *The Cambridge handbook of expertise and expert performance* (pp. 683–704). New York: Cambridge University Press.

Evertson, C. M., & Weinstein, C. S. (2006). Classroom management as a field of inquiry. In C. M. Evertson, & C. S. Weinstein (Eds.), *Handbook of classroom management: Research, practice, and contemporary issues* (pp. 3–16). Mahwah, NJ: Lawrence Erlbaum Associates.

Grossman, P., Compton, C. *et al.* (2009a). Teaching practice: a cross-professional perspective. *Teachers College Record, 111*(9).

Grossman, P., Hammerness, K., & McDonald, M. (2009b). Redefining teaching, reimagining teacher education. *Teachers and Teaching: Theory and Practice*, 15(2): 273–289.

Hammerness, K. (2006). From coherence in theory to coherence in practice. *Teachers College Record*, 108(7), 1241–1265.

Hammerness, K. (under review). The relationship between teacher education program visions and teacher's visions: an examination of three programs.

Hammerness, K., & Darling-Hammond, L. (2002). Meeting old challenges and new demands: the redesign of the Stanford Teacher Education Program. *Issues in Teacher Education*, 11(1), 17–30.

Hammerness, K., Darling-Hammond, L. with Rust, F., Grossman, P., & Shulman, L. (2005). The design of teacher education programs. In J. Bransford, L Darling-Hammond, P. LePage, K. Hammerness, & H. Duffy (Eds.). *Preparing teachers for a changing world* (pp. 390–441). San Francisco: Jossey-Bass.

Hatch, T. (2009). *Managing to change: How schools can survive (and sometimes thrive) in turbulent times.* New York: Teachers College Press.

Janssen, F., De Hullu, E., & Tigelaar, D. E. H. (2008). Positive experiences as input for reflection by student teachers. *Teachers and Teaching: Theory and Practice*, 14(2), 115–127.

Kennedy, M. M. (2006). Knowledge and vision in teaching. *Journal of Teacher Education*, 57(3), 205–211.

KNAW (2009). *Mathematics in primary education: Analysis and keys for improvement* [Rekenonderwijs op de basisschool: Analyses en sleutels tot verbetering]. Amsterdam: Koninklijke Nederlandse Academie voor Wetenschappen.

Koetsier, C. P., & Wubbels, T. (1995). Bridging the gap between initial teacher training and teacher induction. *Journal of Education for Teaching*, 21(3), 333–345.

Korthagen, F., & Kessels, J. (1999). Linking theory and practice: Changing the pedagogy of teacher education. *Educational Researcher*, 28(4), 4–17.

Korthagen, F. A. J., Kessels, J., Koster, B., Lagerwerf, B., & Wubbels, T. (2001). *Linking theory and practice: The pedagogy of realistic teacher education.* Mahwah, NJ: Lawrence Erlbaum Associates.

Koster, B. & Dengerink, J. J. (2008). Professional standards for teacher educators: How to deal with complexity, ownership and function. Experiences from the Netherlands. *European Journal of Teacher Education*, 31(2), 135–149.

Ladson-Billings, G. (1995). Multicultural teacher education: Research, practice, and policy. In J. Banks and C. M. Banks. (Eds.) *Handbook of research on multicultural education.* (pp. 747–759). New York: Simon & Schuster Macmillan.

Ladson-Billings, G. (2001). *Crossing over to Canaan: The journey of new teachers in diverse classrooms.* San Francisco: Jossey-Bass.

LePage, P., Darling-Hammond, L., & Akar, H. (with Guttiérez, C., Jenkins-Gunn, E., and Rosebrock, K). (2005). Classroom management. In J. B. L. Darling-Hammond, P. LePage, K. Hammerness, & H. Duffy. (Eds.) *Preparing teachers for a changing world.* (pp. 327–357). San Francisco: Jossey-Bass.

Maandag, D. W., Deinum, J. F. *et al.* (2007). Teacher education in schools: An international comparison. *European Journal of Teacher Education*, 30(2), 151–173.

Meesters, M. (2003). *Attracting, developing and retaining effective teachers: Country background report for The Netherlands.* Paris: OECD.

Ministry of Education, Culture and Science (2008). *Working in Education 2008: The Netherlands.* The Hague, Ministry of Education, Culture and Science in the Netherlands.

Ministry of Education, Culture, and Science (1999a). *Maatwerk voor morgen: Het perspectief van een open onderwijsmarkt* [Tailor-made for tomorrow: The perspective of an open labor market in education]. The Hague: SDU-servicecentrum.

Ministry of Education, Culture, and Science (1999b). *Maatwerk 2: Vervolgnota over een open onderwijsmarkt* [Tailor-made for tomorrow 2: A follow-up on an open labor market in education]. The Hague: SDU-servicecentrum.

Mullis, I. V. S., Martin, M. O., Kennedy, A. M. & Foy, P. (2007). *IEA's Progress in International Reading Literacy Study in Primary School in 40 Countries.* Chestnut Hill, MA: TIMSS & PIRLS International Study Center, Lynch School of Education, Boston College.

NRC (2006). Think first before acting [Eerst denken dan pas doen]. 8 April.

NRC (2007). Students protest against "New Learning" [Scholierenprotest tegen "nieuwe leren"]. 27 January.

OECD (2007). *PISA 2006: Science Competencies for Tomorrow's World: Executive Summary.* Paris Author.

OECD (2010). *PISA 2009 Results: Executive Summary.* Paris: Author.

Simons, P. R. J. (2000). Towards a constructivistic theory of self-directed learning. In G. A. Straka (Ed.), *Conceptions of self-directed learning* (pp. 155–170). New York: Waxman.

Simons, P. R. J. (2006). How to kill a caricature of new learning [Hoe je een karikatuur van het nieuwe leren om zeep helpt]. *Pedagogische Studiën, 83*(1), 81–85.

Simons, P. R. J., van der Linden, J., & Duffy, T. (2000). New learning: Three ways to learn in a new balance. In P. R. J. Simons, J. van der Linden, & T. Duffy (Eds.), *New Learning* (pp. 191–208). Dordrecht: Kluwer Academic Publishers.

Snoek, M., & van der Sanden, J. (2005). *Teacher educators matter.* Amsterdam: Dutch Association of Teacher Educators (VELON).

Snoek, M. & Wielenga, D. (2003). Teacher education in The Netherlands: change of gear. In L. Barrows (Ed.), *Institutional approaches to teacher education in the Europe region: Current models and developments.* Bucharest: UNESCO-CEPES.

Stokking, K., Leenders, F., *et al.* (2003). From student to teacher: reducing practice shock and early dropout in the teaching profession. *European Journal of Teacher Education, 26*(3), 329–350.

Terwindt, S., & Wielenga, D. (2000). Learning practices in Amsterdam. In D. Willis *et al.* (Eds.), *Proceedings of Society for Information Technology & Teacher Education International Conference 2000* (pp. 1326–1327). Chesapeake, VA: AACE.

Tigchelaar, A., & Korthagen, F. A. J. (2004). Deepening the exchange of student teaching experiences: implications for the pedagogy of teacher education of recent insights into teacher behaviour. *Teaching and Teacher Education, 30*(4), 665–679.

UNICEF (2007). *Child poverty in perspective: An overview of child well-being in rich countries.* Innocenti Report Cards, No. 7. Florence: Innocenti Research Centre.

van der Werf, G. (2006). Old or new learning? Or rather just learning? [Oud of nieuw leren? Of liever gewoon léren?]. *Pedagogische Studiën, 83*(1), 74–81.

van Tartwijk, J., den Brok, P., Veldman, I., & Wubbels, T. (2009). Teachers' practical knowledge about classroom management in multicultural classrooms. *Teaching and Teacher Education, 25*(3), 453–460.

van Veen, K., Sleegers, P., & van de Ven, P. (2005). One teacher's identity, emotions, and commitment to change: A case study into the cognitive-affective processes of a secondary school teacher in the context of reforms. *Teaching and Teacher Education*, 21(8), 917–934.

Veenman, S. (1984). Perceived problems of beginning teachers. *Review of Educational Research*, 54(2), 143–178.

Verloop, N. & T. Wubbels (2000). Some major developments in teacher education in the Netherlands and their relationship with international trends. In J. H. H. S. G. M. Willems, & W. Veugelers. *Trends in Dutch Teacher Education*. (pp. 19–32). Leuven-Apeldoorn, Garant.

Vermeulen, A. & Koopman, P. (2000). *De begeleiding van beginnende teraren* [The Guidance of Beginning Teachers]. Zoetermeer, Ministerie van OC&W.

Villegas, A.M. (2008). Diversity and teacher education. In M. Cochran-Smith, S. Feiman-Nemser & D. J. McIntyre, & K. Demers (Eds.). *Handbook of research on teacher education: Enduring questions in changing contexts*. (pp. 551–558). New York: Routledge.

Wubbels, T., Brekelmans, M., den Brok, P., & van Tartwijk, J. (2006). An interpersonal perspective on classroom management in secondary classrooms in the Netherlands. In C. Evertson, & C. Weinstein (Eds.), *Handbook of classroom management: Research, practice, and contemporary issues* (pp. 1161–1191). Mahwah, NJ: Lawrence Erlbaum Associates.

Zeller, J. T., (2007). Children, let me tell you about a place called Amsterdam. *New York Times*, February 14, 2007.

Chapter 4: Teacher training, education or learning by doing in the UK

Baker, K. (1993). *The turbulent years: My life in politics*. London: Faber and Faber.

Bangs, J., Galton, M., & MacBeath, J. (2010). *Re-inventing schools: And now for something completely different?* London: Routledge.

Barber, M. (2007). *Instruction to deliver: Fighting to transform Britain's public services*. London: Methuen.

Bridges, D. (2007). *Education and the possibility of outsider understanding*. Cambridge: Von Hugel Institute, St. Edmund's College, Cambridge.

Brighouse, T., & Woods, D. (1999). *How to improve your school*. London: Routledge.

Campbell, A. A. (1993). Dream at conception: a nightmare at delivery. In R. J. Campbell (Ed.), *Breadth and balance in the primary curriculum*. London: Falmer.

Claxton, G. (2006). Expanding the capacity to learn: a new end for education? Keynote address, British Educational Research Association, Warwick, 6 September.

Cordingley, P., Bell, M., Evans, D., & Firth, A. (2003). *What do teacher impact data tell us about collaborative CPD?* London: DfES/EPPI/CUREE.

Cullingford, C., & Daniels, S. (1999). *The effects of Ofsted inspection on school performance*. Huddersfield: University of Huddersfield.

Department for Children, Schools and Families (2008). *21st century schools: A world class education for every child*. London: DCSF.

Department for Education and Skills (2005). *A new relationship with schools: School improvement partners' brief*. London: DfES.

Elmore, R. (2005). *Agency, reciprocity, and accountability in democratic education*. Cambridge, MA: Harvard Consortium for Policy Research in Education.

Frost, D. (2005). Resisting the juggernaut: building capacity through teacher leadership in spite of it all. *Leading and Managing, 10*(2), 70–87.

Furlong, J. (2003). Ideology and reform in teacher education in England. *Educational Researcher, 31*(6), 23–25.

Galton, M. (2007) *Learning and teaching in the primary classroom.* London: Sage Publications.

Galton, M. & MacBeath, J. (2002). *A life in teaching?* Cambridge: National Union of Teachers.

Galton, M., & MacBeath, J. (2008). *Teachers under pressure.* London: Sage.

Galton, M., & MacBeath, J. (2010). *Re-inventing schools, reforming teaching: From political visions to classroom practice.* London: Routledge.

Giroux, H. (1992). *Border crossings.* London: Routledge.

James, M., Black, P., Carmichael, P., Fox, A., Frost, D., Honour, L., MacBeath, J., McCormick, R., Marshall, B., Pedder, D., Procter, R., Swaffield, S. and Wiliam, D. (2007). *Improving learning how to learn: Classroom, schools and networks.* London: Routledge.

Jones, S., Beale V., Kogan, M., & Maden, M. (1999). *The Ofsted system of school inspection: An independent evaluation.* London: Centre for the Evaluation of Policy and Practice, Brunel University.

Learmonth, J. (2000). *Inspection: What's in it for schools?* London: Routledge.

Lieberman, A., & Friedrich, L. (2007). Changing teachers from within: teachers as leaders. In J. MacBeath, & Y.C. Cheng (Eds.), *Leadership for learning: International perspectives.* Amsterdam: Sense Publishers.

MacBeath, J. (2006). *School inspection and self-evaluation: Working with the new relationship.* London: Routledge.

MacBeath, J., & Dempster, N. (2008) *Leadership for learning: Making the connections.* London: Routledge.

MacBeath, J., & Galton, M. (2006). *A life in secondary teaching?* Cambridge: National Union of Teachers.

MacBeath, J., & Galton, M. with S. Steward, & C. Page (2008). *The costs of inclusion.* London: National Union of Teachers.

MacBeath, J., & Mortimore, P. (Eds.). (2001). *Improving school effectiveness.* Buckingham: Open University Press.

McCrone, T., Rudd, P., & Blenkinsop, S. (2007). *Evaluation of the impact of Section 5 inspections.* Research report, NFER, April.

National Foundation for Educational Research (2007). *Evaluation of the impact of Section 5 Inspections.* Slough: NFER.

National Foundation for Educational Research (2009) *Teacher resignation and recruitment survey.* London: NFER.

Office for Standards in Education (2004). *A new relationship with schools.* London: Ofsted.

Office for Standards in Education (2006). The first term of the new arrangements. Available at: http://www.ofsted.gov.uk/news/almost-60-of-schools-judged-outstanding-or-good-first-two-terms-of-new-style-ofsted-inspections.

Rosenthal, L. (2000). *The cost of regulation in education: Do school inspections improve school quality?* Keele: Department of Economics, University of Keele.

Scottish Executive (2002). *Standards for Chartered Teacher.* Edinburgh: Scottish Executive.

Swaffield, S. (2007). Light touch, critical friendship. *Improving Schools*, *10*(3), 205–219.

Waterhouse, J., Gronn, P., & MacBeath, J. (2008). Mapping leadership practice: focused, distributed or hybrid? Paper delivered at the British Education Association Annual Conference, Edinburgh, 3–6 September.

Wenger, E. (1999) *Communities of practice: Learning, meaning and identity.* Cambridge: Cambridge University Press.

Woodhead, C. (2002). *Class wars.* London: Little, Brown.

Chapter 5: Hong Kong: Professional preparation and development of teachers in a market economy

Advisory Committee on Teacher Education and Qualifications (ACTEQ). (2003). *Towards a learning profession: The teacher competencies framework and the continuing professional development of teachers.* Hong Kong: Government Logistics Department.

Advisory Committee on Teacher Education and Qualifications (ACTEQ). (2006). *Towards a learning profession: Interim report on teachers' continuing professional development.* Hong Kong: Government Logistics Department.

Advisory Committee on Teacher Education and Qualifications (ACTEQ). (2008). http://www.acteq.hk/category.asp?lang=en&cid=301&pid=237.

Advisory Committee on Teacher Education and Qualifications (ACTEQ). (2009). *Towards a learning profession: Third report on teachers' continuing professional development.* Hong Kong: Government Logistics Department.

Ball, S. (1987). *The micro-politics of the school.* London: Methuen.

Bolam, R. (2000). Emerging policy trends: some implications for continuing professional development. *Journal of In-Service Education*, *26*(2), 267–289.

Bray, M. (2007). *The shadow education system: Private tutoring and its implications for planners* (2nd ed.). Paris: UNESCO, International Institute for Educational Planning.

Burns, T., & Stalker, G. M. (1961). *The management of innovation.* Oxford: Pergamon.

Chan, R. M. C., & Lee, J. C. K. (2009). Teachers' continuing professional development in Hong Kong: are we on the right track? In J. C. K. Lee, & L. P. Shiu (Eds.), *Developing teachers and developing schools in changing contexts* (pp. 71–99). Oxford: Oxford University Press.

Cheng, Y. C., Tam, W. M., & Tsui, K. T. (2002). New conceptions of teacher effectiveness and teacher education in the new century. *Hong Kong Teachers' Centre Journal*, *1*, 1–19.

Chinese University of Hong Kong (2008). http://www.fed.cuhk.edu.hk/handbook/doc-2008.pdf.

Corcoran, T. B. (2006). Helping teachers teach well: transforming professional development. In P. R. Villa (Ed.), *Teacher change and development* (pp. 1–100). New York: Nove Science.

Darling-Hammond, L., & Bransford, J. (2005). *Preparing teachers for a changing world.* San Francisco: Jossey-Bass.

Day, C., & Sachs, J. (2004). *International handbook on the continuing professional development of teachers.* Maidenhead: Open University Press.

Draper, J., Chan, R. M C., & Cheung, C. (2008). Teachers' work life balance in Hong Kong: is there space for effective CPD? Paper given at APERA, Singapore, November.

Draper, J., & Forrester, V. (2009). The induction of beginning teachers in Scotland and Hong Kong: getting it right? *Journal of Comparative and International Education*, *4*(1), 74–86.

Education Bureau (EDB). (2011). Ratio of Graduate teacher posts. Press release LCQ4. http://www.info.gov.hk/gia/general/201111/23/P201111230296.htm.

Education Commission. (1992). *The teaching profession*. Report no. 5. Hong Kong: Government Logistics Printer.

Education Commission. (2000). *Learning for life, Learning through Life: Reform proposals for the twenty-first century*. Hong Kong: Government Logistics Printer.

Education Commission. (2006a). *Progress report on the education reform*. http://www.ec.edu.hk/eng/reform/progress004_pdf_eng.htm.

Education Commission. (2006b). *Education statistics*. Hong Kong: Hong Kong Government Logistics Printer.

EPPI: Evidence for Policy and Practice Information. (2003, 2005a, 2005b). http://eppi.ioe.ac.uk/cms/Default.aspx?tabid=159 (accessed November 19 2009).

Forrester, F., & Draper, J. (2005). The professional formation of teachers in Hong Kong: a dim-sum model? *Teacher Development*, *9*(3), 413–428.

Hargeaves, A. (1994). *Changing teachers, changing times*. London: Cassell.

Hong Kong University. (2011). http://web.edu.hku.hk/programme/pgde/docs/PGDE_Handbook_2011-12.pdf.

Joint Consultation Service Team. (2007). *Provision of consultation service: Revamp of the teachers' IT training framework*. http://www.edb.gov.hk/FileManager/EN/Content_4833/revamp2007_eng.pdf (accessed Nov. 17, 2009).

Leung, F-S. K. (2003). Issues concerning teacher education in the East Asian region. *Asia Pacific Journal of Teacher Education and Development*, *6*(2), 5–21.

Li, S-P.T., & Kwo, W-Y.O. (2004). Teacher education. In M. Bray, & R. Koo (Eds.), *Education and society in Macao and Hong Kong* (2nd edn.). Hong Kong: Kluwer and Comparative Education Research Centre, Hong Kong University.

Llewellyn, J. *et al.* (1982). *A perspective on education in Hong Kong* ('The Llewellyn Report'). Hong Kong: Government Logistics Printer.

Louie, K. (1984). Salvaging Confucian education (1949–1983). *Comparative Education*, *20*(1), 27–38.

Ma, H.-T.W. (1999). Higher education and the labour force. In M. Bray & R. Koo (Eds.), (2005) *Education and society in Hong Kong and Macau* (pp. 127–139). Dordrecht: Springer.

Morris, P. (2004). Teaching in Hong Kong: professionalization, accountability and the state. *Research Papers in Education*, *19*(1): 105–121.

Scottish Office (2000). *A teaching profession for the 21st century*. Vol. 1: the report. (The 'McCrone Report'). Edinburgh: Her Majesty's Stationery Office.

Singapore Ministry of Education. (2009). http://www.moe.gov.sg/media/speeches/2009/10/16/thailand-conference-learning-teaching.php.

Sweeting, A. (2004). *Education in Hong Kong, 1941–2001*. Hong Kong: Hong Kong University Press.

Tung, C. H. (1997). *Policy Programme: The 1997 Policy Address*. Hong Kong: Government Logistics Printer.

Wu, G., & Kwo, W-Y. O. (2003). Teachers' time on teaching and professional development: a comparison of Hong Kong, Macau, Beijing and Shanghai. *Education Research Journal* (Hong Kong), *18*(1), 117–136 (in Chinese).

Chapter 6: Building capacity for sustained school improvement

Barber, M. (2007). *Instruction to deliver*. London: Methuen.

Campbell, C., & Fulford, D. (2009). From knowledge generation to knowledge integration: analysis of how a government uses research. Paper presented to the American Educational Research Association, San Diego.

Earl, L., Watson, N., Levin, B., Leithwood, K., Fullan, M., & Torrance, N. (2003). Watching and learning 3: Final report of the OISE/UT evaluation of the implementation of the national literacy and numeracy strategies. Toronto: OISE/University of Toronto. Retrieved July 25, 2008, from www.standards.dfes.gov.uk/literacy/publications.

Elmore, R. (2004). *School reform from the inside out: Policy, practice, and performance*. Cambridge, MA: Harvard Education Press.

Fullan, M. (2010). *All systems go*. Thousand Oaks, CA: Corwin Press.

Grubb, N. (2009). *The money myth*. New York: Russell Sage Foundation.

Leithwood, K. (2006). *Teacher working conditions that matter: Evidence for change*. Toronto: Elementary Teachers' Federation of Ontario.

Levin, B. (2008) *How to change 5000 schools*. Cambridge, MA: Harvard Education Press.

Levin, B., & Fullan, M. (2008) Learning about system renewal. *Journal of Educational Management, Administration and Leadership, 36*(2), 289–303.

Levin, B., & Naylor, N. (2007) Using resources effectively in education. In J. Burger, P. Klinck, & C. Webber (Eds.), *Intelligent leadership*. Dordrecht: Springer.

OECD (2005). *Teachers matter: Attracting, developing and retaining effective teachers*. Paris: OECD.

Rees-Potter, C, & Kasian, M. (2006). *The impact of the CODE Special Education Project in Ontario schools, 2005–2006*. Toronto: Council of Ontario Directors of Education.

Reeves, D. (2006). *The learning leader*. Alexandria, VA: Association for Supervision and Curriculum Development.

Stannard, J., & Huxford, L. (2006) *The literacy game: The story of the national literacy strategy*. London: Routledge.

van Roosmalen, E. (2007). *CODE Special Education Project 2006–2007: Final research report*. Toronto: Council of Ontario Directors of Education.

Chapter 7: Rethinking teacher education in Australia: The teacher quality reforms

AERA, APA, NCME. (1999). *Standards for educational and psychological testing*. Washington, DC: American Psychological Association.

Arends, R. I. (2006a). Performance assessment in perspective: History, opportunities, and challenges. In S. Castle, & B. D. Shaklee (Eds.), *Assessing teacher performance: Performance-based assessment in teacher education* (pp. 3–22). Lanham, MD: Rowman and Littlefield.

Arends, R. I. (2006b). Summative performance assessments. In S. Castle & B. D. Shaklee (Eds.), *Assessing teacher performance: Performance-based assessment in teacher education* (pp. 93–123). Lanham, MD: Rowman and Littlefield.

Australian Association of Mathematics Teachers. (2006). *Standards for Excellence in Teaching Mathematics in Australian Schools*. Adelaide, SA: The Australian Association of Mathematics Teachers Inc.

Australian Council of Deans of Education. (1998). *Preparing a profession: Report of the national standards and guidelines for initial teacher education project.* Canberra: Australian Council of Deans of Education.

Australian Institute of Teaching and School Leadership (2011a). *National Professional Standards for Teachers. February 2011.* Carlton, Victoria: Ministerial Council for Education, Early Childhood Development and Youth Affairs (MCEECDYA).

Australian Institute of Teaching and School Leadership (2011b). *Accreditation of initial teacher education programs in Australia: Standards and Procedures. April 2011.* Carlton, Victoria: Ministerial Council for Education, Early Childhood Development and Youth Affairs (MCEECDYA).

Australian Science Teachers Association. (2002). *National Professional Standards for Highly Accomplished Teachers of Science.* Canberra: Australian Science Teachers Association.

Black, P., & Wiliam, D. (1998). Inside the black box: Raising standards through classroom assessment. *Phi Delta Kappan, 80,* 139–148.

Cochran-Smith, M., & Fries, M. (2005). Researching teacher education in changing times: politics and paradigms. In M. Cochran-Smith, & K. Zeichner (Eds.), *Studying teacher education: The report of the AERA panel on research and teacher education.* Mahwah, NJ: Lawrence Erlbaum Publishers.

Darling-Hammond, L. (1989). Accountability for professional practice. *Teachers College Record, 91*(1), 59–80.

Darling-Hammond, L. (2000). Teacher quality and student achievement: a review of state policy evidence. *Education Policy Analysis Archives, 8*(1), Retrieved August 2005 from http://epaa.asu.edu/epaa/v2008n2001.html.

Darling-Hammond, L., & Youngs, P. (2002). Standard setting in teaching: Changes in licensing, certification, and assessment. In V. Richardson (Ed.), *Handbook of research on teaching* (4th ed.) (pp. 751–776). Washington, DC: American Educational Research Association.

Education and Training Committee. (2005). *Step up, step in, step out: Report on the inquiry into the suitability of pre-service teacher training in Victoria.* Melbourne: Parliament of Victoria.

Goldhaber, D., & Brewer, D. (2000). Does teacher certification make a difference? High school teacher certification status and student achievement. *Educational Evaluation and Policy Analysis, 22*(2), 129–145.

Grimmett, P. (2009). Legitimacy and identity in teacher education: A micro-political struggle constrained by macro-political pressures. *Asia Pacific Journal of Teacher Education, 37*(1), 5–26.

House of Representatives Standing Committee on Education and Vocational Training. (2007). *Top of the class: Report on the inquiry into teacher education.* Canberra: The Parliament of the Commonwealth of Australia.

Ingvarson, L., Elliot, A., Kleinhenz, E., & McKenzie, P. (2006). *Teacher education accreditation: A review of national and international trends and practices.* Melbourne: Australian Council for Educational Research.

Masters, G. (2009). *A shared challenge: Improving literacy, numeracy and science learning in Queensland primary schools.* Melbourne: ACER.

Mayer, D. (2005). Reviving the 'Policy Bargain' discussion: the status of professional accountability and the contribution of teacher performance assessment. *The Clearing House, 78*(4), 177–181.

Mayer, D. (2006). Research funding in the US: implications for teacher education research. *Teacher Education Quarterly, 33*(1), 5–18.

Mayer, D. (2009). *Conceptualising a voluntary certification system for highly accomplished teachers.* Canberra: Teaching Australia – Australian Institute for Teaching and School Leadership Limited.

Ministerial Council on Education Employment Training and Youth Affairs. (2003). *National Framework for Professional Standards for Teaching.* Melbourne: MCEETYA.

Monk, D. H. (1994). Subject area preparation of secondary mathematics and science teachers and student achievement. *Economics of Education Review, 13,* 125–145.

National Board for Professional Teaching Standards. (1989). *Toward high and rigorous standards for the teaching profession.* Detroit, MI: Author.

Pecheone, R., & Chung, R. R. (2006). Evidence in teacher education: The performance assessment for California teachers. *Journal of Teacher Education, 57,* 22–36.

Rice, J. K. (2003). *Teacher Quality: Understanding the effectiveness of teacher attributes.* Washington, DC: Economic Policy Institute.

Rivkin, S., Hanushek, E., & Kain, J. (2005). Teachers, schools, and academic achievement. *Econometrica, 73*(2), 417–458.

Rockoff, J. E. (2004). The impact of individual teachers on students' achievement: evidence from panel data. *American Economic Review, 94*(2), 247–252.

Sanders, W. L., & Rivers, J. C. (1996). *Research project report: Cumulative and residual effects of teachers on future student academic achievement.* Knoxville: University of Tennessee Value-Added Research and Assessment Center.

St Maurice, H., & Shaw, P. (2004). Teacher portfolios come of age: a preliminary study. *NAASP Bulletin, 88*(639), 15–25.

Standards for Teachers of English Language and Literacy in Australia (STELLA). (2002). Retrieved from http://www.stella.org.au/statements.jsp.

Teaching Australia. (2008). *National professional standards for advanced teaching and for principals: Second consultation paper.* Canberra: Teaching Australia.

The Business Council of Australia. (2008). *Teaching talent: The best teachers for Australia's classrooms.* Melbourne: BCA.

US Department of Education. (2004). *Meeting the highly qualified teacher challenge: The Secretary's third annual report on teacher quality.* Washington, DC: US Department of Education.

Wenglinsky, H. (2003). Using large-scale research to gauge the impact of instructional practices on student reading comprehension: an exploratory study. *Education Policy Analysis Archives, 11*(19), 1–19.

Wilkerson, J. R., & Lang, W. S. (2003). Portfolios, the pied piper of teacher certification assessments: legal and psychometric issues. *Education Policy Analysis Archives, 11*(45). Retrieved on August 30, 2008 from http://epaa.asu.edu/epaa/v11n45.

Wilson, S. M., Floden, R. E., & Ferrini-Mundy, J. (2001). *Teacher preparation research: Current knowledge, gaps and recommendations. A research report prepared for the US Department of Education.* Washington, DC: Center for the Study of Teaching and Policy.

Yinger, R. J., & Hendricks-Lee, M. S. (2000). The language of standards and teacher education reform. *Educational Policy, 14*(1), 94–106.

Chapter 8: Teacher preparation and development in the United States: A changing policy landscape

Abdal-Haqq, I. (1998). *Professional development schools: Weighing the evidence.* Thousand Oaks, CA: Corwin Press.

Altenbaugh, R. J. & Underwood, K. (1990) The evolution of normal schools. In J. I. Goodlad, R. Soder, & K. Sirotnik (Eds.), *Places where teachers are taught* (pp. 136–186). San Francisco: Jossey-Bass.

Andrew, M., & Schwab, R. L. (1995). Has reform in teacher education influenced teacher performance? An outcome assessment of graduates of eleven teacher education programs. *Action in Teacher Education, 17*(3), 43–53.

Angrist, J. D., & Lavy, V. (2001). Does teacher training affect pupil learning? Evidence from matched comparisons in Jerusalem public schools. *Journal of Labor Economics, 19,* 343–369.

Athanases, S. Z. (1994). Teachers' reports of the effects of preparing portfolios of literacy instruction. *Elementary School Journal, 94,* 421–439.

Ayers, J. B. (1988). Another look at the concurrent and predictive validity of the National Teacher Examinations. *Journal of Educational Research, 81,* 133–137.

Baker, T. (1993). A survey of four-year and five-year program graduates and their principals. *Southeastern Regional Association of Teacher Educators Journal, 2*(2), 28–33.

Baratz-Snowden, J. (1990). The NBPTS begins its research and development program, *Educational Researcher, 19*(6), 19–24.

Barber, B. R. (2004). Taking the public out of education: The perverse notion that American democracy can survive without its public schools. *School Administrator, 61*(5), 10–13.

Begle, E. G. (1979). *Critical variables in mathematics education: Findings from a survey of the empirical literature.* Washington, DC: Mathematical Association of America; Reston, VA: National Council of Teachers of Mathematics.

Bond, L., Smith, T., Baker, W., & Hattie, J. (2000). *The certification system of the National Board for Professional Teaching Standards: A construct and consequential validity study.* Greensboro, NC: Center for Educational Research and Evaluation.

Boyd, D., Grossman, P., Lankford, H., Loeb, S., & Wyckoff, J. (2006). How changes in entry requirements alter the teacher workforce and affect student achievement. *Education Finance and Policy, 1,* 178–216.

California State University. (2002a). *First system wide evaluation of teacher education programs in the California State University: Summary Report.* Long Beach, CA: California State University.

California State University. (2002b). *Preparing teachers for reading instruction (K-12): An evaluation brief by the California State University.* Long Beach, CA: California State University.

Cavaluzzo, L. (2004). *Is National Board Certification an effective signal of teacher quality?* (National Science Foundation No. REC-0107014). Alexandria, VA: The CNA Corporation.

Chung, R. R. (2008). Beyond assessment: Performance assessments in teacher education. *Teacher Education Quarterly, 35*(1), 7–28.

Clotfelter, C., Ladd, H., & Vigdor, J. (2007). How and why do teacher credentials matter for student achievement? NBER Working Paper 12828. Cambridge, MA: National Bureau of Economic Research.

Conant, J. B. (1963). *The education of American teachers*. New York: McGraw-Hill.

Darling-Hammond, L. (Ed.). (1994). *Professional development schools: Schools for developing a profession*. New York: Teachers College Press.

Darling-Hammond, L. (2000). Teacher quality and student achievement: A review of state policy evidence. *Educational Policy Analysis Archives*, 8(1). Retrieved June 10, 2008, from http://epaa.asu.edu/epaa/v8n1.

Darling-Hammond, L. (2006). *Powerful teacher education: Lessons from exemplary programs*. San Francisco: Jossey-Bass.

Darling-Hammond, L., & Ball, D. L. (1997). Teaching for high standards: What policymakers need to know and be able to do. Paper prepared for the National Education Goals Panel, Washington, DC.

Darling-Hammond, L., & Bransford, J. (Eds.). (2005). *Preparing teachers for a changing world: What teachers should learn and be able to do*. San Francisco: Jossey-Bass.

Darling-Hammond, L., Chung, R., & Frelow, F. (2002). Variation in teacher preparation: How well do different pathways prepare teachers to teach? *Journal of Teacher Education*, 53(4), 286–302.

Darling-Hammond, L., Holtzman, D. J., Gatlin, S. J., & Heilig, J. V. (2005). Does teacher preparation matter? Evidence about teacher certification, Teach for America, and teacher effectiveness. *Education Policy Analysis Archives*, 13(42). Retrieved June 10, 2008, from http://epaa.asu.edu/epaa/v13n42/.

Darling-Hammond, L., & Sykes, G. (2003). Wanted: A national teacher supply policy for education: The right way to meet the "highly qualified teacher" challenge. *Educational Policy Analysis Archives*, 11(33). Retrieved June 10, 2008, from http://epaa.asu.edu/epaa/v11n33/.

Darling-Hammond, L., & Wei, R. C. (2009). Teacher preparation and teacher learning: a changing policy landscape. In G. Sykes (Ed.), *The handbook of education policy research* (pp. 613–636). Washington, DC: American Education Research Association.

David, J. L. (1994). *Transforming state education agencies to support education reform*. Washington, DC: National Governors' Association.

Dennison, G. M. (1992). National standards in teacher preparation: A commitment to quality. *The Chronicle of Higher Education*, 39(15), A40.

Denton, J. J. (1982). Early field experiences' influence on performance in subsequent coursework. *Journal of Teacher Education*, 33(2), 19–23.

Denton, J. J., & Lacina, L. J. (1984). Quantity of professional education coursework linked with process measures of student teaching. *Teacher Education and Practice*, 1, 39–64.

Denton, J. J., Morris, J. E., & Tooke, D. J. (1982). The influence of academic characteristics of student teachers on the cognitive attainment of learners. *Educational and Psychological Research*, 2(1), 15–29.

Denton, J. J., & Peters, W. H. (1988). *Program assessment report: Curriculum evaluation of a non-traditional program for certifying teachers*. College Station: Texas A&M University.

Denton, J. J., & Tooke, J. (1981–82). Examining learner cognitive attainment as a basis for assessing student teachers. *Action in Teacher Education*, 3, 39–45.

Druva, C. A., & Anderson, R. D. (1983). Science teacher characteristics by teacher behavior and by student outcome: A meta-analysis of research. *Journal of Research in Science Teaching*, 20, 467–479.

Ebmeier, H., & Good., T. L. (1979). The effects of instructing teachers about good teaching on the mathematics achievement of fourth grade students. *American Educational Research Journal, 16*, 1–16.

Feiman-Nemser, S. (1990). Teacher preparation: Structural and conceptual alternatives. In W. R. Houston (Ed.), *Handbook for research on teacher education* (pp. 212–233). New York: Macmillan.

Feiman-Nemser, S., & Buchmann, M. (1985). Pitfalls of experience in teacher preparation. *Teachers College Record, 87*, 53–65.

Feistritzer, C. E. (2005). *Profile of alternate route teachers.* Washington, DC: National Center for Alternative Certification.

Ferguson, P., & Womack, S.T. (1993). The impact of subject matter and education coursework on teaching performance. *Journal of Teacher Education, 44*(1): 55–63.

Fischetti, J., & Larson, A. (2002). How an integrated unit increased student achievement in a high school PDS. In I. N. Guadarrama, J. Ramsey, & J. L. Nath (Eds.), *Forging alliances in community and thought: Research in professional development schools* (pp. 227–258). Greenwich, CT: Information Age Publishing.

Frey, N. (2002). Literacy achievement in an urban middle-level professional development school: A learning community at work. *Reading Improvement, 39*(1), 3–13.

Gill, B., & Hove, A. (1999). *The Benedum collaborative model of teacher education: A preliminary evaluation.* Santa Monica, CA: RAND Corporation.

Glaeser, B. C., Karge, B. D., Smith, J., & Weatherill, C. (2002). Paradigm pioneers: A professional development school collaborative for special education teacher education candidates. In I. N. Guadarrama, J. Ramsey, & J. L. Nath (Eds.), *Forging alliances in community and thought: Research in professional development schools* (pp. 125–152). Greenwich, CT: Information Age Publishing.

Goertz, M. E., Ekstrom, R. B., & Coley, R. J. (1984). *The impact of state policy on entrance into the teaching profession.* Princeton, NJ: Educational Testing Service.

Goldhaber, D., & Anthony, E. (2005). *Can teacher quality be effectively assessed?* Seattle: University of Washington and the Urban Institute.

Goodlad, J. I, Soder, R., & Sirotnik, K. A. (Eds.). (1990). *Places where teachers are taught.* San Francisco: Jossey-Bass.

Goodman, J. (1985). What students learn from early field experiences: A case study and critical analysis. *Journal of Teacher Education, 36*(6), 42–48.

Gray, L., Calahan, M., Hein, S., Litman, C., Severynse, J., Warren, S. *et al.* (1993). *New teachers in the job market: 1991 update.* Washington, DC: U.S. Department of Education.

Haertel, E. H. (1991). New forms of teacher assessment. In G. Grant (Ed.), *Review of research in education, 17* (pp. 3–29). Washington, DC: American Educational Research Association.

Hammerness, K., & Darling-Hammond, L. (2002). Meeting old challenges and new demands: The redesign of the Stanford Teacher Education Program. *Issues in Teacher Education, 11*(1), 17–30.

Haney, W., Madaus, G., & Kreitzer, A. (1987). Charms talismanic: Testing teachers for the improvement of American education. In E. Z. Rothkopf (Ed.), *Review of research in education*, vol. 14 (pp. 169–238). Washington, DC: American Educational Research Association.

Haynes, D. D. (1995). One teacher's experience with National Board assessment. *Educational Leadership, 52*(8), 58–60.

Henke, R. R., Chen, X., & Geis, S. (2000). *Progress through the teacher pipeline: 1992–1993 College graduates and elementary/secondary school teaching as of 1997.* Washington, DC: U.S. Department of Education, National Center for Education Statistics.

Henke, R. R., Geis, S., Giambattista, J., & Knepper, P. (1996). *Out of the lecture hall and into the classroom: 1992–1993 College graduates and elementary/secondary school teaching.* Washington, DC: U.S. Department of Education, National Center for Education Statistics.

Henry, M. (1983). The effect of increased exploratory field experiences upon the perceptions and performance of student teachers. *Action in Teacher Education, 5*(1–2), 66–70.

Holmes Group. (1986). *Tomorrow's teachers: A report of the Holmes Group.* East Lansing, MI: Holmes Group.

Holmes Group. (1990). *Tomorrow's schools: Principles for the design of professional development schools: A report of the Holmes Group.* East Lansing, MI: Holmes Group.

Houston Consortium of Professional Development. (1996). *ATE Newsletter*, April, p. 7.

Houston, W. R., Clay, D., Hollis, L. Y., Ligons, C., Roff, L., & Lopez, N. (1995). *Strength through diversity: Houston Consortium for Professional Development and Technology Centers.* Houston, TX: University of Houston, College of Education.

Howey, K. R., & Zimpher, N. L. (1993). *Patterns in prospective teachers: Guides for designing preservice programs.* Columbus: Ohio State University.

Hunter-Quartz, K. (2003). "Too angry to leave:" Supporting new teachers' commitment to transform urban schools. *Journal of Teacher Education, 54*, 99–111.

Ingvarson, L. (1997). *Teaching standards: Foundations for professional development reform.* Melbourne, Australia: Monash University.

Jett-Simpson, M., Pugach, M. C., & Whipp, J. (1992). Portrait of an urban professional development school. Paper presented at the annual meeting of the American Educational Research Association, San Francisco, April.

Judge, H., Carrideo, R., & Johnson, S. M. (1995). *Professional development schools and MSU: The report of the 1995 review.* East Lansing: Michigan State University.

Kane, T. J., Rockoff, J. E., & Staiger, D. O. (2006). What does teacher certification tell us about teacher effectiveness? Evidence from New York City, NBER Working Paper No. 12155. Cambridge, MA: National Bureau of Economic Research.

Kenreich, T., Hartzler-Miller, C., Neopolitan, J. E., & Wiltz, N. W. (2004). Impact of teacher preparation on teacher retention and quality. Paper presented at the meeting of the American Educational Research Association, San Diego, CA, April.

Kentucky Institute for Education Research. (1997). *The preparation of teachers for Kentucky Schools: A survey of new teachers.* Frankfort: Kentucky Institute for Education Research.

Knowles, J. G., & Hoefler, V. B. (1989). The student-teacher who wouldn't go away: Learning from failure. *Journal of Experiential Education, 12*(2), 14–21.

Koerner, J. (1963). *The miseducation of American teachers.* Baltimore, MD: Penguin Books.

Koerner, M., & Rust, F., Baumgartner, F. (2002). Exploring roles in student teaching placements. *Teacher Education Quarterly, 29*(2), 35–58.

Laboskey, V. K., & Richert, A. E. (2002). Identifying good student teaching placements: A programmatic perspective. *Teacher Education Quarterly, 29*(2), 7–34.

Lanier, J., & Little, J. (1986). Research on teacher education. In M. C. Wittrock (Ed.), *Handbook of research on teaching* (3rd ed., pp. 527–569). New York: Macmillan.

Latham, N. I., & Vogt, W. P. (2007). Do professional development schools reduce teacher attrition? Evidence from a longitudinal study of 1000 graduates. *Journal of Teacher Education, 58*(2), 153–167.

Lawrenz, F., & McCreath, H. (1988). Integrating quantitative and qualitative evaluation methods to compare two teacher inservice training programs. *Journal of Research in Science Teaching, 25*(5), 397–407.

Levine, A. (2006). *Educating school teachers.* Washington, DC: The Education Schools Project.

Lusi, S. F. (1997). *The role of state departments of education in complex school reform.* New York: Teachers College Press.

Lustick, D., & Sykes, G. (2006). National Board Certification as professional development: What are teachers learning? *Education Policy Analysis Archives, 14*(5). Retrieved June 10, 2008, from http://epaa.asu.edu/epaa/v14n5/.

Lyons, N. P. (1998). Portfolio possibilities: Validating a new teacher professionalism. In N. P. Lyons (Ed.), *With portfolio in hand: Validating the new teacher professionalism* (pp. 247–264). New York: Teachers College Press.

Mantle-Bromley, C. (2002). The status of early theories of professional development school potential. In I. Guadarrama, J. Ramsey, & J. Nath (Eds.), *Forging alliances in community and thought: Research in professional development schools* (pp. 3–30). Greenwich, CT: Information Age Publishing.

Mitchell, K. J., Robinson, D. Z., Plake, B. S., & Knowles, K. T. (2001). *Testing teacher candidates: The role of licensure tests in improving teacher quality.* Washington, DC: National Academy Press.

Monk, D. H. (1994). Subject area preparation of secondary mathematics and science teachers and student achievement. *Economics of Education Review, 13*(2), 125–145.

Monk, D. H., & King, J. A. (1994). Multilevel teacher resource effects on pupil performance in secondary mathematics and science: The case of teacher subject-matter preparation. In R. G. Ehrenberg (Ed.), *Choices and consequences: Contemporary policy issues in education* (pp. 29–58). Ithaca, NY: ILR Press.

National Board for Professional Teaching Standards (NBPTS). (2001a). *"I am a better teacher:" What candidates for National Board certification say about the assessment process.* Arlington, VA: NBPTS.

National Board for Professional Teaching Standards (NBPTS). (2001b). *The impact of National Board Certification on teachers: A survey of National Board certified teachers and assessors.* Arlington, VA: NBPTS.

National Center for Education Statistics (NCES). (1996). *NAEP 1992, 1994 National Reading Assessments, Data Almanac, Grade 4.* Washington, DC: NCES.

National Center for Education Statistics (NCES). (2010). *The condition of education, 2010.* Indicator 28, Tables A-28-1, pp. 244–247. Retrieved on November 26, 2010 at http://nces.ed.gov/programs/coe/2010/pdf/28_2010.pdf.

National Commission on Teaching and America's Future (NCTAF). (1996). *What matters most: Teaching for America's future.* Washington, DC: Author.

National Commission on Teaching and America's Future (NCTAF). (2003). *No dream denied: A pledge to America's children.* Washington, DC: NCTAF.

Neubert, G. A., & Binko, J. B. (1998). Professional development schools: The proof is in the performance. *Educational Leadership, 55*(5), 44–46.

Newton, S. (2010) *Preservice performance assessment and teacher early career effectiveness: Preliminary findings on PACT.* Stanford, CA: Stanford Center for Assessment, Learning and Equity.

Orland-Barak, L. (2002). The impact of the assessment of practice teaching on beginning teaching: Learning to ask different questions. *Teacher Education Quarterly, 29,* 99–122.

Pecheone, R., & Chung, R. R. (2006). Evidence in teacher education: The performance assessment for California teachers. *Journal of Teacher Education, 57*, 22–36.

Pecheone, R., & Stansbury, K. (1996). Connecting teacher assessment and school reform. *Elementary School Journal, 97*, 163–177.

Rice, J. (2003). *Teacher quality: Understanding the effectiveness of teacher attributes.* Washington, DC: Economic Policy Institute.

Rodriguez, Y., & Sjostrom, B. (1995). Culturally responsive teacher preparation evident in classroom approaches to cultural diversity: A novice and an experienced teacher. *Journal of Teacher Education, 46*, 304–311.

Ross, S. M., Hughes, T. M., & Hill, R. E. (1981). Field experiences as meaningful contexts for learning about learning. *Journal of Educational Research, 75*, 103–107.

Sandholtz, J. H., & Dadlez, S. H. (2000). Professional development school trade-offs in teacher preparation and renewal. *Teacher Education Quarterly, 27*(1), 7–27.

Sato, M. (2000). The National Board for Professional Teaching Standards: Teacher learning through the assessment process. Paper presented at the annual meeting of the American Educational Research Association, New Orleans, LA, April.

Sato, M., Chung Wei, R., & Darling-Hammond, L. (2008). Improving teachers' assessment practices through professional development: The case of National Board Certification. *American Educational Research Journal, 45*, 669–700.

Schalock, D. (1979). Research on teacher selection. In D. C. Berliner (Ed.), *Review of research in education*, Vol. 7 (pp. 364–417). Washington, DC: American Educational Research Association.

Shin, H. S. (1994). Estimating future teacher supply: An application of survival analysis. Paper presented at the annual meeting of the American Educational Research Association, New Orleans, LA, April.

Shroyer, G., Wright, E., & Ramey-Gassert, L. (1996). An innovative model for collaborative reform in elementary school science teaching. *Journal of Science Teacher Education, 7*, 151–168.

Smith, T., Gordon, B., Colby, S., & Wang, J. (2005). *An examination of the relationship between the depth of student learning and National Board certification status.* Boone, NC: Appalachian State University, Office for Research on Teaching.

Stallings, J., Bossung, J., & Martin, A. (1990). Houston Teaching Academy: Partnership in developing teachers. *Teaching and Teacher Education, 6*, 355–365.

Sumara, D. J., & Luce-Kapler, R. (1996). (Un)Becoming a teacher: Negotiating identities while learning to teach. *Canadian Journal of Education, 21*, 65–83.

Sunal, D. W. (1980). Effect of field experience during elementary methods courses on preservice teacher behavior. *Journal of Research in Science Teaching, 17*, 17–23.

Sykes, G., Anagnostopoulos, D., Cannata, M., Chard, L., Frank, K., McCrory, R., *et al.* (2006). *National Board of Certified Teachers: An Organizational resource: Final report to the National Board for Professional Teaching Standards.* Washington, DC: NBPTS.

Thomas B. Fordham Foundation. (1999). *The teachers we need and how to get more of them.* Washington, DC: Thomas B. Fordham Foundation.

Tom, A. R. (1997). *Redesigning teacher education.* Albany: State University of New York Press.

Trachtman, R. (1996). *The NCATE professional development school study: A survey of 28 PDS sites.* Washington, DC: National Council for the Accreditation of Teacher Education.

Tracz, S. M., Sienty, S., & Mata, S. (1994). *The self-reflection of teachers compiling portfolios for National Certification.* Paper presented at the annual meeting of the American Association of Colleges for Teacher Education, Chicago, February.

Tracz, S., Sienty, S., Todorov, K., Snyder, J., Takashima, B., Pensabene, R. *et al.* (1995). Improvement in teaching skills: perspectives from National Board for Professional Teaching Standards field test network candidates. Paper presented at the annual meeting of the American Educational Research Association, San Francisco, April.

U.S. Department of Education (2002). *Meeting the highly qualified teachers challenge: The secretary's annual report on teacher quality.* Washington, DC: Author. Retrieved from: http://www.ed.gov/news/speeches/2002/06/061102.html.

Vandevoort, L. G., Amrein-Beardsley, A., & Berliner, D. C. (2004). National Board certified teachers and their students' achievement. *Education Policy Analysis Archives, 12*(46), 117.

Walsh, K. (2001) *Teacher certification reconsidered: Stumbling for quality.* Baltimore, MD: The Abell Foundation.

Weiner, L. (2007). A lethal threat to U.S. teacher education. *Journal of Teacher Education, 58,* 274–286.

Williams, B. C. (Ed.). (2000). *Reforming teacher education through accreditation: Telling our story.* Washington, DC: National Council for the Accreditation of Teacher Education and American Association of Colleges for Teacher Education.

Wilson, M., Hallam, P. J., Moss, P., & Pecheone, R. (2007). *Using Student Achievement Test scores as evidence of external validity for indicators of teacher quality: Connecticut's Beginning Educator Support and Training program.* Stanford: SCALE.

Wilson, S. M., Floden, R. E., & Ferrini-Mundy, J. (2001). *Teacher preparation research: Current knowledge, gaps, and recommendations: A research report prepared for the U.S. Department of Education.* Seattle: Center for the Study of Teaching and Policy.

Wiseman, D. L., & Cooner, D. (1996). Discovering the power of collaboration: The impact of a school–university partnership on teaching. *Teacher Education and Practice, 12,* 18–28.

Yerian, S., & Grossman, P. L. (1997). Preservice teachers' perceptions of their middle level teacher education experience: A comparison of a traditional and a PDS model. *Teacher Education Quarterly, 24*(4), 85–101.

Chapter 9: Teacher education around the world: What can we learn from international practice?

Cochran-Smith, M., & Fries, M. (2005). Researching teacher education in changing times: politics and paradigms. In M. Cochran-Smith, & K. Zeichner (Eds.), *Studying teacher education: The report of the AERA panel on research and teacher education.* Mahwah, NJ: Lawrence Erlbaum Publishers.

Organization for Economic Cooperation and Development (OECD) (2011). *Building a teaching profession: Lessons from around the world.* Paris: OECD.

Wei, R. C., Darling-Hammond, L., & Adamson, F. (2010). *Professional development in the United States: Trends and challenges.* Dallas, TX: National Staff Development Council.

Index